Love, Nina

Love, Nina

A Nanny Writes Home

Nina Stibbe

Little, Brown and Company

New York Boston London

Little, Brown and Company
Hachette Book Group
237 Park Avenue, New York, NY 10017
littlebrown.com

First United States Edition: April 2014
Originally published in Great Britain by the Penguin Group, November 2013

Little, Brown and Company is a division of Hachette Book Group, Inc. The Little, Brown name and logo are trademarks of Hachette Book Group, Inc.

The publisher is not responsible for websites (or their content) that are not owned by the publisher.

The Hachette Speakers Bureau provides a wide range of authors for speaking events. To find out more, go to hachettespeakersbureau.com or call (866) 376-6591.

LCCN 2014931140
ISBN 978-0-316-24339-1

10 9 8 7 6 5 4 3 2 1

RRD-C

Printed in the United States of America

Introduction

In 1982, at the age of twenty, I left my home in Leicestershire to take up a job as a nanny in London. I'd not been a nanny before but felt sure it would be a nice life.

And it was a nice life at 55 Gloucester Crescent. The household was made up of Mary-Kay Wilmers and her sons Sam, aged ten and a half who had some disabilities, and Will, aged nine. Also, there was Lucas the cat who was mostly out, and Alan Bennett, who lived across the street and often appeared at suppertime, and other neighbors, visitors and droppers-in.

Except for missing my sister Victoria, I was settled and happy straightaway.

Victoria stayed in Leicestershire, near where we'd grown up, working and living in a nursing home. I missed telling her everything every night, however mundane—the explaining of who was who and what he'd said and she'd said and what that might mean. Not that I very often wanted her opinion on anything, nor she mine, but we'd grown accustomed to a nightly conflab.

If there'd been a convenient phone where she lived these letters would not have been written because I'd have just rung her up. But there wasn't, so I wrote to her and she wrote back and there was something nice about the writing of and getting of letters, so we carried on.

It occurs to me that if Vic had loved London as I did, my letters wouldn't have been so detailed, as she'd have seen everything for herself on little trips. But she disliked London and came to stay only once or twice in all that time and spent those visits twitchy and longing to be home and not noticing the things I wanted her to notice.

These are the letters I sent to Victoria during my first years in London, starting with my arrival at Gloucester Crescent. The letters were often undated or partially dated. I have done my best to get them in the right order, but this was oddly tricky and I apologize if one or two events seem to occur slightly early or late. I apologize too for the things I got a bit wrong. Alan Bennett was never in *Coronation Street* for instance and Jonathan Miller has never been an opera singer as far as I know.

As for spelling, grammar and so forth, apart from some fine tuning, these have been left as they were in the original letters.

I'd like to thank Mary-Kay Wilmers who, in spite of misgivings, agreed to this book being published. Some names have been changed for obvious reasons, but most haven't and I hope the cast will enjoy seeing themselves here.

Nina Stibbe, 2013

Who's Who

(Some of the characters, and their occupations at the time. Some names have been changed.)

VIC: Victoria Stibbe, my sister

MARY-KAY WILMERS (MK): mother of Sam and Will (S&W), deputy editor of the *London Review of Books*

SAM FREARS: Mary-Kay's son

WILL FREARS: Mary-Kay's son

ELSPETH: Elspeth Allison, my mother

GEORGE MELLY: jazz singer, critic, writer

AB: Alan Bennett, playwright, screenwriter, actor

JONATHAN MILLER: theater and opera director, actor

TREVOR BROOKING: footballer (West Ham United)

JEZ: Jeremy Stibbe, my brother

DR. DILLON: doctor at Great Ormond Street Hospital

WILLIE CARSON: jockey, TV presenter

CLAIRE TOMALIN: biographer and journalist, literary editor of the *New Statesman* and the *Sunday Times*

TOM TOMALIN: son of Claire Tomalin, Sam's friend

NUNNEY: Mark Nunney, volunteer helper at the Tomalins'

MICHAEL FRAYN: partner of Claire Tomalin, playwright and novelist

JOHN LAHR: American theater critic and playwright

ANTHEA LAHR: writer

PIPPA: nanny to a family in Primrose Hill

AMANDA: nanny to a family in Gloucester Crescent

RAS WHITTAKER: school friend of Sam's

STEPHEN FREARS: father of Sam and Will, film director

BETSY REISZ (NÉE BLAIR): actress

KAREL REISZ: filmmaker

SUSANNAH CLAPP: friend of MK, worked at *London Review of Books*

CESIA WILMERS (GRANNY WILMERS): MK's mother

MR. MACKIE: Ian Mackie, ophthalmologist

RUSSELL HARTY: television presenter

MICHAEL NEVE: former partner of MK, academic

MARY HOPE: friend of MK

POLLY HOPE: daughter of Mary Hope

GM: Sheila Barlow, my grandmother

THE EVANS: family in Gloucester Crescent

DELIA SMITH: cookery writer and TV presenter

DEBORAH MOGGACH: writer and screenwriter

MAXWELL: my ex-pony

HARRIET GARLAND: friend of MK

RIK MAYALL: actor

ADRIAN EDMONDSON: actor

JOHN WILLIAMS: lecturer at Thames Polytechnic

ANNIE ROTHENSTEIN: second wife of Stephen Frears, artist

MR. JOHNSON: former boss

STELLA HEATH: student at Thames Polytechnic

PETER WIDDOWSON: lecturer at Thames Polytechnic

BRIAN HOOPER: former British Olympic pole-vaulter

VICKI JOYCE: lecturer at Thames Polytechnic

PETER M: lecturer at Thames Polytechnic

PETER H (PH): Peter Humm, my personal tutor, lecturer at Thames Polytechnic

PB: Peter Brooker, lecturer at Thames Polytechnic
LES DAWSON: comedian
MOLLY O: Victoria's horse
NICK NICHOLS: visiting lecturer (from San Diego State University)
TOM STIBBE: my brother
GORDON BANKS: England goalkeeper (ex–Leicester City)

I
MOVING IN
1982–1984

55 Gloucester Crescent
London NW1
September 1982

Dear Vic,

It's fantastic here, the house, the street, London. You can hear the zoo animals waking up in the morning.

Mary-Kay is funny. Nothing bothers her much—except she can't stand having too much milk in the fridge (they have skimmed).

Her and Sam and Will all have the same basin haircut. Apart from that, she's quite fashionable. She swears a lot (f and c), and reminds me of Elspeth, but not an alcy.

She loves hearing about you lot, so do S&W. They remember everything I tell them and they often ask about you all by name.

Yesterday MK asked, "So, is it Victoria who plays the violin?" and I spat out my tea laughing. Honestly, Vic, they're always laughing. I feel so happy here.

People come round loads. Some real weirdos. The other night one of them laughed at my ponytail (very short and a bit sticky-out). I saw her reflection in the French windows pointing.

I told Mary-Kay later, "I saw (that woman) pointing at my ponytail and smirking."

MK said, "Oh, she's just an idiot and you're more of one for caring."

That's what she's like.

Love, Nina
PS Who's George Melly? I'm in his room.

⌒

Dear Vic,

Being a nanny is great. Not like a job really, just like living in someone else's life. Today before breakfast Sam had to empty the dishwasher and Will had to feed the cat.

Sam: I hate emptying the dishwasher.
MK: We all do, that's why we take turns.
Will: I hate the cat.
MK: We all do, that's why we take turns.
Sam: Anyway, Will, the cat hates you.
Will: Don't talk shit, Sam.
Sam: Don't say shit in front of the new nanny. (*Drops cutlery onto the floor and shouts, "Trevor Brooking"*)
Will: Don't say Trevor Brooking in front of the new nanny.

Sam had porridge (made by me in a pan). Tea, no sugar. Pills.

Will had grilled tomatoes with garlic (he made it himself, except for lighting the grill) and tea, three sugars.

MK had hippie bread (not granary), toasted. Earl Grey, one eighth of a spoon of sugar.

Lucas had Go-Cat (chicken flavor), water.

We are very near the zoo, but they never go there. And nearish to Madame Tussaud's but they never go there either. They never do the things you'd imagine. Apparently only people who don't live in London do all that stuff. Real Londoners just go to secret places that tourists don't know about, like Hampstead Heath. Our closest, Monopoly-wise, would be Oxford Street (green) or Euston Road (blue). But the funny thing is, how near *everything* is. You could walk pretty much anywhere. Distances seem further on the underground because you go all round the houses and not just from A to B.

Hope all's well with you.

Love, Nina

PS Jez lives up the road in halls of residence and his college (UCL) is very close to MK's office on Gower Street, which is quite near Oxford Street.

∽

Dear Vic,

Took Sam to Great Ormond Street Hospital for his regular check up with Dr. Dillon. Sam gave his name to the receptionist as Willie Carson.

She said, "Take a seat, Mr. Carson."

Just when I began to worry that we'd miss our turn—Sam having given the wrong name—Dr. Dillon popped his head out and called Willie Carson.

Dr. Dillon: So, Sam, how have you been?
Sam: Can't complain. You?
Dr. Dillon: I'm well, thanks.
Sam: Jolly good.

On the way out of the consulting room:

Sam: By the way, I'm ditching the name Willie Carson.
Dr. Dillon: Oh, I rather like Willie Carson.
Sam: You obviously don't watch *Question of Sport*, then.

Sam is excited to have found out Dr. Dillon's first name (Michael). He can't wait to go back to Great Ormond Street. He's planning to say, "How are you, Mike?"

Sam: I'm going to say "How are you, *Mike?*"
MK: Sounds like a good plan.

(*Sam chuckles.*)
Me: It's three months away, you might forget.
MK: He won't.

After hospital, we had lunch in Boswell Street. Sam had Spaghetti Napoli. MK had pasta with butter and garlic. MK was annoyed that the napkins were bitty. Sam ate half of his napkin by accident. It matched his Napoli (red).

Tonight at supper:

Sam: I like people with higgledy faces.
Will: What, like Picasso?
Sam: I've never seen him.

That made Will think about a teacher at school, Miss X, who his mates all call "Boss-eye."

Will: All my friends say she's cross-eyed but I've never noticed her eyes.
AB: You must be a mouth-looker. We are all either an eye-looker or a mouth-looker.
Will: I'm an eye-looker.
AB: You can't be or you'd have noticed this woman's eyes.
Will: I'm an eye-looker, except when it comes to teachers. You never look them in the eye.
Sam: I'm an eye-looker.
MK: I'm a shoe-looker.

Love, Nina
PS I think I'm a mouth-looker.

∽

Dear Vic,

Mary-Kay is skinny (not *too* skinny). And therefore is always a bit chilly and has to wear cardigans and socks. Her legs and even her feet are slim, and therefore she has to take care with shoe styles, or they can look clompy. Everything has a consequence.

The kitchen is where we are most of the time. It's a big room with a long table in one half and a sofa and telly in the other. Mary-Kay and Will like to sit on the back of the sofa with their feet on the seat bit. And me and Sam like to sit in the proper place. We watch *Coronation Street, The Young Ones, Question of Sport, University Challenge,* sports, snooker, football.

The walls are covered in ancient plates (blue and white mostly) and pictures—one of a cyclist, one of a man holding a fish by its tail, and a cutting of an old uncle of Mary-Kay's who was a conductor in the USA (music, not bus) and a woman from the olden days in the worst shoes and perfect squares for teeth. And a very nice one of a black ship on blue water.

A massive dresser, like a Welsh but bigger, all covered in trinkets and pretend fruit, little animals and people and little cups and in each little cup a little thing.

Most of the plates we use for food, and mugs, are antique. Some chipped, some nice, some spooky. I have a favorite plate, white with dark blue rim. If Mary-Kay gets that one she says, "How did I get the hideous plate?"

The knives and forks are giant. Some are white-handled (not to go in dishwasher).

Our usual places at the table for supper: Will at 11. Sam at 12. MK at 1. AB at 9 and me at 3 (rectangle clock face). AB tries to go in Will's place sometimes because he likes to be in the middle. Breakfast we all go wherever...apart from only Sam in Sam's place.

Mary-Kay and Sam have chairs they prefer. Sam's is a big square one with great curly arms and MK's has a bar underneath that she can rest her feet on. I've got to admit, hers is nice foot-rest-wise, and once you've been in it nothing else feels as comfy. It's a well-designed chair.

There are two tall lamps. MK hates it if these aren't on and it's the first thing she does when she comes down, unless I've switched them on, which I try to. There's a plastic tablecloth which Sam hides food under and a great clanking bread bin.

The floor is planks of wood with gaps, so if you drop 50p it might go down (for ever). Sometimes slugs come up in the night. I've never seen this but MK says it's a horrible thing to come down to first thing. It's a common feature of this type of floor.

Wooden shutters at the window. You have to shut them or people walking past can look in. I don't always remember to and people do (look in). If that happens, we always look out at them and it's strange.

My rooms (two adjoining) are the nicest, I think. I have a giant mirror, like out of a posh pub. The surround is ornate and painted bright orangey-red. I've got a bed in my bedroom, but I like sleeping in the mirror room, so have got a mattress in there too. I have a window to the front that looks over the street and a window at the back which looks over the gardens.

Love, Nina

∾

Dear Vic,

Thanks for George Melly information. He sounds nice, but I'm sorry to tell you that he doesn't live here anymore—he used to (before Mary-Kay did). But there are famous persons living in the street—inc. Jonathan Miller (ex-doctor, now opera singer).

Yesterday I cooked a stew (four hours—oven lowest). AB came for supper.

AB: Very nice, but you don't really want tinned tomatoes in a beef stew.

Me: It's a Hunter's Stew.
AB: You don't want tinned tomatoes in it, whoever's it is.

Who's more likely to know about beef stew—him (a bloke who can't be bothered to cook his own tea) or *The Good Housekeeping Illustrated Cookbook*?

MK has shown me how to do stir-fried cabbage. Fry an onion and garlic (always garlic, garlic, garlic), add some fine shredded cabbage, fry and add soy sauce (at the end). It's lovely but you're always thirsty after.

Also, been cooking porridge for Sam. This morning, at breakfast, I dropped his porridge bowl ("sam's porridge bowl" printed round rim). It smashed and he was very upset. I felt awful. It was a gift. If only it had been Will's (porridge bowl)—he doesn't like his bowl (or porridge). And Sam loves dwelling on that type of tragedy whereas Will doesn't.

Will: Don't worry, Sam, you can use my porridge bowl.
Sam: Don't be stupid—it's got "Will's Bloody Porridge Bowl" written on it.
Me: No one will know.
Sam: I'm not using it. I'm going back to mashed potato.

Love, Nina

⌒

Dear Vic,
Shocked to hear that Sam and Will had never had Toffos, so I got some for after school and put them on the radiator to soften up (Sam doesn't like chewing chewy things).

Sam: (*suspicious*) Are they toffees? I don't like toffee.
Me: Not as such.

Sam: Why are they called Toffos, then?
Will: Cos they're for toffs.
Will: (*chewing, thinking*) Actually, they're just naked Rolos.

AB at supper again. He must get bored writing plays on his own all day and comes round for a laugh with Mary-Kay.

Will told us about his school-friend X.
Will: He's got a swimming pool. An Ink Spot.
Sam: What? Full of ink?
Will: No, the name refers to the shape.

Then Will began to tell us about food's journey through the human intestine "from table to toilet." AB said it wasn't an appropriate subject for suppertime. But when S&W went up, AB, still eating (rice pudding), began as follows:

AB: X has got crabs, apparently.
MK: Who has?
AB: X.
MK: Oh dear.
AB: He's been fucking the cleaner.
MK: Oh.

Neither of them seemed bothered—or surprised. AB just carried on eating rice pudding, and as soon as it was polite MK ground the coffee beans (noisy). Unfair that Will wasn't allowed to discuss "from table to toilet" when they can talk about crabs. Typical AB.

Hope all well at The Pines. Bad news you're doing nights.

Love, Nina
PS What are crabs exactly? (I know roughly.)

Dear Vic,

Firstly, about your boss walking around in the nude... I don't think it's anything to do with him being Swedish or Norwegian (first you say he's Swedish, then you say he's Norwegian). They only do that for the sauna etc. They're quite reserved apart from in the sauna. I have heard that in the sauna they find the sight of bikini/trunks embarrassing whereas they don't even notice nudity. And, no, Mary-Kay would NEVER dream of walking round in the nude—she doesn't even use the downstairs toilet.

I'm trying to work out who it is (with the crabs). There are two Xs. X who comes round here a bit. And X from down the street. I just can't imagine X from down the street—he's so polite. I'm guessing it's the other X. But you never know.

Yesterday, X (the first X) came round to drop something off for MK and seemed completely normal (not a care in the world). He said he was starving and cooked himself a fried egg (in olive oil). Would someone with *crabs* go round to someone's house and cook a fried egg?

Now I'm wondering, maybe it's the polite X after all. Or a totally other X that I've not met. It's a common name.

Would it seem bad if I asked MK who it is? I think it would. She'd wonder why I wanted to know.

Glad to hear you're almost finished night duty. I can imagine it. All those sleeping old people in that spooky old house with that ticking clock. Been telling S&W about it all. They love it (especially the ghostly ticking of the grandfather clock).

Love, Nina

PS Why watch horror films if you're scared? Why don't you read a funny book, or play chess?

Dear Vic,

Mary-Kay's favorite color is a greeny-blue, not bright, but like a eucalyptus leaf.

Will likes blue in general, but red for Arsenal. Sam likes red, but not for Arsenal.

I like the same greeny-blue as MK, only brighter.

I dyed my plimsolls that exact color. I mixed two Dylons together, one green, one blue. I did them in the washing machine (according to instructions) with a granddad shirt and some grayish T-shirts of Sam's. They all came out lovely. Then MK started to notice that everything was coming out of the wash a bit greeny-blue.

MK: How come everything's going green?
Me: You mean greeny-blue?
MK: Yes.
Me: I dyed a few things.
MK: Can it stop now?

AB suggested running the cycle through on hot to flush the dye out, which I'll do. I hope it won't put her off the color.

I got new shoes (£10) but hate them (sketch below—you can have if you like, size 6). I can never find shoes that I like, only plimmies and they feel so flat and hot. Shoes embarrass me. I go barefoot a lot, which is better.

Had to go to Golders Green to get new shoes for Sam.

Me: Right, we're off to Brian's.
MK: Aren't you going to put some shoes on?
Me: No, I hate my shoes.
MK: Well, get some nice ones.
Me: I never see any.
MK: Have a look in Brian's.
Me: Brian's is only for kids.
MK: First bare feet, then kids' shoes, then adult shoes. One step at a time.

Hope all's well with you. Sorry to hear about the gum bite...good job she had no teeth, but horrible anyway. Told S&W and they were horrified and now quite scared of the old lady opposite.

Love, Nina

⌒

Dear Vic,

Great news about TB. Don't worry about the double-denim, it's just a phase.

Mary-Kay has a new boyfriend too. His name is D— but Sam calls him "Floppy Hair" (because he has floppy hair)—or "Floppy" for short. I find him (Floppy) embarrassing because he's so nice (all the time) but you can't just ignore him because he's always engaging you in conversation. He's tall and handsome with dark black shiny hair, like a horse's mane flopping over his eyes, and when he sits down he adjusts his trousers with a little upwards tug. But I don't think he's ever fully comfortable trouserwise, he's forever at them. MK doesn't do the polite thing of pretending not to notice. She looks at him and says, "Are you all right?" and he doesn't even know he's doing it.

He's ruining our Saturdays with gloomy Bob Dylan drowning out *World of Sport*. I can tell MK doesn't like him (Floppy) that much. Coming down into the kitchen on his first (public) visit, he stopped on the stairs and gazed out of the window into the garden (mossy slabs and two small trees).

Floppy: What kind of trees are those?
MK: They're just *trees*. (Which, in her language, is like calling someone a fucking twat. She ought to knock it on the head really.)

Last night they went out for dinner. Floppy hung around the kitchen while MK got ready. Sam and Will and me were quite excited about the date.

MK wasn't excited at all. She did wear her silky jumpsuit thing though and at least looked nice.

As they left the house and went into the street we called goodbye from the door.

Will: Have a nice time.
Me: Bye.
Sam: (*loud*) Get in there, Floppy!

Love, Nina
PS Could Mr. T not watch horror films on his own? Anyway, I didn't think old people liked horror.

∽

14

Dear Vic,

Went to a party last night with the helper from the Tomalins'. In a dark house in Mornington Crescent and grim-looking people all swigging from cans. I hung around in the kitchen (the only room with a light on). A fat boy called Colin suddenly tipped a packet of Trill (birdseed) into his mouth. He finished the pack, washed it down with a can of Long Life and burped. Everyone clapped and laughed. Then the boy threw up into the sink and everyone clapped again.

Told Sam and Will the birdseed story. I thought it might show them that you shouldn't perform degrading acts to get attention, even if you're fat. They thought it was excellent.

Will: I'm going to do that when I grow up, it's cool.
Sam: I am, but not with birdseed.
Will: It has to be birdseed, that's the point.
Sam: I'm going to do it with something nicer, like Quavers.
Will: You already do.

Will worries about nuclear war. Everyone's told him it'll never happen but, once it's mentioned, it sticks in his mind. He's a bit like you in that respect. Mary-Kay has suggested we stop talking about it altogether (nuclear war). Not that we ever did talk about it much anyway—but it crops up on *The Young Ones* and other comedies. MK has Sellotaped some pages together in his encyclopedia so he can't accidentally turn to that section (War, nuclear).

Sam is envious of all the attention Will's getting over the nuclear war anxiety. He says he's got an anxiety too, he can't say what it is, only that it's a lot worse than Will's.

MK: How can we reassure you if you won't say what it is?
Sam: It's been in the news.
Will: Is it to do with West Ham?

Sam: Fuck off, Will.

Will: Only trying to help.

Hope all well at The Pines. Congratulations re patio. It sounds great. Fresh air always good.

Love, Nina

~

Dear Vic,

Had a v. nice time with Elspeth.

It's usually extremely embarrassing, mixing people like that. And it was, but it wore off quite quickly. Mary-Kay said Elspeth seemed like fun. Elspeth didn't say anything about MK seeming like fun (MK keeps that sort of thing hidden until you know her a bit better) but did say MK was pretty and that she had nice objects about the place. Elspeth loved the house (bookshelves and pictures and that it's in London).

Me: My mum thought you were pretty.

MK: Rubbish.

Me: She did, and she said you had nice objects around the place.

MK: That's nice of her.

Me: So?

MK: So what?

Me: What did you think of her?

MK: She seemed like fun.

On the negative side, I found out something about Elspeth that I didn't know before. She snores, not loud but piercing, and rolls about in bed all night like a Labrador trying to get comfy. In the morning she remarked that she'd had a great night's sleep and I told her that

16

she'd snored and rolled around all night and therefore I hadn't (had a great night's sleep) and she laughed and asked if AJA had told me to say that.

Me: Why would he tell me to say that?
E: Because he says that every morning.
Me: He says it because it's true.

She hadn't thought of that.

Anyway, we had a great time and E was nostalgic about London and took me to an old marketplace that used to be better than it is now and a park where she used to walk you in your pram. We were going to visit an old neighbor of hers in Hamilton Terrace but Elspeth decided against it at the last minute due to suddenly remembering something.

Went to National Gallery instead. E got the giggles at a painting of a few nudes having a classical/ancient picnic (grapes and goblets). It wasn't the nakedness but the fact that they looked so stupid (the nudes) having the picnic (in the nude). And in trying to explain why it was funny, she set me off. We had to leave because we were spoiling it for everyone else who didn't find it funny. People hate it when other people laugh in a gallery.

Make sure you tell her you know all about the gallery thing and the snoring.

Love, Nina

Dear Vic,
I'll be in Leics on 24th December.
Saturday: Mary-Kay came home with an eight-foot-tall Xmas tree.

She'd carried it up from Inverness Street with one of the market blokes. We had a lot of problems getting it up. MK thought the stem was too long (she called it a stem, it was actually a *trunk*).

> MK: Someone will have to go to the Millers' and borrow their saw. (*We ignore her.*)
> MK: Who's going? I've just lugged the tree home.
> Will: Not me.
> Sam: I'm not going.
> MK: (*to me*) Looks like it's you, Nanny.

I said I'd go if Sam came with me. When we got there (only a few doors up) we had a scuffle on the doorstep. When Jonathan Miller answered the door, I pushed Sam in front of me and he blurted out, "The nanny wants to borrow the saw."

When we got home, MK asked what JM had said. I said he'd said, "Don't forget to bring it back." MK looked at the ceiling (which in her language means "fucking idiot").

And I felt bad because JM hadn't actually said, "don't forget to bring it back." He'd said something like, "Well, good luck, take care"— something friendly and supportive and really didn't deserve the ceiling look. I said he'd said, "don't forget etc.," to make sure we *would* actually give it back—seeing as I'd been the borrower. I know what it's like when you borrow a thing on behalf of someone else.

Anyway it's up now all covered with little angels and balls and beads and lights (the Xmas tree). It looks brilliant. The best I've ever seen in real life.

See you on the 24th.

Love, Nina

PS Great that you're having lessons, but not sure Mr. T is the best instructor. He never sleeps and he's eighty-nine.

Dear Vic,

Sam and me are bickering a lot at the moment. Yesterday I pranged the car on England's Lane—only slightly and decided not to mention it to MK. I said to Sam, "I'm not going to say anything about it to Mary-Kay—so don't you mention it, OK?" And he agreed.

MK grilled lamb chops for supper and Sam found them too chewy but MK wouldn't let him off them. So, because he was mardy about that, he snitched on me about the car prang.

Sam: Nina crashed the car on the way back from the Lahrs'.

MK: (*surprised face*).

Me: It was just a tiny bump.

Sam: She told us not to tell you.

Me: It was a slight bump on the bumper.

Will: Whatever happened to "honesty is the best policy"?

Me: That's what bumpers are for anyway—bumping.

AB: Bumpers *were*, probably, originally designed to take bumps.

MK: Well, how bad is it? Do we need to get it fixed?

Me: No, it's nothing.

AB went outside to look and came back saying it was "livable with."

Got my own back on Sam a bit later. I could see a lump under the tablecloth where he'd hidden his chewy chops (usually I'd ignore it). "What's that lump there, Sam?"

Sam not allowed any pudding (banana custard) due to hiding the chops.

Checked the car this morning, just a few black lines like it's been clawed by someone with mascara on their fingernails. That makes it sound bad—it's not that bad. I know you're going to make a joke about me needing driving lessons. But London's crammed with parked cars and sometimes you have to nudge them gently out of the way when you drive off.

Love, Nina

⌒

Dear Vic,

I have promised I'll feed Lucas the cat every day and clean out the crusty food bowl if we can change his name (to Jack). I'm not keen on the name Lucas. It reminds me of Mrs. Lucas. You might not remember her. She was that nice, but quiet teacher at Gwendolyn Junior School.

She taught us how to draw a detailed map of Great Britain by drawing a woman in a bonnet riding a pig. I'll never forget the awful picture she drew on the board as an example. The woman's face represented North Wales and had to be quite contorted to give the right contours, and the pig she was riding (South Wales) had to be equally so. Both with mouths open as if shouting. Devon was the pig's knobbly leg and Cornwall its trotter. The Southeast, inc. London, was its back leg and bum.

She didn't seem to have a plan for Scotland at all.

She also told us to remember Italy as a boot, America a turtle and France a homemade biscuit. Says a lot about her homemade biscuits. My homemade biscuits are more like Poland.

Anyway, I used to notice Mrs. Lucas driving to school in the morning. She was a nervous driver, chest up to the steering wheel, face at the windscreen, in second gear the whole way. I used to feel sorry for her when we overtook her as she waited too long at junctions with cars queuing up behind, bibbing.

Anyway, that's why I don't like the name Lucas. I hate having to feel sorry for people. So the cat is now called Jack.

Saw Joan Thirkettle (newsreader) the other day (short fringe) and the posh bloke from *Rising Damp* (handsome black bloke)—he has this really slow walk.

Love, Nina

⌒

Dear Vic,

I've made friends with two nannies nearby. Pippa and Amanda.

Pippa calls herself an "au pair" as opposed to nanny—don't know why. It could be that "au pair" sounds younger and her being a bit older (about twenty-four). You can tell Pippa spends ages choosing what to wear and has an endless supply of different-colored trousers (including a striped pair and a pair with flowers embroidered down one leg).

Amanda is nice and funny (and thinks I'm nice and funny) and she loves Sam and Will and thinks they're nice and funny too and they like her—plus she always wears the same old jeans.

If Amanda pops round here without Pippa, she tries not to sit near the window. I think this might be because Pippa is a bit tyrannical and doesn't want Amanda popping round here on her own (without Pippa). One day though, Pippa popped round on *her* own (except for a small baby called Julian). It was unplanned—she suddenly peered in at the kitchen window going, "Yoo-hoo." I asked Pippa (politely) not to shout at the kitchen window in future, but to ring on the doorbell like everybody else. She never fully recovered from the telling-off. Then baby Julian needed something and she had to go. She had the stripy trousers on which never quite work at the back and it looks like a trompe l'oeil.

Also, on the friend-front, there's Nunney, the Tomalins' new helper volunteer (time was up for the old one). He's very confident and jokey

21

which is good for Tom but will take a bit of getting used to. Nunney has the annoying habit of suddenly laughing *at* you though—which can be disconcerting. For instance, to make conversation, I asked him if he had any hobbies and he burst out laughing as if I'd said a hilarious punch line. I must've looked shocked because he then said, "Sorry, no, I don't have any hobbies. Do you?" and of course I said, "No, not really." So that's how it'll be with this helper. Seems a bit like hard work.

To be fair he did tell a funny thing about himself. On his first night having supper with Claire and Michael and Tom, there was a plate of smoked salmon as a shared starter with lemon wedges and when the plate was passed to Nunney he just ate it (all) and said, "Lovely."

Claire said, "Oh, that salmon was meant for all four of us, never mind." And they moved on to the casserole, which Nunney was too full for.

Anyway, I think he'll be good for Tom. And if not, he's only here for six months.

Love, Nina

PS Also on the friend-front, Misty C from Robert Smyth School is at college in Roehampton and Helen from Jez's sixth form is at college in West London.

∽

Dear Vic,

Mary-Kay keeps being ambushed (her word) by a loose paving slab on the crescent near the house. It's this slab that, when you step on it, squirts water at your foot (if it's been raining) and trips you up in general. I say "you" but it actually mostly happens to MK. I asked her why she doesn't sidestep the slab and she said it's never the one she thinks it is. I keep saying I'll mark it with a blob of green paint, but never do.

Sam was due to go to Ras's for tea. Ras's mum asked if there was anything Sam doesn't eat. I said he had the usual prejudices for his age (which isn't exactly true but I couldn't be bothered to go into detail). You'd think she'd know anyway, they've been friends since toddler age.

Me: Ras's mum wants to know if there's anything you don't like.
Sam: Shoes with shoelaces.
Me: She meant food.
Sam: I don't like Brazil nuts or trout-fish.
Me: Oh no, she was planning a trout-fish and mixed nut risotto.
Sam: Shit.

Played a little trick on Nunney, which seems bad now, but at the time was funny. There was a note on the sideboard from Claire saying about putting a casserole in the oven at such and such a time and temp and I added at the bottom "and please groom Miranda (the cat)." Later:

Nunney: I've told Claire I'm not prepared to groom the cat.
Me: Oh, what did she say?
Nunney: She was fine about it.

We all played Buckaroo, which Sam got for Xmas, but none of us like the bit where the mule bucks (too shocking) except Nunney, who says if Sam doesn't want it (Buckaroo) he'll take it round to 57. Me and Will have advised Sam not to let go of Buckaroo so soon.
Love, Nina
PS Jez says it wasn't Mrs. Lucas who drew the map of England as a woman in a bonnet riding a pig. It was Mrs. Curtis. I think he might be right but I am sure Mrs. Lucas was the nervous driver. He says Mrs. Lucas always walked to school.

Dear Vic,

I can't pass on Mr. Blunt's letter to Jonathan Miller just at the moment—I think I'm in his bad books. It's partly that I asked him if he was an opera singer and everyone laughed (because he isn't one and although being an opera singer is fine, apparently it's ridiculous if someone thinks you are but you aren't). Can't decide if this is insulting to opera singers or to anyone who isn't one.

Also, I think J Miller is bearing a grudge over the loss of his saw at Xmas. He never mentions it but I know something's on his mind.

Me: (*to MK*) I think Jonathan Miller hates me.

MK: What?

Me: I think Jonathan hates me.

MK: I shouldn't worry about it.

Me: *I shouldn't worry about it?* That means he does.

MK: I'm sure he doesn't *hate* you.

Me: It's your fault, making me borrow the saw and then losing it.

MK: I didn't lose the saw—you did.

Me: No, *you* did and now he hates me.

It's the injustice of it that bothers me. I tried my hardest to keep the saw safe, but nothing's sacred (in this madhouse).

I think MK was miffed because Jonathan Miller said, "Don't forget to bring it back," because she hates being bossed about. He didn't say it but it's too late to tell her that now.

Love, Nina

Dear Vic,

Will goes to a posh school. One friend there is a distant relative of Ian Fleming the writer (the one that has the Ink Spot pool, I think).

Sam and Will love nostalgia. It doesn't matter how ordinary a thing is, if it occurred more than a month ago, they discuss it in glowing terms and great detail. Sam especially has a good memory for detail.

Will: Do you remember when that dog nicked your sausage roll?
Sam: (*laughs*) Yes, do you?
Will: I've just mentioned it.
Sam: Do you remember when Stibbe scored that header at the Astroturf?
Will: (*laughs*) Yeah, it was an own goal.
Sam: Yeah.
MK: Didn't you remember all this yesterday?
Will: No, Saturday.

Mary-Kay has a new (boy)friend called H—. She can hardly bring herself to say the word (H—). It isn't only the name H—she has a problem with. She's just funny about names and like so many things, once you know she's funny about it, you start to see why and then you're funny about it. I tested her on names she finds it easy / difficult to say.

Me: H—?
MK: Difficult.
Me: D—?
MK: Difficult.
Me: Geoffrey?
MK: Difficult.
Me: Michael?
MK: Easy.

Me: Stephen?
MK: Easy.
Me: Jack?
MK: Difficult.
Me: Alan?
MK: Enough, shut up.

My theory: some (lots of) men's names sound like toilets, penises or wanking. Have you noticed?

Will and me both have head lice. Sam is lording over us because he's clear as a bell. MK's having the overnight lotion same as us, to be on the safe side. We look terrible. All greasy-haired. And we stink. AB was a bit put off at supper and said not to scratch or shake near his plate.

See you soon.

Love, Nina

∽

Dear Vic,

Met Mary-Kay at John Bell pharmacy in Wigmore Street. Approaching the car where MK had parked, we saw a traffic warden (bloke) writing a ticket.

MK: (*calling out*) Hullo, warden (*walking quickly*), I'm here now.
Traffic Warden: (*placing ticket*).
MK: (*takes ticket and offers it back to the warden*) I was only a minute late.
TW: (*backs away, avoiding ticket*) I'm sorry, madam.
MK: But I'm here now.
TW: The ticket is issued, I'm afraid.
MK: (*points to litter bin*).

TW: I'm sorry, madam.
MK: It seems unsporting...
TW: I'm sorry, madam.
MK: In this weather (*sunny*).
TW: (*smiles*).
MK: Well, you smiled, that's something.
TW: (*laughs*) Yes, madam.

Driving away:

MK: He was handsome...didn't you think?
Me: I didn't see him in that light.
MK: In what light did you see him?
Me: Authoritative.
MK: Yes, and handsome.

Later we were talking about buddleia (the horrible purple-flowered shrub that grows out of neglected masonry in places like Highfields):

AB: It can be nice, in the right place.
Me: I don't like it—it grows out of derelict houses.
MK: Only if it has to.
AB: It's very attractive to butterflies.
MK: (*to me*) There you go, butterflies like it.
Me: But it grows out of cracks and guttering.
MK: (*pleased*) Butterflies and squalor.

Hope all's well with you.

Love, Nina

Dear Vic,

Of course he's *the* Alan Bennett. You'd know him if you saw him. He used to be in *Coronation Street*. He's got a small nose and Yorkshire accent.

He's very nice. He says, "don't be daft" etc. He's getting quite famous now (probably more so than Jonathan Miller actually) but he's not bothered about it. He's very interested in history, but he's rubbish on nature (like MK) although he is very outdoorsy and does like it (nature) for walks etc. (unlike MK).

When he comes over for supper he does this tiny short doorbell ring, hardly a ring at all, he just touches the bell and it makes just the beginning of a ring. That's him. Minimum fuss.

Once, late at night, when I was on my own, I thought I could hear someone creeping around in the house (burglar or worse). I got myself so scared I rang AB and asked him to come over. He came over straightaway (his mac over his pajamas) holding his brolly. He had a good look around. There was no one. I was so embarrassed I almost wished there was. I said, "I feel such an idiot." And he said, "Don't be daft."

Love, Nina

PS Everyone passes with Brown School of Motoring (BSM). Really, Mr. Brown has never had a fail. The thing about Mr. T is he's on medication and he indicates right and left by HAND. I've seen him. You need someone with a normal, modern car (and techniques), not a Hillman.

∽

Dear Vic,

A man from Camden Council came round to notify us. He was only a bit older than me but acted very official and mature. He talked about "forthcoming essential street works" and gave us a typed page. He was formal and wouldn't chat or be at all light-hearted (unlike the traffic warden the other day).

MK: So, will there be digging?
Young Man: A certain amount.
MK: Machines?
YM: I expect so.
MK: Will it be noisy?
YM: Do you go out to work during the day, madam?
Me: Why? Are you about to offer her a job?
YM: I'm not authorized to make appointments.

Later at supper:

Me: (*to AB*) Did a young man come to you?
AB: Not today.
Me: We had one to warn us of street works.
AB: (*very interested, turns to MK for more*) Oh, what?
MK: Some digging and stuff.
AB: Why didn't the young man come and warn me?
Me: It's not your side.
AB: But things travel across.
MK: Not the young man though, apparently.

AB returned to the subject after pudding.

AB: I can't think what road works could be necessary.
Me: It's not *road works*, it's *street works* (*I fetch the typed page*).
AB: Oh, yes, it says here *street works*, you're right.
He never believes what I say—without proof.

29

I remembered the wobbly slab that splashes and trips people (especially Mary-Kay).

Me: Someone should've told the man about the wobbly slab.
MK: (*hands up*) Yes! I thought that when he was here.
Me: Why didn't you mention it?
MK: Enough was enough.
Me: I'll bring it up.
AB: You can't just lift paving stones willy-nilly.
Me: I meant bring it up in conversation.

Hope all well with you. Good luck with quiz. You might want to brush up on football and pop. They always ask about those. And about Mark Twain.

Love, Nina

∽

Dear Vic,

Told MK about this under-the-sink cupboard bin thing they have where Pippa lives.

Me: You open the cupboard door and the bin lid lifts off and you can just toss rubbish in and shut the door again.
MK: (*seeming unimpressed*) Oh.
Me: It's really good.
MK: How is it better than the one we've got?
Me: Well, you don't have to touch the bin lid with your hand.
MK: I don't like those hidden bins.
Sam: Me neither, I like things out in the open.
AB: Very Brechtian.

So we'll carry on with the swing-top even though the swingy bit has disappeared (must've fallen in) and it's just a big hole. MK doesn't care about having all our peelings and fag ends on display.

On the subject of "au pair" Pippa. I think she might be leaving her job. Keeps hinting but not saying. I can tell she wants me to ask. No chance.

Love, Nina

∽

Dear Vic,

Ben came to visit me. Mary-Kay opened the door to him. Later she said, "Well, he looked a bit—you know."

I said, "A bit what?"

And she said, "You know."

So I said, "I suppose so."

She could have meant anything—you're guessing half the time.

Sam has finally told us what his anxiety is—it's that the queen might have an intruder at the palace. We said she'd already had one and he could stop worrying. He said he was worried she might have another—a copy-cat intruder. When we all laughed and he realized it wasn't a bad enough anxiety, he switched to being anxious about Shergar (will he ever be found?). He's always up on the news.

Mary-Kay has been to the USA. And you'll never guess what she brought back as a souvenir. A duvet cover. I couldn't believe it. To go all that way and get yourself a duvet cover. I said it was very nice. It was OK—stripy like a bloke's shirt, but nothing special considering. I said, "Did you get anything else?"

She said, "Yes, I stocked up on headache pills."

Also, while in the USA she tried a new kind of sandwich, an American sandwich—bacon, tomato, and lettuce (BLT).

Remember the woman that laughed at my ponytail? Well, she was here again last night. This time she laughed at the supper and said it was the first time she'd "appreciated the qualities of Heinz Ketchup." Then she asked who'd cooked it.

Horrible Woman: Who was responsible for the delicious supper (*looking at S&W*)?
Me: I was.
HW: Oh! I am sorry. I'd assumed it was one of the boys.

This morning I said something to MK.

Me: HW didn't think much of my turkey burgers.
MK: Well, it wasn't your best-ever supper.

That annoyed me — it was MK who bought the turkey mince in the first place (S&W are supposed to have gone low-cholesterol dietwise now since Stephen turns out to be high) and apparently turkey mince is helpfully low. Anyway, the horrible woman only came round because she wanted to tell MK about the fellow she's having an affair with — MK mostly calls men fellow or chap, sometimes bloke, but never guy (or man, come to think of it).

Me: She deserved those turkey burgers then, two-timing cow.
MK: No one's that bad.

Funny hearing about your old ladies and their baths. You should try washing Sam's hair. He hates it and gets more and more annoyed, and struggles as though you're trying to drown him and he shouts for Trevor Brooking (throughout the rinsing) plus you're having to be very careful not to get soap in his eyes.

Mary-Kay has started washing her hair over the kitchen sink (when she's in a hurry). I know because she keeps the shampoo in the cupboard above the sink by the sunflower oil. I'm hoping one day she'll pick up the wrong bottle.

Love, Nina

PS *Do Not* practice in Dad's car. It veers to the left. I drove down the M1(Leics to London) and my arms were killing me the day after, it's like you're on a permanent hairpin bend just keeping it in a straight line. I stopped at the services (Newport Pagnell) and a bloke advised me not to drive it any further.

∽

Dear Vic,

Last night Betsy and Karel Reisz came round. I cooked a chicken and Betsy brought a cake. At supper Betsy kept saying, "Beautiful, beautiful" (about the roast chicken).

MK: Aren't we due a break from mashed potatoes?
Betsy: No, Mary-Kay—it's all lovely, really beautiful. I love carrots done this way (*boiled in sugary water with cornflour added at the end, then sprinkled with fresh chopped parsley*).

Will had his carrots raw, but even he admitted the cooked ones looked good.

Betsy's pudding cake was very nice. Sam almost choked on a bit of tinfoil she'd accidentally left on it. But apart from that, it was really delicious (American style, homemade).

Karel and Betsy are proof that nice people don't have to be embarrassing. I was just thinking that (aren't they nice etc.) and I was feeling pleased with Betsy's appreciation of the supper (esp. after the turkey burger snub), when Betsy accidentally ruined it... well, her and MK.

Suddenly, Betsy said, "You know, Mary-Kay, you should have someone come in and clean, it'd really make a difference."

"Yeah, I know," said MK.

"I think Carmelita could come over, I'm sure she could use the extra cash, I'll ask her," said Betsy.

"Great," said MK.

The thing is, I think I'm supposed to do it (the cleaning). Well, a bit. I only *don't* do it because MK isn't bothered—if she had said something I'd have hoovered up or something (though to be honest I've never seen a hoover anywhere). MK never mentions the mess or seems to care. She washes up and tidies up etc. and the boys fill and empty the dishwasher. I just do the cat bowl.

Anyway, I think it's settled (about the cleaner starting). I feel that guilty/annoyed mix.

Love, Nina

‿つ

February

Dear Vic,

OK, I *know* Jonathan Miller isn't an opera singer. I told you a while ago, it was a misunderstanding. I knew he had something to do with opera (people were always saying, "Have you heard Jonathan's *Rigoletto?*" to each other) and he's got a very deep voice. I just put two and two together. Anyway, I know he's not. He's a doctor (a writer-doctor and opera-director).

Mary-Kay has started hanging around with a friend called Susannah. She's very nice.

S&W like her a lot. I suppose she seems really nice compared with me and MK because she's so nice-mannered and not sarcastic, and she's pretty.

But...she wears this startling eye makeup, even S&W have commented...thick black eyeliner—*under* the eye. The liquid type that only professionals can (or should) do. I was on the brink of saying something about it to MK (like it's a shame Susannah spoils her nice face with all that black on her eyes) but thought I'd better not—seeing as they're such good friends. Plus it would've sounded like I meant something else.

Then—fucking Ada—last night MK came downstairs ready to go out and was all done up the same! She looks even worse than Susannah. Susannah sort of pulls it off. Somehow it goes with the whole of her. But it's all wrong on MK. I wish I'd said something earlier. Too late now.

I was v. pleased to get a Valentine card—it said, "Baby I dig you." I don't know who sent it but it was posted in this area. So I know it wasn't you.

Also, I *sent* one to Tom Miller (JM's son) who's very nice and handsome. It was an ostrich (B&W photo—he's a photographer). He'll have no idea it was me.

Carmelita (cleaner) started today. She did nothing but clean for about three hours. She had one cup of tea, which she sipped as she worked. She won't chat (too busy). MK was really pleased when she got home and had a good look at all the clean areas and surfaces and sniffed the air (floor polish) and said, "Hey!" She could tell I was a bit annoyed.

MK: Isn't it nice?
Me: It's OK.
MK: Don't know what you're so mardy about (*with her black eyeliner on*).
Me: I feel guilty about the cleaning.

35

MK: Well, you don't need to. Yes, it would have been nice if, occasionally, you'd tidied up just a bit. But you do all the important stuff—you idiot. And you feed Lucas.

Me: You mean *Jack*.

MK: Yes, Jack.

So it's OK and I can just be glad that, once a week, it's going to smell of floor polish and the mouthpiece on the phone will have been wiped with a J cloth.

Love, Nina

∽

Dear Vic,

Noticed a skip in the crescent today, up the posh end. Will and me like skips and Sam was interested to see his first ever skip. So we went to have a look at it. It was quite a big one. I thought it would be funny to put Sam in it (the skip), so I did. We were all laughing and Sam's laugh was echoing around inside the skip.

Sam: There's a thing in here.

Me: What is it?

Sam: I don't know.

Him saying that made me think I'd better get him out, but it was difficult because when I tried to lift him out he seemed about ten times heavier than when I lifted him in. And it was deep, plus we were laughing a lot and that weakens you (as you know from the near drowning at St. Margaret's). Will was helpful and offered to get into the skip himself and help from the inside, but I wanted at least one of them *not* in the skip. But in the end, Will had to.

Will: Shall I get in?

Me: No.

Will: Shall I fetch Jonathan Miller? (*We were just along from his house.*)

Me: No!

Will: Bennett?

Me: No!

Will: Nunney?

Me: No, we've got to do this ourselves.

Will: So, shall I get in then?

Me: OK.

Anyway, Will got in and they both got out and I said not to tell Mary-Kay. Later AB said he'd seen us "messing about with Ursula Vaughan Williams' skip."

MK: Nicking stuff out of it?

AB: Chucking stuff in, from what I could see.

MK: Chucking what in?

Sam & me: Nothing.

Will: Rubbish from the street.

Good old Will, he always knows what to say, which is amazing when you think he's only nine.

AB wouldn't stop going on about the woman whose skip we'd been messing around in.

AB: She's the widow of Ralph Williams.

Me: Who?

AB: The composer.

Me: A composer called *Ralph*?

AB: Have you never heard of *The Lark Ascending* (*hums tune*)?

Sam: I know that one, it was on *Bugs Bunny*.

I'm doing lots of cooking too, and beginning to get the hang. The worst thing is knowing when a thing is going to be done. How do you know? A chicken seems to take forever. I know the "juices have to run clear" when you stab the leg, but they never do (run clear). So my chickens can be a bit dried out, but at least they're not going to kill anyone. The secret is to baste them with oil.

Love, Nina

⁓

Dear Vic,
Will is fed up with an overly strict teacher being a bit horrible. I suggested that whenever the teacher is being shouty, Will should imagine him naked on the toilet.

MK: Why does he have to be naked? Couldn't he just be on the toilet?
Me: Oh, yes. I meant just on the toilet.
MK: (*weary*).
Me: I didn't mean to say naked.
Will: (*head in hands*) Aargh!
MK: Now look what you've done.
Me: (*to Will*) Sorry, forget him being naked, just imagine him on the toilet, but fully clothed.
Sam: But with his trousers down.
Will: Too late, I can't get the picture out of my head.
MK: (*shaking head*).
Me: Is he the maths teacher?
MK: Just leave it.

AB is back and came over just for pudding because he'd had a late snack with Coral. Coral is a friend who AB likes a lot who seems to always be saying funny/clever things that make AB laugh. He says Coral's as sharp as a tack. And it's a bit "Coral said this" and "Coral said that" at the moment.

This Coral is an actress but I'd never heard of an actress called Coral, so it occurred to me that AB was just saying it funny and it was actually *Carol*—I thought it might be the actress Carol Drinkwater (TV wife of Christopher Timothy in *All Creatures Great and Small*) though I couldn't imagine her being "sharp as a tack."

Me: Is it Coral, or Carol?
AB: Coral, Coral.
Me: Like the color?
AB: Well...like the marine organism.
Me: It's nice.
Will: It sounds a bit sharp.
Me: Yes, like coral.
Sam: Yeah, the marine orgasm.
AB: Org-an-ism.

I wonder if AB will tell the funny/clever Coral about Sam calling Coral an orgasm.

Love, Nina

∽

Dear Vic,

Mondays are very busy now. I have to go and collect the cleaner (Carmelita—she lives with Karel and Betsy in Belsize Park). And Monday is always Jez's day for laundry (he only has lectures first thing), so he's always waiting on the doorstep with his laundry bundle when we get back.

Jez and Carmelita get along very well. Jez makes her laugh. He asks her if ours is the messiest house she's ever seen and whether she thinks a nanny might usually find time to clean up just a bit and stuff like that and Carmelita laughs. I've asked him to stop highlighting my failure to clean, but their friendship seems to be built around it. She loves him and pretty much never stops laughing when he's around, whereas when he's not, she's quite serious.

At supper tonight, extra people came round (Granny Wilmers, the Reiszs, the Lahrs and a lone woman called Caroline) and it was my new recipe for Florida coleslaw versus AB's watercress and orange salad.

I'd made my salad to go with the supper. AB just turned up with his, unasked.

His is just a bag of plain watercress, one chopped-up orange, with a bit of olive oil and some ground pepper. My coleslaw is:

Shredded cabbage
Grated carrot
Onion
1 tin of mandarins
4 large spoons salad cream
Chives

I think more of mine (salad) would have gone if the two salad dishes had been anonymous—everyone looks up to AB these days since all his success on telly, so they're not going to ignore his salad. Seeing such a lot of my Florida coleslaw left in the bowl, AB made one of his usual food pronouncements, "You'd be better off with mayonnaise or yoghurt, and perhaps not the tinned oranges."

My God, Vic, MK has started driving like Mrs. Lucas from Gwendolyn Junior. She stayed in second gear all the way along

Arlington Road and then changed into third for a maneuver (which, in case you don't know yet, is the wrong way round). Plus, she's right up against the steering wheel. Must be the new car (Saab). Hope so.

I said to her, "I think you have your seat too far forward." And she said, "I have to, otherwise my feet don't reach the pedals."

It can't be right. Are the Swedes a tall race?

Love, Nina

$\backsim$

Dear Vic,

You're not going to like this, but I'm telling you anyway.

It's about Lucas (aka Jack) the cat. At first, I thought I quite liked him, but began to get sick of his food/food bowl. Because the thing with cats (as opposed to dogs) is you don't have much to do with the actual cat, just the food and the bowl and the leftovers and assorted worries—he hasn't been fed/let in for his food/let out...he's got fleas/flu/dehydration. Plus, there's the thing about them prowling round killing baby birds. Plus, I have assumed much of the responsibility for him since insisting on a name change (from Lucas to Jack).

Saw a notice in the newsagent:

CAT WANTED
Adult cat wanted (neutered) by lonely elderly cat lover
(Mornington Crescent).
Have recently lost my old Tom.
Telephone xxx

Memorized it approximately, told Mary-Kay.

MK: So what are you waiting for?

Me: Shouldn't we discuss it with Sam and Will?

MK: And have someone else beat us to it?

Me: OK.

Rang the old cat lover and was about to take Lucas/Jack round to Mornington Crescent when Will came in.

Will: What's in the box?

Me: Lucas.

Will: Did he die?

Me: No, he's going to live somewhere else.

Will: Are you trying to tell me he died?

Me: No, he's alive, but someone else needs a cat more than we do.

Will: Have you had an offer for him?

Me: Yes.

Will came with me to the woman's house. She took to him (Lucas/Jack) straightaway and said he was handsome. She liked his "mittens." Will and I felt quite proud of him.

Woman: (*stroking Lucas/Jack*) What's his name?

Me: Jack.

Will: Lucas.

Woman: Jack Lucas?

Me: Yes, Jack Lucas.

Woman: Hmm, I'll call him Johnny.

Pause while the woman strokes Lucas and says, "Hello, Johnny."

Woman: (*to Will*) I've just lost my best friend.

Will: Was it a cat?

Woman: Yes, it was Johnny.

Will: I'm sorry.

Woman: (*proud*) He was eighteen.

Will: What's that in cat years?

Woman: Eighteen.

Will: Oh.

Woman: If he'd been a dog he'd have been a lot older.

Will: Oh, sorry.

Later:

AB: So Lucas has gone, then?

Sam: Lucas Bunt the big fat runt.

AB: Sam! That's not very nice.

Will: Yeah, Sam, don't speak ill of the departed.

Sam: Sorry.

Will: Anyway, he's called Johnny now.

Sam: *Johnny?*

Me: It *does* feel strange without him.

MK: Rubbish.

Sam: I don't want him to be in Mornington Crescent being called Johnny—I want us to get him back (*dramatic gesture, head in hands*).

AB: That's only natural—knowing someone else wants him changes your feelings toward a thing.

MK: Doesn't me.

Will: Hey, Sam, it's just like Buckaroo.

Sam: (*serious*) Oh God! Don't mention Buckaroo.

Me: Well, we warned you.

Sam: They play Buckaroo night and day round there now.

Me: Perhaps we could borrow it back.

Sam: Lucas or Buckaroo?

Love, Nina

Dear Vic,

No. I don't worry about Sam much. Mainly because MK does the worrying and keeps it to herself. It's no good two people worrying about the same thing unless they want to go on about it and we don't (unless there's a practical angle and there usually isn't). Have done a few experiments with different foods to see if they make a difference and they don't. Except porridge which is good in every way.

I think Will worries when we rush off to Great Ormond Street. Usually what happens is Sam gets a very (very) high temperature and seems extremely ill and we zoom off and when we get there Sam suddenly seems OK enough for the docs not to be worried and they say we can go home again. And we're there thinking, Bloody hell!

Last time we went to GOSH Sam had been (very, very) ill at home and then, when we got to GOSH, he seemed quite a bit better. I said to him, "Make sure you're still ill when the doctor comes." I know that sounds terrible, but it's how it is. You want the doctors to see it. He doesn't put it on and they need to see it. Then later, in the lift on the way up to the ward on a trolley after they'd admitted him, he suddenly sat up and seemed fine and I pushed him back down again, I was so frazzled. He keeps reminding me of that. He says I said, "No fucking way."

I do worry about his eyes though (my number one concern). Mr. Mackie (eye doc, Scottish) is brilliant. We go there whenever we're worried and always come away feeling reassured. Sam doesn't cheat his eye tape for a while afterward either. He's a bit mad though (Mr. Mackie) and says funny things. Last time he asked if we knew anyone called Marigold and we said no and he said it seemed such a nice name and wondered if it was still in use as a girl's name. And he said it a few times (Marigold) until we changed the subject.

Another time he advised us to always have our photograph taken in front of a flight of steps (or stairs) and focus just above the photographer's head, slightly to the right. To get the best-looking portrait.

Overall, with Sam, though, it's not like looking after someone ill. He just is ill occasionally and usually at night unfortunately.

Pippa's eyebrows have gone wrong. She's been plucking from the top, which you should never do—it ruins the natural line (apparently). The rule is: only pluck from underneath. If you pluck at all, which I don't.

Hope all's well with you. Sorry to hear about curling-tong burn, always a risk with hot instruments (and early morning usage).

Love, Nina

∽

Dear Vic,

My April Fool joke on S&W didn't go to plan. It was based on Elspeth's old "there's an elephant in the garden" but scaled down for a very small garden.

Me: Oh my God, there's a sheep in the garden.
Sam: (*looks out*) It's probably a cat.
Will: (*goes to French window*).
Me: There's a sheep in the garden.
Will: What are you on about? (*Pause. S&W go about their business.*)
Me: OK, it's an April Fool's joke.
Sam: So there *isn't* a sheep?
Me: No, it was an April Fool.
Will: It was rubbish.
Me: My mum used to say there was an elephant in the garden and we always fell for it.

Will: But you said sheep.

Me: It's a smaller garden.

Sam: An elephant would've been better than a sheep.

Will: An elephant would've been cool.

Me: But a sheep is more believable.

Will: You should've said elephant.

Sam: Yeah.

Said I'd do Bolognese (Sam likes it). Fried up some turkey mince and added a jar of Dolmio. Pippa always does it like that and it seems OK. (No AB, he's in Egypt or Yorkshire or somewhere miles away and no chance of turning up and criticizing the turkey Bolognese.)

At supper:

Sam: (*digging about in his food*) You said Bolognese.

Me: Yes.

Sam: (*inspecting*) Is this Bolognese?

Me: Of course.

Will: (*digging about*) Wait a minute, is it *turkey* Bolognese?

Me: Does it taste like turkey?

Sam: Yes.

Will: Yes.

MK: Is this what happens when Bennett's away?

Told S&W about how I like cold toast.

Me: I like it cold with butter and marmalade.

Will: Why?

Me: Makes me think I'm in a hotel.

Will: Or prison.

Sam: You don't have toast in prison.

Will: What do you have?
Sam: Porridge.

Love, Nina

∽

April / May 1983 (General Election soon)

Dear Vic,

It's the total opposite here—they all absolutely HATE her guts (they call her *Mrs.* Thatcher). When they see her on the telly someone will say, "Look, Mrs. Thatcher." In a disgusted-but-interested way.

MK and AB used to be Labour but they've gone over to the SDP. Sam and Will used to both be Labour, but now Sam's gone over to the SDP. Stephen is Labour (apparently) and hasn't gone over so far. Sam and Will are taking the General Election very seriously. They want to know how you lot are all going to vote. I've said you're all Ecology to keep it neutral.

Yesterday Sam asked if the SDP will win the election.

Me: It's unlikely.
Sam: (*worried*) I might switch back to Labour.
Will: You can't keep switching—I'm Labour, you're SDP now.
Sam: I want to switch back to Labour.
Will: You can't.
Sam: Yeah, I'm going to. I'm Labour again.
Will: You've got an SDP strip in your window.
Sam: I'll take it down.
Will: I'm ringing Mum. (*Will rings MK*) Sam, Mum wants to talk to you.

After the phone call:

Me: What did MK say?

Sam: She said I should stay true to my beliefs.

Will: Whatever the hell they are.

Me: What are your beliefs?

Sam: I believe in Paolo Rossi.

Love, Nina

PS Nunney's to and fro to Ickenham to do with the Labour Party. Knocking on doors, asking people about their intentions and trying to convince them over, if necessary.

⌇

Dear Vic,

Will's got a cold, so was at home groggy. This has been our day.

Will: What will I do when you go to do Sam's drops?

Me: You can either come with me or I'll ask Amanda to come and sit with you.

Will: How will you get there?

Me: Depends whether you come or not.

Will: If I come?

Me: Car.

Will: If just you go?

Me: Um, car.

Will: So, car then?

Me: I could walk, but that would take longer and Amanda might not have time.

Will: So car then?

Me: I could walk quickly—or we could both walk, it's such a nice day and might clear your head.

Will: I've lost interest. Just tell me when we're going...or not going.

At school gate:

Will: Can I come in?
Me: No, you're ill, wait here.

In the playground:

Sam: Is Will in the car?
Me: No, we walked, he's at the gate.
Sam: Can we go and see him?
Me: No, he's ill.
Sam: But he walked here.
Me: For a bit of fresh air.
Sam: Can't I just say hello to my own brother?
Me: No, he's ill, he doesn't want bothering.
Sam: Is he not seeing visitors?

Outside:

Will: Huh! Nice of Sam to totally ignore me.

At home:

Will: I feel better now—can I go and call for Robert?
Me: No, he's off school with a sore throat.
Will: I'm off too.
Me: But you're both supposed to be ill.
Will: I feel better.
Me: He might not.
Will: Why are you isolating me?
Me: Because otherwise I look irresponsible.
Will: You *are* irresponsible.

Me: I don't want to *look* irresponsible.

Love, Nina

∽

Dear Vic,
Mentioned to MK how much I hate the fishmonger.

Me: I don't like the fishmonger.
MK: How can you not like the fishmonger?
Me: I just don't.
MK: What's wrong with him?
Me: He's tricky to do business with.
MK: Like fish.

Discussing this further:

MK: It's not him, it's you.
Me: No, it's him.
MK: It's the way you approach.
Me: Like what?
MK: Barefoot for a start.

I don't agree. I think the fishmonger is deliberately difficult with anyone who doesn't know much about fish—i.e. me. He abuses his power.

Later, we were watching a film and some music came on the telly and we agreed we didn't like it.

Sam: I hate this music.
Will: Me too.

Sam: I hate it when music does that.

Will: What?

Sam: Comes on in a film and makes the film seem sad.

MK: I think it's meant to be happy.

Me: But it's that film-style happy that actually seems sad.

Sam: Yeah.

Me: I hate emotional music.

MK: More or less than you hate the fishmonger?

Love, Nina

∽

Dear Vic,

Had tea at the Lahrs' as usual yesterday. I don't know why it's always so nice. It just is. There's John Lahr and Anthea and their son Chris—a good friend of S&W and goes to Anna Sher (children's theater company) with them. Usually Karel and Betsy, plus an assortment of other people.

The tea itself is a mixed bag. The cake/cookies are nice (Betsy?) and the people are nice, probably due to being mostly American, although Anthea isn't (American) and is the nicest of all. But the tea (beverage) is always revolting, like tree-bark, and goes like dishwater if you put milk in. It's either that or orange squash or milk—in a beaker.

John always brings things up for discussion round the tea table. And everyone joins in with their view. Even me. He likes to know what everyone's been doing. He means what films or plays have they seen or, failing that, what telly or books. And then he likes to know what you thought of it (the play, film, book, whatever) and he really is interested in whether you thought the actor/actress was funny or not.

He wears a jacket (either tweedy, beige, cord, or checked), even inside. You never see him without one even on a warm day. Unless he takes it off, briefly, but then he's got it over his shoulder with his finger in the loop thing. Also, he's just written a book about the playwright Joe Orton who used to live on Saffron Lane in Leicester, near the Pork Pie library.

Anyway. They're nice and we like going there and they love MK and always say how clever and sweet she is. She'd die if she heard.

Ring me on Tuesday. Definitely going to Greece. I know it's a bit last minute, but would you want to come?

Discuss on phone on Tuesday.

Love, Nina

PS Anthea says I have the nicest feet she's ever seen and she marvels at my ability to not wear shoes. She thinks it's a wonder I don't stub my toe. I didn't tell her that I do (stub my toe). I just took the praise.

∽

Dear Vic,

It's a hard-water area, not bleachy tasting, but makes fluffy hair less so (good for me but bad for someone with coarse, thick hair). Some people have water filter jug things but they're a bit of a faff, to be honest. You have to keep topping them up and it's easy to forget. Also, if you pour quickly, the water comes out of the top (i.e. not filtered) so what's the point. Plus, if everything else in your house is all charming and junky, why would you want an ugly plastic jug? You wouldn't.

Been trying out a side ponytail. Quite short, but at the side (low). It's OK but can't decide if it's stylish or strange.

MK: What's happened?
Me: I'm trying a side pony.
MK: How's it going?

Me: Can't tell if it looks strange or stylish.
MK: It could be neither, or both.

Will played a good trick on Sam and me. The lights and telly went off.

Will: (*shining a torch around*) Shit, a power cut.
Me: Did you just turn the lecky off?
Will: What makes you think that?
Me: You went into the utility room *with a torch* just before the lecky went off.
Will: I had a premonition and went for a pee.

Sam and I went to 57. Saw a basket of clean washing all neatly folded with a pair of Nunney's boxer shorts on top (stripy, ironed). I threw them at Sam, Sam threw them back and they ended up out of the window (second floor). They were meant to drop down onto Nunney and Tom in the garden but they caught on a tree branch.

Then yesterday went to National Gallery with Nunney. He likes it there (the big scenes). After we'd looked at all the art, he tricked me into hanging off a high wall by the entrance steps and pulled my trousers down. Loads of people around. Me in Mickey Mouse pants.

Me: How could you do that in a public place?
N: I took no pleasure in it—simply a taste of your own medicine.
Me: I was vulnerable.
N: That's when to strike—as you know.

Hope you're well. Try to come down soon. Or I'll go there.

Love, Nina

May 1983

Dear Vic,

AB has started bringing a little can of beer round with him (lager).

Me: Why don't you bring a few cans over and leave them in the fridge?
MK: He can manage them one at a time.
AB: They *are* cold to carry.
MK: Wear gloves.

Will got new trainers. White with green. I liked the box.

Me: I'm going to keep this box.
MK: What's this keeping boxes thing?
Me: It's just one box.
MK: You kept one the other day.
Me: That was a bag.
MK: Boxes, bags—are you planning to run away?

Jez gave Sam a sexy pen. Press the top and the woman's bra disappears. We all like it and keep pressing the top to see the bra disappear.

MK: Don't take it to school.
Sam: Why not?
MK: Your teacher will confiscate it.
Sam: What do you mean?
MK: She'll take it from you.
Sam: She won't want it.

Mr. Mackie, Sam's eye doctor, has suggested I consider a nose job (he's got a friend who's a plastic surgeon in the same consulting suite and he'd be happy to make an introduction, he said). Mr. Mackie thinks I'd be very pretty if I sorted my nose out. Told Nunney. Nunney thinks it's unimpressive of Mr. Mackie to try and drum up business for his mate and that people shouldn't fuck about with what nature's dealt them—unless it's life-threatening.

Me and Jez back 14th/15th. I'm going to teach him to drive. Have already done dummy run in Saab, but he's not insured to switch ignition on unless we're off the public highway, which you can't be in NW1. They don't have driveways. Except AB, and his is occupied.

Love, Nina

∽

Dear Vic,

We're considering canceling the milkman and getting cartons with the main shop. AB is trying to put us off, saying we should support the milkman (at all costs), otherwise there might not be any milkmen. The milkman here wakes me up every morning earlier than necessary, clanking his bottles and revving his float. I wouldn't be that sad to see him go actually. But I know what AB means, they are a good thing, checking on old people. Noticing milk that's gone off on the step because someone's had a fall and not got it in, type thing.

MK hasn't had a milk bill since 1981 and if she ever bumps into the milkman on the step, she tells him and he says he'll look in the book. Still no bill comes. Maybe someone else is paying. Like someone else was feeding the cat.

We have those stubby little milk bottles too. I think they're everywhere now. The days of the long slim bottles are gone. Remember the ones with embossed writing on (Kirby & West)?

55

Maybe it's the stubby little bottles that are driving people to get cartons with the main shop? Are cartons any nicer than the not so nice bottles? No.

Sam accidentally tipped Tom out of his wheelchair going up a curb. He came home all dramatic.

Me: What's up?
Sam: It's really bad, Tomalin's wheelchair bumped into a moped and fell over and Tom fell out in the street and the moped went on its side.
Me: Oh dear, was Tom OK?
Sam: Yeah, I think so, he wasn't hurt.
Me: Poor Tom. Poor you.
Will: Poor moped.

Fifteen minutes later:

Sam: Shall we go and check on him?
Me: Tom?
Sam: Yeah, see if anyone's helped him up.
Me: What? He's still there?
Sam: Probably, maybe, I don't know.
Me: What, you left him there?
Sam: Yeah, I came to get you.
Me: But, Sam, you've had a peanut butter sandwich.

Tom was at home. He'd shouted, been helped up and wheeled himself home. He thought nothing of it (he was worried about Sam).

Love, Nina

⟡

Dear Vic,

Pippa brought new boyfriend round to show him off. S&W liked him because of what was written on his T-shirt. Will ran upstairs and put on *his* funny T-shirt (*Registered piss artist*) and the new boyfriend said he'd seen one like that before. Thoughtless.

Pippa seems keen. Can't see why. He seems pleased with himself and pushes his glasses up on his nose all the time with his hand. Unnecessarily. It's one of those habits that you don't realize you're doing but drives other people mad and can cause blackheads (all the nose touching). Then yesterday she told me that he has this thing. He has to masturbate every night or else can't get to sleep.

Me: God!
Pippa: Yeah, but to be fair, he does it himself.
Me: What, and do you, you know, at all?
Pippa: No, we don't.
Me: But you're boyfriend and girlfriend?
Pippa: The relationship is culture based, I don't even have to shave my legs.

Told Mary-Kay about him/it.

Me: He can't get to sleep unless he's ejaculated.
MK: Oh, *that!*

Love, Nina

PS Me and S&W have a new code. If we think someone's annoying we tap our fingertips on the table. It's so funny, esp. when MK's mates are round. They go on about this, that and the other and we tap our fingers and laugh. MK even said one time, "What's this finger tapping thing?" and we said, "Nothing," but laughed.

I told Helen about it which was a real shame and I regretted it because later she was talking to MK about Django Reinhardt (the Belgian guitarist with only seven fingers in total) and, though it started out interesting, it dragged on and on and I wanted to do the finger tap to S&W but Helen knew the code so I couldn't. Will managed a half-tap thing, which meant the same. But the rule is not to tell anyone about these things. Apart from you. Obviously.

~

Dear Vic,

Hope you got pc from Rhodes?

Helen had good knowledge of how to *be* abroad in that kind of place. For instance, you try to blend in and not wear short shorts but long shorts or a skirt and you don't smoke except with a coffee or Metaxa. She learned how to say certain phrases (in Greek) just in case, but never needed to use them. Except "Can we share one between us please?"

HH: You have to blend in when abroad.
Me: I did live in France for six months.
HH: But France is France and Greece is Greece and they're worlds apart.

Which is true.

Rhodes town is the oldest inhabited medieval town in Europe and altogether foreign. The writing, heat and smells, all very foreign. The modesty thing is confusing—on the one hand you can't really wear short shorts, but there are images of Priapus (Greek god with a huge erect penis) everywhere—key rings, pens, postcards, jewelry, bottle openers, statuettes, shoehorns.

A man told us that every new building in Greece now is left slightly incomplete, usually the roof and plumbing, because when a building's finished the owner pays some kind of tax. I wish the bloke hadn't told us that. Helen never stopped pointing out pipes and exposed workings and saying how the tax was ruining the skyline and how people should do something.

Helen put the vegetarianism on hold due to Greece being so limited in veggie choices. We had breakfast every morning at the widow's café (χήρα καφενείο) where the widow cooked floppy bacon and eggs with bread and honey (μέλι). I wished Helen knew how to say, "Please can you cook the bacon for a bit longer?" But she couldn't work it out and we decided to put up with it floppy.

The widow had some green herby stuff growing out of a Shell can, which turned out to be oregano, and two hens in an upside-down supermarket trolley called Elvis and Athena (both females).

Walked into the countryside—saw some goats eating watermelons with stained pink mouths. At nights Helen had lots of cocktails and got quite tipsy. One night she confided in me that she feels she let her parents down by not being a doctor.

HH: I feel I could have achieved more for them. I could have been a doctor.
Me: Are they doctors?
HH: No, but they're bilingual and love opera.
Me: Well, you speak Greek and you're vegetarian by choice.
HH: I suppose.

Then she went quiet and ate so many pistachios, her thumbnail was bruised the next day.

Anyway, it was all great. Hot sun, nice sea, arid countryside, history, sardines, and cheap sandals. And very foreign, which I loved.

Love, Nina

PS Have got you some worry beads. You fiddle with them when you're doing nothing and worrying. People fiddle with worry beads a lot in Greece. They find it soothing. It's instead of biting their nails.

∾

Summer 1983

Dear Vic,

They came home from France, MK and Will both brown as berries. Sam not brown but glad to be home and back to normal, needed a trim.

Pippa is harvesting carrots and beginner's veg in the garden with the kids she looks after. She's surprised we don't do any (kitchen gardening) here and keeps going on about it.

> Pippa: Blah and blah get such a thrill growing their own carrots.
> Me: That's nice.
> Pippa: Have you tried gardening with Sam and Will?
> Me: They're too busy. Will's writing a novel and Sam's an actor.
> Pippa: But they seem to watch a lot of TV.
> Me: For inspiration.
> Pippa: The snooker?

I was defensive and annoyed but I did also think to myself, "Why can't I work for a family like hers who enjoy growing carrots etc.?" It's all telly and books at 55 and no one wants to set foot outside unless it's to go somewhere. There's Pippa munching away on homegrown radishes and making little vegetable people and entering fetes and winning Nanny of the Year, while I watch the snooker and loiter in a car park with a ball, some delinquents and Tom Tomalin.

AB came over after supper tonight. Didn't want any leftover pie.

Too excited for some reason. Then left early. I thought he might've been dressed up. But his dressed up is the same as his not dressed up, so who knows?

Me: Was Bennett a bit dressed up?
MK: No, he's always like that.
Me: His collar looked crease-free.
MK: I never look below the chin.

Hope all's well with you. The R Patel thing is amazing, sad/happy (poignant, like a short story).

Love, Nina
PS Sorry to hear about the prang. The thing to say to yourself about prangs is, "It could've been a lot worse," which it always could (and sometimes is). And it's all part of the learning.

∽

Dear Vic,

Exciting this evening. AB came over with Russell Harty. And even though it was a strange time to be having a cup of tea, we had one. No one mentioned supper because it seemed too early, but we had chocolate digestives. Russell Harty was funny and told a joke but wouldn't take his coat off. His joke was about Shakespeare and an actor playing Ophelia (none of us understood it except MK and she smiled and tutted).

Then we all told him our jokes.

Will: Bald man/comb/I'll never part with it.
Sam: Two pilots/loop de loop.
MK: You have acute paranoia/I came here to be cured, not admired.

61

AB: Doctor, Doctor / we needed the eggs.

Me: I meant to say pass the salt / manipulative bitch, you've ruined my life.

Anyway Russell Harty was cleverer and thinner than he seems on telly and said "doodah" (meaning "thing") which we all liked. But wouldn't take his coat off—as previously mentioned.

Love, Nina

PS Marks & Spencer chocolate digestives. Very crunchy, but you can feel the grains of sugar.

～

Dear Vic,

Misty has shaved. She did it to surprise her boyfriend but he doesn't like the look of it. Says it's not how he expected(?). She's philosophical but says the itching (regrowth) is driving her mad. She's using a calming powder. And has advised us never to do it (shave). Says if she could turn the clock back she would (turn it back).

Discussing bathroom routines: Misty said she shaves her legs (the whole leg) every other day. Pippa doesn't bother with legs but is religious re armpits. I've not bothered with armpits since living in France where *not* shaving was the norm. Misty says I shouldn't be influenced too much by what I saw there, especially as I live in England where men hate hairy women and would prefer them totally bald (bar the head). I *am* influenced though, especially as the armpit is such a tricky area to tackle with a razor.

Thought of the time Misty had breakfast with Pippa. While everyone else was eating Rice Krispies, Pippa sat shaving her legs with a Bic, dry, there at the table. Misty said it put her off her breakfast.

Which reminds me: we're all envious of your outing to the

Weetabix factory, not that anyone of us is a big Weetabix eater, but MK likes outings and S&W like factories.

MK: Lucky them.
Will: What will they see?
MK: Weetabix.
AB: At various stages of the manufacture.
Will: Cool—it's like *Charlie and the Chocolate Factory.*
Me: They might win a lifetime supply of Weetabix.

MK asked me to get some Odor-Eaters for Will's trainers. I hate it when I have to get embarrassing stuff like that. I said Will should get his own Odor-Eaters but he says he hates going into Boots full stop and says he'll just put them on the window sill. I asked Will why he hates chemist shops. He couldn't quite put it into words. I guess it's the potential embarrassment. It would be that for me (seeing someone you know with a wee sample or a personal problem).

MK: Have you got the things for Will's stinky trainers?
Me: I've powdered them.
MK: Powdered them? What with?
Me: I bought some talc.
MK: If you bought talc, why not the trainer things?
Me: They're out of stock in Will's size.

Next day MK pulled a pack of enormous Odor-Eaters from her bag.

Me: They look too big.
MK: You cut them down to size.
Me: (*to MK*) Sounds like a job for you.

Enjoy the Weetabix factory outing.

Love, Nina

∽

Dear Vic,

Took two pillows in a bin liner to Parkway laundrette (extra-large load). Sam had done a bit of sick on them (not enough to ruin them but too much to ignore).

The laundrette woman said the filling might perish in the wash, but worth the risk to save them. They came out clean but clumpy. Laundrette woman said they might fluff up with a tumble dry. They did a bit, but not to their former fluffiness and shape. They weren't very nice anymore, but smelled nice (Daz). Anyway, somehow they ended up on Mary-Kay's bed. MK brought them down to show and discuss.

MK: What are these?
Me: Pillows.
MK: Yes, but why have I got them? Where are my usual ones?
Me: Sam's probably got your usual ones.
MK: So what are these?
Me: I think they might be the ones I laundered.
MK: Laundered?
Me: Took to the laundrette.
MK: Are they washable?
Me: Not as such, but it was kill or cure.
MK: It was kill.

If it's me shopping, I buy Daz for the smell and comfort (a tiny drop) but MK always gets Persil, which I dislike. It smells like overripe melons. Plus I'd prefer a washing line outside but it's not the done thing here. We have a Sheila Maid in the utility and a tumble dryer.

Pippa has a new hair thing.

Me: Have you been swimming?
Pippa: (*dripping wet hair*) No, why?
Me: Your hair's wet.
Pippa: No, I'm using a wet-look mousse.
Me: Why?
Pippa: My hair always looks best when wet.

Later:

Me: Pippa is using a wet-look mousse.
MK: What looks wet?
Me: Her hair, she thinks it looks nice wet.
MK: Can't she just wet it?

I'm going to say that exact thing to her if it crops up again.

Told MK about Pippa thinking you have to put one leg up on the toilet to insert a tampon (because the woman in the diagram does). MK said it seemed reasonable.

MK's been wearing a half-cardi/half-shawl thing. It's cozy-looking but aging.

Hope you and co. are all well.

Love, Nina

∽

Dear Vic,

Can't tell if Michael Neve is mentally ill or just unusual. On the one

65

hand he reads the LRB and is a doctor of something, on the other he turned up today in the middle of the morning and asked if he could play a record he'd just bought from the Record and Tape Exchange on Camden High Street.

(*MK's sitting room. Music blaring.*)
Neve: (*singing along with the record*) "Little Red Corvette, baby, you're much too fast"—it's excellent, isn't it?
Me: It's OK.
Neve: He's saying, "slow down baby" to this chick—they're about to fuck in the car.
Me: Right.
Neve: Does your friend like it (*meaning Carmelita, on the stairs with a brush*)?
Me: That's Carmelita, the cleaner.
Neve: Yes, I know, does she like Prince?
Me: How should I know?
Neve: "Little Red Corvette, baby, you're much too fast" (*singing & dancing*).
Me: Do you want a cup of tea?
Neve: "Little Red Corvette, baby, I shoulda known, Little Red Corvette"—no tea, darling, I've got to go to work.
Me: OK.
Neve: I just wanted to share this fucking genius song with you (*puts record on again*).

Afterward, I wanted to let Carmelita know that Neve is MK's friend, not mine. Carmelita lives with Karel and Betsy and I don't want a bad reputation with them. They like me. They even said I was "a good thing." Plus they're friends of the Lahrs who think I have nice feet.

Me: That was Michael.

Carmelita: Yes.

Me: He's a friend of Mary-Kay's.

(*Carmelita nods.*)

Me: He's not *my* friend; he's Mary-Kay's.

Then Jez turned up.

Me: Oh, here's Jez.

Carmelita: For washing machine.

Me: Yes.

Carmelita: Your brother.

Me: And very good friend of Mary-Kay's as well.

(*Carmelita smiles.*)

Love, Nina

PS The LRB—not just about books, but a brainy take on world events etc. You have to be a PhD to get it, or at least a professional intellectual.

∽

Dear Vic,

At the weekend there was talk of one of us driving Will over to see a school friend in Barnsbury in Islington. This boy says he's got a spider the size of a satsuma. It's in a giant ice cube in the freezer.

Will wanted to see the spider but doesn't like the boy that much and neither me nor MK could be bothered to drive to Barnsbury just for the spider viewing. Except that I was curious about the place (Barnsbury), thinking it might be some huge house (it isn't, it's a posh part of Islington with narrow pavements and no parking).

AB thought it was just a ploy to get people round his house. MK agreed, but thought it "quite commendable."

Apparently putting things in ice cubes is a good way of making fake things appear real. So it was possible/likely that the giant spider is a plastic one like the one Will has looked at and considered buying in Harvey Johns (toy shop). Told Will this and he agreed it might not be worth going to Barnsbury. Later he rang the boy in Barnsbury and asked outright if the spider was plastic. The boy admitted it straightaway and even said he'd bought it from Harvey Johns. Will was very satisfied. We all were.

Didn't go to Barnsbury. Went to Harvey Johns.

Pippa has got a new friend called Vie. Not Vi as in Violet, but pronounced Vee as in the French for "life." So she's got Mel the beautician and now this Vie the actress.

She's doing a version of *Swan Lake* (Vie is) where they chuck water at each other and the swan breaks someone's arm on a canal bank (a bringing it bang-up-to-date thing). Audience participation. Pippa says if you don't wear a shower cap you might get a soaking. I reminded her that her hair is wet already via the wet-look mousse. She explained that wet-look hair is actually bone-dry to the touch. It just *looks* wet, so when she goes to see the *Swan Lake* thing, she (of all people) will have to wear a shower cap. Real wet on wet-*look* equals frizz (i.e. dry) like a double negative.

Love, Nina

PS The hair mousse is called Wet-Lookz. She used to use Studio-Line but it gave her crispy curls.

⌒

Dear Vic,

Do you like the typewriter? MK has given it to me (lent). It's crap—you should see it. I like having it but the thing is, using it, I can't think. Like now, I'm trying to write to you but can't get going on a letter. Short on news.

Yours sincerely,
Nina Stibbe

$\sim$

Dear Vic,

Yes, the typewriter is a bit of a disaster. The secret is to learn to type without having to look at the keys, then you can just type as you think, not keep thinking where's the T, etc.

To be honest, I'm trying to write a novel. Have just read an excellent one and think I could easily write one (semi-autobiographical). Was just about to show AB a little synopsis and a few pages when Amanda (nanny up the street) asked me if I'd ask AB if he'd watch her do a bit of acting and give her some tips. She's trying to get into drama school and has been turned down once already and wants to get it right this time. She's very passionate about it (getting into drama school).

AB agreed to watch her (he said, "Don't know why she's asking me, I'm hopeless"). But he likes Amanda and wanted to help so he came over and they did it in the kitchen. I had to be there too (unfortunately). She performed a bit from a play where a young woman strays into the servants' area and sees the butler's muddy boots and has a sexual awakening and rejects her father. Something along those lines (Swedish).

I couldn't help laughing a bit.

Amanda: It's not meant to be a comedy.
Me: It's nerves.
AB: Come on, Nina, be fair.

Then she did another scene from a different play. During her lines she fiddled with a flower for added drama.

Amanda: I'm going to pull the petals off this flower to show I'm in turmoil.
AB: Right-o!

She was a woman on drugs whose son confronts her and calls her a "dope fiend." I was reading the son's lines and I had to say, "You're a dope fiend," and then she has to go off on a rant. It was strange having Amanda in the kitchen ripping the flower and shouting at me in an American accent and AB sipping his chamomile tea.

Because it was a Tuesday, MK came home early and she stood on the stairs for a moment, listening. I could see her feet. I called her to come down.

MK: What's going on?
Me: Amanda is acting for AB.
MK: Why?
Me: She wants tips for her audition.
MK: Oh, I see. Here's one, stop shredding that flower.
Amanda: It's a prop.
MK: It's not working.

I've no idea how good Amanda was at the acting, but AB was encouraging anyway, and said he'd write a reference for drama school (saying what an asset she'd be with her enthusiasm and ideas). She's going to the audition soon. So we'll see. She's decided to ditch the flower.

Once all the fuss has died down, I'll show AB ch. 1 of my novel.

Talking of dope fiends...Mary-Kay has asked me if I can give her "a bit of grass." She meant cannabis. I was shocked and said it wasn't my thing. God, Vic, I don't want *her* turning into a dope fiend, things are going well for her, with the LRB and everything. I hope she doesn't go down that road—imagine her and AB puffing away on a bong every night.

It might be the influence of X (the crab man). I think he might be a bit druggy.

Love, Nina

⌒

Dear Vic,

Still working on my semiautobiographical novel. Not as easy as I thought. The problem is all the explaining you have to do. Your story gets overwhelmed with detail. Stupidly told Pippa that I was trying to write a novel and now she always asks, "How's the novel going?" with an expression of boredom on her face. And sometimes says, "What's it about?" or "Am I in it?"

Pippa: I'll *never* write a novel or play.
Me: Most people won't.
Pippa: No, but I won't on principle.
Me: Why?
Pippa: Because of what happened to my friend Tony.
Me: What happened to him?
Pippa: He wrote an amazing TV series and sent it to the BBC and they sent a letter back saying thanks, but no thanks.
Me: You have to learn to accept rejection.
Pippa: Yeah, but then, a couple of years later, the very thing he sent in came on the telly.
Me: What was it?
Pippa: *Taxi.*

71

I didn't ask who Tony was. Couldn't be bothered.

You have to have a very clear idea of the end before you start and then work toward that end. Discussing it with Will (who is always working on a novel):

Will: I just write and see what occurs.
Me: You should have a plan.
Will: My plan is to see what occurs.
Me: But a reader will look for clues and signals.
Will: I am the reader.

Love, Nina

⌒

Dear Vic,

Both Mary-Kay and Nunney believe there's no such thing as an accident when bad things happen (accidentally) to me, i.e. my toothbrush slipping and cutting my gum. Told Nunney (I'd cut my gum by accident) and he said, "No such thing as an accident." Meaning I injured my own gum deliberately. Presumably so I could tell him and get some attention and sympathy.

Told MK.

Me: Nunney says there's no such thing as an accident.
MK: I'm aware of that idea.
Me: Do you think there's no such thing as an accident?
MK: Sort of.

But the next day, it's a 100% accident when she throws her car keys in the bin and we're digging through bits of saucy kitchen roll, fag ends and potato peelings (and teaspoons as it turned out).

Someone drew something on our wall with a penknife or stick. MK thought it was a heart. I went and looked and saw a penis (scratched into the brick).

Me: I think it's meant to be a man's penis.
MK: I thought it might be a heart.
Me: How?
MK: An upside down one.
AB: Like mine.
(*Will goes out to look.*)
Me: People don't usually draw hearts on walls.
MK: I might.
Sam: I'd never draw a heart or...the other thing.
Will: (*returns*) It's definitely a dick.
MK: It looks more like a heart.
AB: You'd think they'd label it.

(AB phones later to say he saw it on the way out. It's a penis.)
Earlier this week. A boy in UCS uniform flicked the Vs at me while I was waiting to pick Will up from school. I flicked them back.

Will: What did the boy look like?
Me: Your height, dark hair.
Will: Blue rucksack?
Me: Yes, crossing near the pasta shop.
Will: I think it was me. Dammit.
Me: Why dammit?
Will: He sounded cool.

Amanda has another drama-school audition looming. This time she's doing a modern piece about a female serial killer. She rehearsed at the table with our Kitchen Devil. It was the most gruesome thing I've ever seen (but a monologue, thank God). Mary-Kay came home and caught the tail end—piling body parts (lemons) into a sack (M&S bag).

Me: Another audition.
MK: I see.
Amanda: (*waving knife about*) I'm a serial killer cutting up a body.
MK: (*to me*) You could find her the Millers' saw.

At Primrose Hill Pippa surpassed herself showing-off-wise. She did a whole gym routine starting with a one-handed cartwheel and ended with a back bend and kick over. It was based on an Olga Korbut routine including the cheeky facial expressions that used to please the judges. No one was interested except in a horrified way. On the plus side, her beret fell off and we all saw the clips.

Love, Nina

∽

Dear Vic,
    Day out in Brighton. Boring overall.
    The best bit was when we went into an antique shop and Misty picked up a pickle fork with a pretty green jewel on the end.
    "How much is this pickle fork?" she asked the antique man.
    The man said it wasn't a pickle fork but a runcible spoon.

Misty: What's a runcible spoon?
Man: One of them in your hand.
Misty: But what's it for?
Man: Pickles and such.

It was only one pound fifty, and even though Misty likes spoons and liked the little jewel, she couldn't buy it, not knowing what a runcible spoon was. Then, on the way out, an old woman in the alleyway offered to tell our fortunes. I declined. Partly because she looked so horrible and partly because I had my palm read last week by Sam. It went something like this:

Sam: (*studying wrong side of my hand*) I see you're going to have a baby.
Me: When?
Sam: About 1988.
Me: That's too soon.
Sam: 1989, then.
Me: Too soon.
Sam: Bloody Nora, 1990, then.
Me: Still too soon.
Sam: All right, 1995, but it's twins.

Anyway, as we walked away from the antique shop, the old woman shouted after us, "You didn't want the spoon, then?" I said she must have been looking in through the window, but Misty wanted to be frightened (that's how boring the day was).

Anyway, Brighton is quite nice. Arriving at railway station is good. It's downhill into town and you feel energetic, striding down to the sea front—as opposed to an uphill walk at the start of a place. But then, before you get anywhere charming, you're surrounded by W H Smith and Boots and people wanting a haircut and you might as well be in Loughborough.

Beach disappointing and the whole place pleased with itself for no real reason.

I won't mention my Brighton thoughts to Nunney. Sussex University is in his top three for university next year.

Love, Nina

Dear Vic,

Sam had this thing at the Tomalins' made by a friend of the family who goes round a lot and makes corner shop puddings. It's basically a load of Maryland cookies all sandwiched together with some kind of cream or ice cream or dream topping. She also does hot chocolate that you drink through a Wispa bar.

Funny about the giraffe thing. Similar here. A while back Sam took part in a class assembly (Romans) which "went wrong" because they all mixed up their lines and the teacher felt "a bit let down."

This week:

Me: (*to Sam*) How was school?
Sam: It was OK but someone said "Rome."
Me: Rome?
Sam: Yes, and it all came back to me.
Me: What did?
Sam: (*quietly*) The assembly.
Will: (*to Sam*) You're not raking that up again, are you?

Later:

MK: What's up with Sam?
Me: He had a flashback to the Roman assembly.
MK: Oh dear.
AB: The Ides of March.

Pippa came round with a window box, nice (with a heart cut out). Her boyfriend made it at woodwork night class. I have to admit it's nice. She's going to paint it (green) because she hates wood.

Me: How can you hate wood?

Pippa: I don't hate wood, I just hate the grain.

Will: The grain *is* the wood.

Pippa: The Scandinavians respect wood.

(*Will, puzzled, looks at me. Taps side of his head.*)

Will: What have Scandinavians got to do with it?

Pippa: I'm just saying they like wood.

Will: Why?

Pippa: Do I have to have a reason for stating a fact?

Will: No, but it's helpful in a conversation.

She doesn't like the grain but owns a shirt with a wood-grain pattern. Didn't mention it. Don't want her to think I notice her clothes.

Love, Nina

∽

Dear Vic,

Had smoked salmon with bread and butter (and lemon and pepper) at supper followed by my veg soup. The salmon was too nice to have anything after, esp. veg soup. Should have done it the other way around. Mary-Kay made the good point that starters always seem nicer due to you being hungry, but even allowing for that, the soup was like a lot of mushed-up overcooked veg—which it was.

AB disagreed with MK and said starters *are* always nicer. He sometimes orders two starters (instead of a main course) in a café, partly to get the nicest things and partly not to get overstuffed.

I'd done a fruit pie for pudding (blackberry and apple) using a tin of Morton's pie-filler. I admitted it was out of a tin but didn't say it was blackberry and apple. AB likes real blackberries but they make him nostalgic about blackberrying in the lanes. So, to avoid a whole lot of disappointment (and his blackberrying anecdotes), I said the pie was apple and raspberry. Pie fillers all being pinkish-purplish, could be any flavor—they are what you think they are, basically. Apart from apricot, which is bright orange and could only really be apricot (or carrot).

Anyway AB said it wasn't bad for a tinned pie-filler, but said it tasted more like blackberry. Which I thought was quite impressive (AB for detecting blackberry and the pie-filler for tasting of blackberry).

AB did his chicken curry and rice round here the other day (he had a load of cooked chicken to get rid of). I have to admit, it was very nice and only used one pan.

Cooked chicken (chopped up)
Single cream
Curry powder
Grapes—cut in half (or raisins if you don't have grapes)

That's it. Heat it up. No herbs (only what's in the curry powder, if any). It's similar to Dad's Chicken Muck-up, only easier. He got it out of a magazine.

I gave a couple of pages of my semiautobiographical novel to AB.

Me: Did you read my thing?
AB: Yes, it was funny.
MK: What's it about?
AB: I'm not sure.
Me: Are you being discreet?
AB: No, I just can't quite describe it.
Me: So you *didn't* read it?
AB: I did. I'm not sure what it's about. A bunch of literary types doing laundry and making salad—or something.
Me: I think I've given you a letter to my sister by mistake.

I was joking, but "many a true word spoken in jest" because, when he gave it back to me, it did seem very similar to one of my letters to you. Anyway, AB thought it was funny and that's the main thing.

Thanks for sending Moussaka recipe. Will try out, but with turkey mince.

Love, Nina

∽

Dear Vic,

Nunney thinks I should go to university. And I agree and MK agrees. It's a funny thing because I was pretty much told that I'd never be allowed to go to university because of leaving school too soon and that only people who slog it out till they're eighteen are allowed. Nunney says, one, I'm too bright not to go and, two, the universities are desperate for anyone these days. So, I have decided to study for an A level (English Lit) so I can. Have enrolled with C— College to sit exam next June. I have to study all on my own.

I didn't have a clue how it all worked. Thank God Nunney has just done his (A levels and applications). In fact, he's done his A levels twice because of not doing quite well enough the first time to go to the university of his choice (which is *not* Oxford or Cambridge by the way).

Nunney: So have you got all the books on the syllabus?
Me: The what?

I.e. I didn't even know what a syllabus was. It's just a list of books that you have to study but they call it a syllabus rather than book list.

Nunney is going to read the books (on the syllabus) at the same time as me so we can discuss (study). When he looked down the list of books (syllabus) he said, "You're on your own with *Seamus Heaney—Selected Poems.*" He said that because he's not a huge fan of poetry, but I think he'll read them anyway—I hope so. We'll cross that bridge when we come to it. We're starting on *Return of the Native* by Thomas Hardy (of *Far from the Madding Crowd* fame).

Have told S&W all about my plans. Will laughed when I said my ambition was to be a proper student. He just thinks of *The Young Ones.*

Hope you are well. I hope Miss H is recovering on the Ripple bed.

Love, Nina

⌒

Dear Vic,

Mary-Kay's good friend from university has just come back to the UK from South Africa (Mary Hope). She's very nice (in a good way). She smokes, even when eating sometimes. Not that she continually takes puffs, or takes long puffs, she just lights up a lot. It's a habit from the 70s.

Her fingers are like sausages at the moment (temporarily) because they're swollen for some reason, possibly an allergy. She loved being in South Africa except they couldn't get SR toothpaste and of course they abhorred the situation.

I mind Mary's daughter Polly sometimes while Mary sorts out their new house and her life. She's buying a house just behind us on Regent's Park Terrace. Mary Hope often says she's pleased that the three children (S, W & Polly) get along so well. The thing is—they don't. I get along with Polly (very grown-up and funny), but she finds S&W tedious.

Mary will arrive to collect Polly and ask, "Have you had a super time?" and I'll say, "Yes, they've all had a great time." And Polly will say under her breath, "Except William's a complete idiot." And

Will'll say, "Yeah, and she's so boring." And Mary will say, "Marvelous, sounds like you've had a super day."

Good about you giving up fags.

MK's trying to cut down. She used to smoke Camels or some brand like that. Then went on to Silk Cut Extra Mild. And tried just holding it and pretending to take puffs. Anyway, now Mary Hope is back, MK's lost her will-power and now smokes as much as ever (about 5–6 per day). I smoke about 5 per day (Silk Cut ordinary). Nunney smokes Camels in the soft pack or Marlboro Lights. He can blow a ring inside a ring. Did 3 the other night.

We have all agreed—we must try not to blow smoke near Sam, it's bad for his eyes etc.

Hope this letter doesn't drive you back to the ashtray.

Love, Nina

∽

Summer 1984

Dear Vic,

I won't mention cigarettes this time.

Mary Hope has given Mary-Kay a box of sugar lumps. They weren't very expensive (you could see the price).

MK: (*admiring pretty box*) Ooh, thank you.
Mary H: I thought it was pretty.
MK: It is, very.

MK and I and everyone else all agree it's one of the nicest things we've ever seen, especially considering the price. For a start the box is lovely with a little green and yellow parrot and the sugar lumps are brown and all lumpy and rough. I've started taking sugar again just to have a lump.

MK had a European soup called Gazpacho at a friend's dinner party. It's a chilled (i.e. freezing cold) soup made of peppers and tomatoes, garlic and olive oil. MK said it was nice, but a bit too cold.

It's a thing you can only have in the summertime. One, because it's chilled and, two, because you need seasonal tomatoes. But it's very simple and easy to make (in the whizzer). I decided to make some using a recipe that came from the wife of the Spanish Ambassador (via Pippa), so bona fide. I couldn't believe the amount of olive oil you were supposed to put in, so I only put half the amount and it came out a bit thick.

Nunney tried a spoonful.

Nunney: Ugh, that's horrible.
Me: That's the Spanish Ambassador's Gazpacho.
Nunney: It's liquidized salad.

Other cold soups include lettuce, beetroot, cucumber. All the salad things basically. But you should only have them in summer. I'd rather soup was warm, to be honest. You don't expect a soup to be freezing cold, it's a mind-set thing.

Had to go to Chamberlaine's to get a puncture-repair kit. MK's bike has a persistent flat and I want to ride it to Parliament Hill Fields to go in the Lido with the nannies. No one at 55 is any good at bicycle maintenance, but AB is brilliant and just as long as you give him prior warning, he'll get the bike upside down in the hall before supper. He seems to like it.

In Chamberlaine's the bloke asked if I needed any help. I said I was going to get a friend to fix the tire. The bloke was very nice and said he'd show me how to do it, then I'd be independent for the rest of my life (puncturewise). I thought about it for a moment but decided I'd rather AB did it. I told the bloke at Chamberlaine's I might pop back later for the lesson. But didn't.

Later on AB came round and fixed the tire.

AB: (*checking the inner tube*) There's nothing wrong with the inner tube.
Me: So is it the tire itself?
AB: No, it's just that someone's let it down.

Then at supper we all tried to guess who (if anyone) might have let MK's tires down.

Sam: Arthur Scargill.
AB: He wouldn't.
MK: There's only one person I can think of.
Me: Who?
MK: You!
Me: Me?
Sam: Yeah, Stibbe.
Me: Why would I?
Will: For a laugh.
Me: Hang on, it was me who went to Chamberlaine's to get a puncture-repair kit and booked Bennett to come and repair it and delayed the stir-fry while he Swarfega'd his oily hands and so on and so on.
AB: The remedying of chaos, a classic psychopathic trait.

Anyway, it's fixed and we're all happy and Mary Hope popped in just in time to see us all admiring the sugar lumps again.

Love, Nina
PS I might get you a box of the nice sugar lumps. Lovely box.

Dear Vic,

Sam is much better, thank God. Last week he couldn't even listen to the cricket (had to keep 100% calm) and had both eyes taped. Poor Sam, it was horrible.

Jez came over and read him a few chapters of Enid Blyton (he calls her *Enoch* Blyton) while his washing went through. I had to read the same chapters all over again after he'd gone because he changed the story. ("I can't allow you to go to Kirrin Island today, you see children there's bad news I'm afraid, Timmy has passed away, he fell into the hands of smugglers and they spoke in their rough common voices to him and he simply died of shock" — and so on.)

I tried reading him a bit of Thomas Hardy (killing two birds).

Me: Shall I read you a bit of the thing I'm reading?
Sam: What's it called?
Me: *Return of the Native.*
Sam: Is it by Enid Blyton?
Me: Yes.
Sam: All right, then.

It didn't work because neither of us knew what was going on and reading it aloud only made it worse.

Sam: What's happening?
Me: I think they're doing a play.
Sam: Who is?
Me: I don't know.
Sam: Can we go back to the Barney Mysteries?

Sam loves having visits from Neve, Nunney or Jez. But best of all

Karel Reisz, who just arrives and things are immediately better for everyone and he doesn't even want a cup of tea.

This afternoon Karel came over and asked Sam what his news was. To my annoyance, Sam told Karel about the turkey burgers (how they all hated them). It's annoying because MK keeps buying turkey mince and what the fuck else can I do with it? I told Karel that it wasn't me (it was MK) buying the stuff. I don't want him thinking I go round buying things they hate and forcing them to eat turkey burgers against their will. Karel said it sounded as though I was doing a great job (with the mince, and in general). And he meant it.

Later I mentioned it to MK.

Me: Can you stop getting the turkey mince?
MK: What's wrong with it?
Me: I can't make anything nice with it.
MK: It's versatile—simply use it in place of beef.
Me: You've memorized the pack.
MK: Yes, giving advice on use.

Anyway, green tagliatelle and Edam cheese tonight. AB disappointed. He was expecting a stir-fry (with turkey).

Went to British Museum with Nunney. The best thing is the building itself. Some significant things in there (mummies, genuine Roman statues etc.) and some insignificant things that are just very, very old. i.e. Egyptian toothpick. The displays are a bit overwhelming and not actually as interesting as MK's kitchen dresser.

Re chewing gum: Try Wrigley's Juicy Fruit (yellow pack). Keeps flavor more and doesn't interfere with other things. But beware, it makes you feel hungry (due to stomach expecting something) and you might turn to biscuits.

Love, Nina

PS Chaucer. Have you ever read it? Fuck. It's a whole other language and meant to be hilarious, but it's grim and annoying.

∽

Dear Vic,

Everyone keeps saying how great yoga is and that we should all go and learn to relax and let go of things that are thwarting us in life (i.e. turkey mince) and breathe properly and stretch and so on.

I haven't been overly keen up to now.

Me: Do you ever do yoga?
MK: No, but I hear it's very good.
Me: So why don't you go?
MK: I expect I shall at some point.
Me: Me too.

Pippa says she has changed beyond all recognition relaxation and stresswise since she started yoga classes. She said she drove to yoga in Haringey and afterward couldn't drive home—too relaxed—and had to sit in the car and listen to *The Archers*. Now every time she hears the *Archers* theme tune, she returns to that deep-relaxed state. Like Sam hearing the word "Rome," only the opposite.

I'll think about going (to yoga). But I'm not sure I want to be that relaxed. I am who I am and I might not do so well as a relaxed person.

Drove Sam's friend Ras home. Took him to the door and saw a paper note Sellotaped to the stained-glass porch door: "This beautiful stained-glass is very old & fragile, please close doors gently."

Both Sam and me admitted that the note made us want to slam the door very hard. Sam said he felt horrible for thinking that. I didn't. I think it's normal to think like that and that's why I'd never write a note like that. You're asking for trouble. Like when people write "Handle with care," what do they think people are going to do? Handle with care?

Talking of notes: have you noticed I've started writing in green pen? Apparently it's more authoritative than blue, but in a nicer way than black. MK writes in different colors. I used to think her notes in red were mardy, but they just seemed that way due to being in red. Which just goes to show the power of the color. Will writes in capitals a lot and it seems as though he's shouting. Although Sam writes big and seems like he's shouting too.

I notice that people often write my name without a capital at the start. It shows because of capital N being so strong compared with little n. I sometimes worry about what that might mean.

Hope all's well with you.

Love, Nina

⌒

Dear Vic,

Decided to try the yoga after all. Partly because Nunney thinks it would be good for me and partly because of wanting to slam the Whittakers' antique stained-glass porch doors. Which I even dreamt about doing.

Me: I dreamt about slamming that glass door in the Whittakers' porch.
Sam: Oh God!

Yoga was OK except the woman running it made it as embarrassing as possible—flamingo pools and greeting the sun etc.—but the worst bit was at the end when we had to wind down (on the floor) with harp music (apparently the harp being played by the breeze, not by a human hand). The yoga woman said, "Feel every part of your body, one part at a time, tense...and relax," and then she listed all the body parts. Tense...and relax. "Tense...and relax your toes...your ankles...your calves...(blah blah)."

And then she said "your genitals," which I thought was unnecessary (though inevitable given the rest of the hour).

I wasn't planning to bring up the yoga at supper (knowing where it would lead), but MK had remembered I'd gone and was very interested to hear all about it (you never know what's going to interest her) and of course I said about the tensing and relaxing of body parts.

Me: Then she said "your genitals."
MK: Well, I suppose if she'd mentioned everything else...
Me: She could've just said "every part of your body" and left it at that.
MK: Yes, but once she'd started the list...
Me: I would've skipped over it.
AB: Then it would've been an elephant in the room.
Will: What would?

To move us along from the genitals, AB said he'd seen some impressive sheepdog trials on a footpath walk through the dales and Sam said "Come by" a few times at funny points. Then we had a debate about bath towels. They come out of the dryer all fluffy and soft, but are less absorbent than if they dry on the rack thing and end up hardish. MK and Will like them soft, but Sam and me like the less fluffy result.

Me: The fluffy ones don't do the job as well as the hard ones.
MK: What job?
Me: Drying.
MK: Their job is to be fluffy.

Me: No, their job is to quickly absorb water.
MK: The yoga hasn't helped, then.

Love, Nina
PS I still think they should have a washing line outside.

∽

Dear Vic,

Still reading *Return of the Native* by Thomas Hardy. It's long and it's not like reading *The Thorn Birds* where you just rattle through and no one's going to ask you any awkward questions. Reading like this (for A level) you have to read thoroughly and get right into the world of the story you're reading.

Nunney keeps saying stuff like, "When Hardy tells us Eustacia has raven hair and she comes from Budmouth, he's telling us that she is a sensual woman and sexually active." Funny to think that without knowing the literary code you might miss those important messages. And funny to think what you might be saying without meaning to (if you wrote a book). Explaining this to Will made me think he might be some help later (studyingwise).

Me: You have to understand the world that the story exists in.
Will: You mean the context.
Me: Sort of.
Will: No, it is the context.
Me: Have you heard of Seamus Heaney?

Love, Nina
PS Nunney's time is up volunteering at the Tomalins.' I think he's sad but not showing it.

Dear Vic,

Nunney's time volunteering at the Tomalins' is up. He's grown to like them, especially Tom. The new helper (Nunney's replacement) arrived at 57 yesterday.

Me: What's he like?
Nunney: He won't be here long.
Me: Why?
N: He's on drugs.

It rang true. We'd seen him earlier being shown the ropes. Shirt unbuttoned to the waist, chunky belt. Yawning and disinterested. Like a grotty Jim Morrison.

Anyway, this morning, he's *gone*. Nunney had to drive him home late last night.

MK: So Nunney drove him out of town?
Me: Yep.
MK: What was so bad about him, apart from the chunky belt?
Me: He was a druggie.
MK: Ooh—a druggie.
Me: So Nunney'll be at 57 for a bit longer.
MK: Yippee!

Went to play cricket/football in Regent's Park. S&W joined in an already-going game and Will scored a goal after about five seconds. Sam came off the pitch mardy.

Me: What's up?
Sam: Will *had* to score, didn't he?

Me: Be pleased for him.

Sam: He's such a show-off.

Me: Well, you go and score, then you can show off.

Sam went back on the pitch and straightaway the ball deflected off his leg and went in.

Walking home, reliving their goals:

Will: Look at that cloud in the shape of the World Cup.

Sam: You're always showing off, Will.

Me: He's just looking at the sky.

Sam: Anyone can do that.

All the way home Sam looked for a better cloud than Will's. When we got home, he'd trodden in dog shit.

Sam and me went to 57 and (to celebrate Nunney staying on) put some little plastic soldiers into the salad Claire had prepared for supper (lamb's lettuce). Was amazed to see a pie, also prepared by Claire for supper, had the cooking instructions piped onto the top *in mashed potato* (gas mark 4 for 30 mins). Imagine being such a good and thoughtful cook that you can do that. I might have a go on my next shepherd's pie. Only problem being that the cooking instructions would be to myself. Still, it would impress S&W and MK.

Nunney came round after supper.

N: Thanks for the soldiers in the salad.

Me: It was our way of saying we're glad you're staying.

N: Well, thanks.

Love, Nina

PS Nunney being next door-but-one is better than him not being...syllabuswise and every other thing-wise.

Dear Vic,

Will's started saying "son of a bitch." Now Sam's picked it up. Will loves swear words and picks up imaginative stuff from school. Sam's always a bit behind.

Sam: What does sonofabitch actually mean?
Will: Son of a bitch.
Sam: Is it bad?
MK: Bad to be one, or to say it?
Sam: Either.
Will: Both.
MK: Well, better to say it than be one, I guess.
Sam: What actually is one?
Will: A total bastard.
AB: But, Sam, it's not a very nice thing to say.
Sam: Who asked you, you sonofabitch?

MK has asked if I would like to go to Switzerland with them for New Year. I said yes.

Me: Will I like it?
MK: I can't promise it'll be the most fun you've ever had.
Me: Why?
MK: You should never promise things like that.
Me: Will I like it though?
MK: I expect it'll be OK.
Me: What will I do?
MK: What you always do—only in Switzerland.

We'll have to take the train because Sam doesn't fly due to an oxygen thing. So a long journey (good for the syllabus).

Went for an early Christmas gathering at Pippa's. She had Xmas, music going (pop and classical) and her friend Mel (trainee-beautician) doing mini facials and manicures etc. on a trestle table (bargain prices). Pippa herself didn't have a treatment.

Pippa: Are you going to have a manicure?
Me: I don't think so.
Pippa: Me neither—it's all just a substitute for sex.

I was going to have an oatmeal facial until she said that.

Mel, the trainee beauty therapist, has one black tooth (2nd incisor) and kept having fag breaks.

Which reminds me. A nut broke my tooth (a walnut, not a person). Had to go to Mr. Jivanjee of Parkway for a filling. Thank-you letters and cards stuck on the walls of the surgery. One read:

Dear Mr. Jivanjee. Just wanted to thank you for your kindness regarding my phobia during my recent root-canal treatment. Many thanks. Mrs. P Smith.

PS If you found a Hush Puppy, brown, size 7 in the surgery, it belongs to me.

Love, Nina

⁓

Dear Vic,

Got a box of chocolates from Nunney for Xmas. Bright blue box with gold writing. I was really pleased with them. I liked the box and thought I could put something in it after the chocolates are gone, something important and to be saved. Will liked it too, being a big fan of boxes of chocolates. Sam thought a video would have been preferable.

Later on, at 57, I noticed the same type of box of chocolates sitting on their round table and it came out that Nunney had got the same (but smaller) for the Tomalins' lodger, Susan (pretty, clever, booky, from Budmouth?). Turns out they're quite pally.

This completely ruined my box of chocolates and I felt dejected. One small consolation being that hers was a lot smaller than mine. Told MK the whole thing and how I was feeling (which I wouldn't normally do in quite so much detail).

MK: "Dejected"—what does that mean?
Me: Annoyed.
MK: Why?
Me: Well, he's bought the same for her at 57, but smaller.
MK: (*shocked*) For *Claire*?
Me: No, for Susan the lodger.
MK: Oh well, your box was bigger—he likes you more.

Then a thought occurred: maybe Nunney's going to ask Susan the lodger to read *Seamus Heaney—Selected Poems* with me (she's the type). Thing is, I quite liked Susan before Nunney bought her the same chocolates. But now I don't so much and even feel a bit angry (with *her*). Mostly, I'm annoyed to have been maneuvered into this pathetic position.

1. I don't like chocolates that much, particularly not ones in boxes.
2. I don't care who anyone buys chocolates for and people can just do what they want.
3. BUT, if someone buys me chocolates as an affectionate thing, then they shouldn't fucking buy the same for someone else.
4. Or they shouldn't let me find out.

I might have to go mardy about it in order to avoid the offer of literary help from someone I now dislike.

Said to Will he could have my box of chocolates, but he said not to drag him into it and just took the truffles.

Everyone's raving about AB's *Englishman Abroad* about the spy. To be honest, I didn't think much to it. On the other hand, Nunney has given S&W a video of *Fawlty Towers*—which is fantastic.

I asked AB to write a get well soon for GM. He did. He wrote: "Nina tells me you're a bit poorly at the moment. I hope you'll soon be feeling better. Alan Bennett." Plus a little caricature of himself. Look out for it on her mantelpiece.

It turns out that Mary Hope (sausage fingers) is allergic to the metal in her knitting needles. They did a series of tests on her (pricking with common allergens). It's amazing what you *could* be allergic to. GM says she's allergic to her hoover handle and has to put a plastic bag over it.

You could have allergies you don't even know about (yet).

Love, Nina

⌒

Jan 1984

Dear Vic,

Happy New Year. Re Switzerland:

Granny Wilmers' helper in Switzerland is a relative of Alec Douglas-Home (not Cardinal Hume, as said in postcard). But we weren't supposed to go on about it. I wouldn't have gone on about it anyway because I'd never heard of him (even now I have, I wouldn't).

Granny W's helper was quite nice, except when I had to trim Sam's hair (getting in his eyes) she stood right by us and criticized my method. Not that she's a hairdresser; she's just an ordinary posh person who's been taught to share her opinions with all and sundry.

Helper: You should snip at the fringe in an upwards motion (*finger snips to demonstrate*).
Me: I always snip in a sideways motion and it comes out fine.
H: You'll get a curtain-effect if you do that.
Me: We like that effect.
H: Does Sam have any say in it?
Me: (*to Sam*) Are you happy with the usual, or would you like *a whole new style?*
Sam: (*alarmed*) Trevor Brooking.

Then at supper MK asked what had happened to Sam's hair—meaning it didn't look very good. The helper didn't hear, thank God. She was in conversation with Beverley about how to make the perfect crouton (very hot fat, stale bread, even-sized cubes).

Me: (*quietly to MK*) Don't slag off Sam's hair in front of the helper.
MK: Why?
Me: She criticized my technique.
MK: Well (*gesturing with her hand to Sam—who looked like one of the Midwich Cuckoos*)...
Me: I know, but don't say anything else. I'll deal with it when we get home.
MK: Why not just let her sort it out now?
Me: NO!

Granny W couldn't stand it that I wore a T-shirt (and no sweater). She kept thinking I must be cold and said that it made her feel cold seeing me looking so cold (with bare arms and feet). So she gave me a sweater. Nice color, but not really me (ruff neck). I decided to wear it to be polite and grateful, knowing I'd never ever wear it again. I was very hot in it but kept it on and boiled.

MK and Will went skiing every day (all day), then spoke about it at supper. MK's skis were called Hot Head with a flame emblem. I had a go. It was MUCH harder than I expected. I slid into a car park (fast). You need to focus. Apart from the skiing and the hot sweater, had a great time (winter wonderland etc., famous people, cows).

Thanks for lovely things. Hope you liked yours.

Love, Nina

PS New Year's resolutions. Mine: to interrupt people speaking less. Sam's: to learn to do shoelaces. Will's: to write a novel. MK's: to interrupt more.

∽

Dear Vic,

MK Wilmers. She's kept her maiden name. S&W Frears.

Sam does NOT like being called Sammy. Some people do call him Sammy but it pisses him off. "Sammy" offenders include:

His friends' mothers
Anna Sher (she started it when he was smaller and didn't mind)
Woman in dry cleaner (as above)
Mrs. Boyce (just assumes anyone small called Sam likes to be called Sammy)
Claire Tomalin (sometimes, but happy to be corrected)
Susannah Clapp (being nice, putting a Y on)
Frances the physio (same as Mrs. Boyce)

I'm going to call mine Jack and/or Eve. I like Sam, but obviously couldn't have that now and quite like Frenchy-sounding names only they can seem sexual/pretentious.

Will's middle name is Emanuel (QED). Sam's middle name is Newton, from Isaac Newton.

Me: Why Newton?
MK: Isaac Newton.
Me: Why not Isaac, then?
MK: You use surnames when naming after someone.
Me: I was named after a midwife's first name.
MK: You were named after an acquaintance.
Sam: Was Isaac Newton an acquaintance?
MK: Not of mine.
Me: I was going to be called Belinda till the midwife turned up.
MK: *Belinda*—crikey!

Finally finished *Return of the Native* by Thomas Hardy.

Hope all well at the Pines. Tell me about Sister S and Conan the Barbarian.

Love, Nina

∽

Dear Vic,

Will told us that his English teacher asked the class if they knew any English idioms. Will's friend C put his hand up.

Teacher: Yes?
C: My brother.

Teacher: Carry on, "My brother..."
C: My brother...is an English idiot?

That got us talking about idioms and phrases and so on.

Sam: Every cloud has a silver outline.
Will: Lining.
Sam: Oh yes, beg your pardon.
Will: Anyway, I don't believe every cloud has a silver lining.
MK: Why?
Will: They don't.
MK: But philosophically?
Will: No, some things are 100 percent total shit.

I kept quiet during all this because I've never got the hang of idioms, proverbs, phrases, adverbs, etc.

Then we were saying how some people are friendly and some grumpy and horrible. S&W and me saying some people just are grumpy by nature, MK saying most people are OK.

MK: People are only horrible if they're hungry or unhappy.
Will: That could be anyone.
MK: Yes.
Will: Everyone.
MK: Yes.
Will: At any time.
MK: Yes.
Sam: They just need a banana.
MK: Exactly.

Love, Nina

Dear Vic,

Syllabus news: Me and Nunney have moved on to *A Winter's Tale*, a comedy by W. Shakespeare. It's ridiculous and more annoying than *The Return of the Native* by Thomas Hardy. A bloke imagines his wife has been unfaithful with his friend so he banishes her and she apparently dies. He soon realizes he made a mistake and is miserable for sixteen years—till the wife comes back to life.

Saw Nunney on a bench near the top of Primrose Hill all wrapped up in a big coat reading a book. I was pleased to see him until I saw he wasn't reading *A Winter's Tale* by William Shakespeare—as per the syllabus—but a book called *One Hundred Years of Solitude*.

Me: (*shocked*) That's not on the syllabus.
Nunney: No, I know. Susan recommended it—it's very good.
Me: So are you not going to bother with *A Winter's Tale*, then?
N: Of course I'm going to bother, but I'm reading other things too.
Me: Fine.

Leaving the park (mardy) I saw Pippa. She's looking after a dog called Charles. Pippa told me about an incontrovertible law that states this type of dog (King Charles Spaniel) is allowed the freedom of the land and can go wherever they want, even if no (other) dogs are allowed. I remarked that Amanda's family have the same type of dog only a bit older and she has never mentioned this special spaniel law. Pippa said it's up to the individual owner/handler to assert their rights (or not).

Pippa: So no one can ask me to remove Charles from this park.
Me: But dogs *are* allowed on Primrose Hill.

Pippa: Yes, but even if they weren't, Charles *would* be.

Me: But they *are*.

Pippa: I know.

Me: Sounds like you want to take him where no dogs are allowed.

Pippa: Yeah, but where?

Told Mary-Kay about Pippa being keen to assert Charles the spaniel's right to go wherever he wants. MK said it was understandable. MK's very understanding of unreasonable behavior but quick to judge other types. MK told us about a bloke she knew who would leave his wallet around in cafés hoping someone would try to nick it so he could defend it. She was understanding about that too, saying sometimes people just want something to happen and that's not always easy these days.

Carol from C— College has written a supportive letter: "Dear A Level Student (Eng Lit)." The letter suggests that remote A level students read some poems by Thomas Hardy (to help us "understand the man behind the pen" with a view to understanding the novel on the syllabus). And says that much reading beyond the set texts (syllabus) is supportive of a student's learning of the texts.

I was a bit annoyed to read this. I thought it was just the syllabus, now it turns out we've got to read lots of other stuff connected with the five different authors as well. Fuck. I'm not going to get anything else done in life.

Got some of Hardy's poems out of Holborn library as per the letter. Most of them are rubbish and do not help me understand him. They make me think of him as wallowing and moaning and wishing for the olden days and that he hadn't been such a cunt to his wife.

Which I already knew from the introduction to *The Return of the Native*.

I did like one bit from a poem about miserable weather (his favorite topic after the olden days): "the sky frowns whitely in eye-trying flaps."

Hardy means the sky was white and hurt your eyes even though it wasn't very bright. The idea is loaded with symbolism. We are so used to gloom, even a white sky tries our eyes.

Also while I was there (library), borrowed a recording of a bloke reading Chaucer in the Old English. Nearly wet myself listening.

Ring me to make a plan.

Love, Nina
PS Beginning to hate Hardy's pea-shaped head.

Dear Vic,

Still little clusters of stuff around from Xmas. You wouldn't believe what people gave them—you'd think they didn't even know them.

One lot:

Sam: xylophone (multicolored)
Will: xylophone (silver)
MK: mini candelabra (red candles, small)

Another lot:

Sam: lunchbox with Yummy written on
Will: lunchbox with Grub written on
MK: Amaryllis bulb, pot, bag of soil (instructions)

Another lot:

Sam: book on cricket by a famous cricketer
Will: My first book of gardening
MK: decorative bell & jar of olive paste

MK was also given a camellia by a bloke (with roots). Fake-looking pink flowers. Half expected the other shrubs to attack it for being blousy.

MK: How's the camellia doing?
Me: Unhappy.
MK: What causes unhappiness in a camellia?
Me: Fluctuations.
MK: In?
Me: Temperature, light.
MK: Fuck, we're supposed to stop the sun from going down.

Love, Nina

‿

Dear Vic,

Having a break from Shakespeare. Reading *One Hundred Years of Solitude* by G. García Márquez. I wish it was on the syllabus, it's marvelous. You'd love it, I'm sure.

When I've finished, I'll go on to *Romeo and Juliet*—I know the basic plot already. Will reminded me—it's like *West Side Story*. Not that Will knows *West Side Story* as such, but MK does, and has mentioned in passing that *West Side Story* is based (loosely) on *R&J*.

Daren't say (to MK or Nunney) how much I don't like Shakespeare. Don't find it funny or exciting. It might have been funny etc. years ago, before modern comedies, but now it's weak and *A Winter's Tale* doesn't even seem like a comedy. The poor little son dies of a broken heart and the baby daughter is left in the woods to die and the wife spends sixteen years as a statue. Also, another bloke gets killed by a bear and it's all because of this king being jealous. Maybe Shakespeare is saying that jealousy is bad, but it's not very funny.

It's like Chaucer. People always going on about how rude and funny it is because someone farts.

Sam is rehearsing for his school play. School doesn't usually encourage him to take part (which makes MK furious) but this term Sam's fought his corner and got a speaking part. We're all very excited and proud.

He has to shout, "Boudicca, Boudicca, Queen of the Iceni," a few times rhythmically and run with a spear.

We're disagreeing over the pronunciation.

Will says it's Bo-a-da-see-er. And I agree.

Sam insists it's Boo-dicca (because that's how Miss Whatnot says it).

AB says there's always been debate on the subject.

MK says Sam must know, and gives Will, me and AB a shut-up look.

Have taken photos of Sam in his costume. Will send when developed.

Pippa has given S&W some sunflower seeds (to plant, so that they could grow sunflowers). Now she keeps asking how they're doing. Have decided to say that we planted them, they grew a bit, then they got eaten by slugs. Just to shut her up.

Glad holiday was good. Josie H. sounds like a marvel. Write a longer letter telling me everything.

Love, Nina

Dear Vic,

Have applied to two polytechnics in London. Thames Polytechnic and North London Polytechnic.

Also, Mary-Kay asked one of her mates—at the University College (UCL)—to interview me.

I went to see Professor Ettrick yesterday. I won't be going to University College! I couldn't understand what he was saying. Either he was using words I don't know, or mumbling. Plus he had a foreign accent. I wanted to say something outstanding to make up for my lack of education, but it turned out to be impossible. He was wearing a fez.

One of the polytechnics will be fine anyway. UCL was aiming a bit high, bearing everything in mind. But it's where Jez goes, so that would have been funny. Though he's in science and I'd have been in English.

Nunney and I are going great with the syllabus (still on *Romeo & Juliet*). Nunney enjoys the punning and humor in *R&J* and keeps saying how clever it is (in context) and now he's reading *The Elizabethan World Picture* by E. M. W. Tillyard, because it gives a picture of the Elizabethan world so that you can really get what Shakespeare was saying.

I might not bother with it.

Love, Nina

∽

Dear Vic,

Some new people have moved into the crescent and put lace curtains up at the windows (where there used to be Venetian blinds). A kind of half-curtain. They're the talk of the Crescent. Everyone keeps saying, "What about those curtains!"

Mary Hope says they're Jardiniere—very popular in Portugal—

she knows about fabrics (worldwide). They're not curtains as such, more of a window dressing. More like underwear than curtains.

Even Claire Tomalin, who usually wouldn't bother mentioning things like that, said, "What bizarre curtains!" Jez thinks they're very "Mike Leigh." Neve thinks they're outrageous. Will says they're poncy. Mary-Kay says it's up to them what they have at the windows but thinks they're a bit pointless. I hate them. Sam thinks we're all being horrible.

Went to Delancey for breakfast with Mary-Kay and S&W and AB. AB and MK and Will were lingering and Sam and I got bored and left before them. Sam waved at the window as we went past. MK did this funny wave (whole hand up salute).

Later, I asked her about it. "What was that wave you did in Delancey?"

"Oh, yes, I thought it was rather good—it's a new one, I got it from Betsy."

I told her we prefer the elbow on the table finger wiggle.

Me: I find the whole waving thing embarrassing.
MK: But surely waving is less embarrassing than *not* waving, if someone's waved at you.
Me: That's with hindsight.
Sam: You could nod.
Will: Nodding's risky—it has meanings.
Me: God, what meanings?
Will: Funny stuff.
Me: How do you know?
Will: My friend has an uncle who nods for "it."
Me: Whose uncle is this?
Sam: I bet it's the one with the Ink Spot swimming pool, it's always him.

Nunney has told me it's rude of me to not say goodbye at the end of my phone calls (with him). I don't know if it is.

I told him it's unnecessary and implied. Sound like MK.

Love, Nina

∽

Dear Vic,

Will got 89% for a science test (The Water Cycle—an annotated illustration).

Will: My picture was OK, but I dropped a percent for drawing a smiley face on my sun.
Me: What's wrong with a smiley face on the sun?
Will: It's not scientific.
Sam: What's a water cycle?
Me: An underwater bike.
MK: Don't tell him that.
Sam: It's not scientific.

Amanda phoned to see if S&W wanted to go round and watch the film *Ring of Bright Water* at the Evans's house. Sam's not keen on that kind of film (sad ending). He likes comedy/action. Will likes all types of film (except romance), but not keen on the Evans's little dog.

Sam: Will I like film?
Me: Yes, but it's a bit sad.
Sam: Does someone die?
Me: Not exactly.
Sam: An animal?
Me: Well, yes.

Sam: A dog?

Me: No.

Sam: A cat?

Me: No.

Sam: A gerbil?

Me: No, it begins with O.

Sam: Ostrich?

Me: No.

Sam: Give in.

Me: An otter.

Sam: Notter begins with N.

Claustrophobic in their telly room with curtains drawn and the dog and the feeling of not being able to move about. So we came home.

MK: What happened to the movie?

Sam: The otter died at the end.

MK: That was quick.

Sam: Nina told us the ending.

MK: (*to me*) Remind me not to go to the movies with you.

Later, at bedtime. Will has read *My Side of the Mountain* and thinks it's great. I offered to read it to Sam.

Sam: Is it any good?

Me: I think so—Will liked it.

Sam: What happens?

Me: This ten-year-old boy is fed up with urban life in New York and goes to live in a hollowed-out tree in the Catskill Mountains.

Sam: Then what?

Me: He just lives there with his pet wild bird, eating berries and making tea.

Sam: Then what?

Me: Well, I'll read it to you, and you'll hear.

Sam: I want it over and done with tonight if possible.

Love, Nina

∽

Dear Vic,

Granny (Wilmers) came over. She came down into the kitchen very slowly, holding the banister (low high-heels/suspicious of wooden steps). Sam impatient at the bottom of stairs, tapping and tutting, said, "Come *on*," under his breath.

Sam gave her a brief hug when she arrived at the bottom step and went back to the snooker. Will hugged her and lifted her up (little feet dangling off the floor like in a cartoon).

I laughed. Will laughed. MK smiled. Granny shrieked.

"Ooo, Villiom, put me down!" (c. Russian).

Sam: What's so funny?

Me: Will lifted Granny up.

Sam: Why's that funny?

Me: It's funny when people lift people up.

Granny W: Perhaps it's funny . . . *once*.

Sam says he's decided to take up the violin (again) and MK had to write a note to the school's music teacher.

MK: What am I to say in this note?

Sam: Just that it's OK.

MK: What's OK?

Sam: Me doing the violin.

109

MK: Well, why wouldn't it be?

Sam: If you didn't want to pay the fees.

MK: Oh, what's the violin teacher's name?

Sam: Mr. Violin.

MK: Mr. *Violin?* Are you kidding?

Sam: Not violin, *Niolin,* Mr. Niolin (*tutting*).

MK: What—it rhymes?

Will: Just write Dear Sir.

Found out later his name is Mr. Nyman.

Love, Nina

PS Window cleaner is out of prison. Came and did the windows. Later, MK and me discussed whether we should get window locks.

∽

Dear Vic,

Will wanted to know the difference between Priceless and Worthless.

MK: Worthless—has no worth. Priceless—has no price.

AB: (*reading from dictionary*) Worthless—without practical value or merit. Priceless—of inestimable worth, beyond value.

Then AB started reading the dictionary and calling out odd words. Then Will got it off him and he started reading out odd words and laughing. It seemed annoying, but then I had a go and could see the appeal. I love the dictionary now—you should try it (if you're bored).

Sam was invited to supper at the Tomalins'—his first ever (official, evening) meal there. Told him that Claire had rung to ask him to bring a potato with him. Will and me thought it was hilarious when Sam set off with a potato in one hand and his football cards in the other.

Later:

Me: What did Claire say about the potato?
Sam: She thinks you're confused.

One of MK's friends brought a load of plums round in a Fine Fare bag, thinking—wrongly—we'd like to make some jam.

Me: Are you going to make the jam?
MK: I thought you might.
Me: I've never made jam.
MK: There's a first time for everything.
Me: I'm not inclined.
MK: Perhaps you could send Sam round to 57 (the Tomalins') with them.

Her way of telling me she knows about the potato trick on Sam.

Thanks for the roast beef recipe. Not sure if I'm up to it (meat in one piece like that).

Keep up the good work with Mr. T.

Love, Nina

⌇

Dear Vic,

Will and me reading *Diary of Adrian Mole*.

Inspired to write our own diaries. AB says everyone should (write a diary) but not to bother with issues, i.e. the news, just the day-to-day stuff (that's what will interest you in years to come).

Helen came to stay, so had to go to Camden Market. A busker playing the didgeridoo drowned out poor blind man who always sings "You Fill Up My Senses" quietly in a less good spot (acoustically).

Helen bought a second-hand eggcup in the shape of a hen and a sachet of MSG from the herb man. She's hankering after strong flavors now she's turned to vegetarianism.

Me: Look what Helen got.

MK: Not sure MSG is good for you.

HH: I find food very bland—I've become a veggie again.

MK: Why?

HH: Health reasons.

MK: I'm not sure MSG is good for you.

HH: I know, but it adds flavor.

The roast beef was OK. Fifteen mins wasn't enough and had to put it back in. V. bloody. MK said I should have had the oven hotter. It was OK. Will quite liked it. Sam put it straight into his meat hiding place and Helen had a bean-burger she'd brought with her in tinfoil.

Thank God AB wasn't around to witness. It turns out that his dad is/was a butcher in Leeds, hence him (AB) being a bit of a know-it-all cookingwise.

Mary Hope has *The Delia Smith Cooking Guide* and likes the no-nonsense approach. They're all going mad for the pâté (kipper?).

From Granny (Stibbe) I got six dishes (Susie Cooper), pretty but shallow. And a set of egg coddlers.

Made some coddled eggs with S&W. Will liked the procedure (season before cooking and the twisty tops) but I can't see what's so good about them. How are they any better than ordinary boiled eggs? Designed for wimps (scared of shell).

Love, Nina

Dear Vic,

Weave-perm at Flickers on Camden Road (Jade's solution to wispy hair). It turned out badly. Had it cut very short straightaway the same day—different hairdresser shop—so as not to offend Jade. Jade's real name—Sally.

Nunney says I look like David O'Leary (Arsenal) in my new hair (short, a bit bouffant).

Me: Nunney says I look like David O'Leary.
Will: Yeah.
Sam: Why d'you want to look like him?
Me: I don't *want* to.
MK: She didn't go to Flickers and ask for a David O'Leary.

Photo in the kitchen of MK with a feather cut in 1978. She looks much better with the feather cut (than with the bowl cut). Plus a bowl cut is hard to maintain, i.e. you need two hands to style it, which you don't have if you're holding a hair dryer, which you are when styling.

Sam's osteopath thinks swimming could help his posture. We made a plan to go to Swiss Cottage pool.

Sam: I don't want to go swimming.
Me: It'll be good for you.
Sam: Can you go swimming if you have a cut finger?
Me: No, but you haven't.
Sam: But could you?
Me: Depends how bad.

Swim day, yesterday. Guess what—Sam cut his finger.

Sam: I didn't do it on purpose.

Me: Tell that to the police.

Sam: Don't ring the police.

Me: Dialing...

On the plus side, he couldn't practice violin with the plaster on his finger. He's playing the violin quite a lot at the moment. It sounds horrible and it makes the rest of us sick to hear it. But MK won't let us say anything negative because he's having a go and that's the main thing.

Love, Nina

⌒

Dear Vic,

A man came to reupholster a little chair (that no one sits in) opposite the sofa. It was all worn out with gray fluff bursting out. The upholsterer was a true craftsman and held curved needles in his mouth etc.

He put a note in his windscreen ("Working at 55") but kept going to the window to check for wardens. He asked me to watch out for wardens too. I said I would do my best but I couldn't commit 100%. The wardens are very quick and ruthless in London, especially round here.

The chair reupholsterer ate his packed lunch in his van. Two hard-boiled eggs. I saw him cracking the shells on the dashboard. No drink. Later, I told him about egg coddlers (him an egg lover). Not interested.

Chair looks nice now. Greeny-blue fabric with tiny red teardrop shapes. Still no one sits in it though. Wrong position and low. It's a small Queen Anne, the upholsterer said, "a smashing chair." He also said the dining chairs were a mix of Hitchcocks and Sheratons.

Weekend at Mary Hope's house in the Cotswolds. It's lovely. The house is yellow stone with big windows. The garden is lovely and there's a tree (cherry?) on the lawn that has one long branch that's a perfect shade for a table. Mary has propped it up with a post. The villages around are all antique shops and tea rooms.

The journey was eventful. First we almost missed our train from Paddington because I forgot it was Paddington and thought it was St. Pancras (Paddington is further away tubewise).

Will saw a field of cows from train window.

Will: (*worried*) Oh God, a field full of dead cows.
Me: They're not dead.
Will: They look dead, their heads are down.
Me: They're just resting.
Will: I thought they only did that in barns or if they had a baby.

Then I almost left Sam's machine on the train at Didcot Parkway. No, I DID leave Sam's machine on the train and the train guard came running off with it. Luckily the train had arrived early, so wasn't rushing off again.

The train guard wanted a lot of acknowledgment for his action and when I didn't thank him enough (I thanked him twice, very enthusiastically) he said to S&W, "Make sure you help your mum," and Will said, "She's the nanny," and the guard said, "Well, you can tell your mum all about your adventures," and Will said, "The nanny doesn't like us to tell our mum stuff like that." The guard was less jolly after that. He reboarded the train and gave me a dirty look.

Mary Hope did sorrel soup again (a bit sour tasting, but you'd probably get used to it if you had it enough). Polly made South African doughnuts (nice). There's a swimming pool in the garden that no one ever seems to want to go in. And when I mentioned going for a swim they looked at me as if I was being silly.

Caught S&W watching a video called *Best Bit of Crumpet out of Denmark.*

Love, Nina

༄

Dear Vic,

One of the weirdos in the street keeps telling everyone she's going to sue the council for pruning her shrubs without permission. Previously a bushy screen, now a few brutal twigs (her words). Council pruners mistook the property for one of theirs due to the front garden containing a mattress, two tires and other people's dustbins. And they pruned the shrubs.

A writer called Deborah Moggach lives on that side of the street. I can see her tapping away writing her novels. I took a batch of Elspeth's poems for DM to assess. To be honest, I thought the poems were very good, poetic and clever, and that DM wouldn't mind the distraction, seeing as she's there all day tapping away.

DM was very happy to look at them and said they showed talent and said that Elspeth should keep writing and that she might send a batch to a certain poetry magazine. DM thinks everyone should write (if they want to) and sometimes being noticed is more about luck than anything else. When I told Elspeth all this she seemed pleased, but not as pleased as I thought she would be. Later, she admitted she was drunk when she wrote her poems and that she *only* writes when drunk and has to be as drunk as possible.

I said it didn't make the poems less valuable (you can tell I'm studying literature). Just that being drunk put her in the mood to write poems, that's all. And that I had a feeling Thomas Hardy might be a bit that way . . . and look at how much people love his poems (though not me).

Then Elspeth confessed that all she did was a kind of translation

116

thing of existing poems. Paraphrasing, line by line, using the thesaurus. So her poem "The White Cat" stems from someone else's poem, "The Brown Dog" type thing. She said it was cheating and she couldn't carry on.

I have attempted the paraphrasing thing and it's really tricky. Much harder than thinking up poems from scratch actually. Imagine finding a poem, searching through the thesaurus, while drunk, translating and scribbling it all down. She deserves the Nobel Prize for poems.

"The Violin"

Violin, I hate your sound,
Scritchy and nervous and sad.
You remind me of a pigeon
(Dusty and old and bad.)
I only like your shape and that,
Compared with a piano,
You're simple to cart about,
And easier to throw.

See. I just wrote that straight off (1 minute).

Love, Nina

∽

Dear Vic,

Rang Swiss Cottage about swim times. Told S&W and friend the options.

Me: (*to Will and friend*) Do you want a normal swim or a life-saving class?

Will: (*after some discussion*) Normal swim.

Me: Not the lifesaving class for under-13s?

Will: No, normal swim.

Me: Wouldn't you like to do lifesaving?

Will: Not at Swiss Cottage.

Me: Where, then?

Will: Well, I wouldn't mind saving someone's life in a real life scenario.

Me: You wouldn't know what to do unless you'd had the lesson.

Will: I would, I'd chuck my scarf at them.

Sam: Yeah, but what if they weren't an Arsenal supporter?

Will: I'd still do my best.

Sam: You're supposed to form a human chain.

Will: That's in a fire.

Sam: No, in a fire you bob down.

Went Swimming. Got home.

MK: How was the swim?

Sam: It was OK.

Will: Great.

Me: Great.

Sam: Except I'm never going to trust her again.

MK: Why?

Sam: She pushed me in.

MK: (*a bit shocked*) You pushed him in?

Me: I had to.

MK: Why?

Me: He didn't want to go in.

MK: Surely that's a reason *not* to push someone in?

Will: Unless it's Sam.

Sam: Anyway, I'll never trust her again.

Will: I haven't trusted her since 1981.

Sam: You didn't meet her till 1982.

Will: Well, there you are.

MK: (*to Sam*) So did you have a nice swim once she'd pushed you in?

Sam: It was OK, but my trust is lost.

Love, Nina

∽

Dear Vic,

Saw some graffiti today—"Be Cool, But Care." Pointed it out to S&W. I started to explain what the author was trying to say but S&W said they knew straightaway what the author was trying to say.

Will: We know what he's saying.

Me: It might have been a *she*.

Sam: Was it you?

They looked out for more graffiti, hoping to see some sweary stuff, but only found "Elliot Gould is a sissy."

Sam told us of some "really bad stuff" near Anna Sher. He couldn't remember how it went, only that Chris Lahr told him it included the "three worst words in the English language." We considered driving over that way to see it, but we thought it might have been washed off since Tuesday, with it being so rude and near Anna Sher.

Will: Why do people do graffiti?

Me: To express their views.

Will: But no one knows it's your views.

Me: That's one of its benefits.

Will: Oh yeah, you can write anything.

Me: Sort of, but it is illegal.

Will: Wicked.

Will was writing about Henry the Eighth for school homework and wrote Anne Boleyn as "Amber Lynn."

Will keen to go to judo club on Albany Street. I think he wants to go because his friend does it. Trying to put him off. Nunney thinks it'll be good (to go). MK says it's up to Will.

Love, Nina

PS Will loves it when people say "Cheerio," not that he likes it when people leave, just that he likes the word.

∽

Hi, Vic,

Parked in the Tomalins' disabled spot (very briefly). Found bossy note under the windscreen wiper (from Nunney). I thought the note might be a "Want to go to the movies?" note, so I was annoyed when it was a telling off for parking in their spot.

Next day, I put a photograph of Nunney on the toilet under Claire Tomalin's windscreen wiper. Nunney is cross about it and has refused to tell me what happened, i.e. did Claire find it? Or did he see it there and manage to remove it?

Me: What happened?

Nunney: I'm not indulging you.

Me: Did Claire find it?

Nunney: Can you just not do stuff like that?

Me: It's funny.

Nunney: It's not.

This is the problem. To me, it is funny. The bawdy nurse in R&J isn't funny, the Wife of Bath isn't particularly funny, but a photograph of Nunney on the toilet is. Especially when it's on the windscreen of the Volvo of the Literary Editor of the *Sunday Times*.

Preparing for interview at North London Poly. Can't have a training session with Nunney because of our row over the photograph of him on the toilet. I don't feel like apologizing. So had preparation session with Mary-Kay.

Me: I'll have to pretend to admire Shakespeare and like Hardy.
MK: Just be yourself—but don't wear that green thing.
Me: I don't want to blow it by looking like a philistine.
MK: Just talk about the plays you've read—a bit.
Me: OK. I just hope they don't ask me about Queen Mab or the bawdy nurse.
MK: The rule is: prepare for it and it won't happen.

Which is what happened. I was all ready to talk about Queen Mab and the bawdy nurse etc. but the only thing the bloke asked me (about the syllabus) was: "How does Hardy make you feel?"

I was tempted to say annoyed and bored, but said INSIGNIFICANT. I think it went down very well. We'll see.

Will liked the judo. Wanted to show us some of the moves after supper. Got Sam in a headlock and sort of flipped him. Sam did a bit of wee.

Love, Nina

∽

Dear Vic,
Pippa came round with a *different* dog. The previous dog (Charles

the King Charles Spaniel) has gone back to Somerset. Now she's dogsitting a retired greyhound (for two weeks). He's called Ted Hughes (Ted for short) because he looks like Ted Hughes—which he does (a bit).

I'm not sure Pippa likes Ted Hughes as much as she liked Charles. Ted Hughes not having the same freedom rights as Charles and being retired.

S&W didn't take to Ted Hughes. Sam said he was "even worse than other dogs" and Will said he was weird, but admitted he was tall. Pippa was just pleased we were all talking endlessly about Ted Hughes (the dog) and kept prolonging it with more snippets about Ted's amazing life. Ted Hughes is fifty-six in dog years and apparently has a chronic dry cough from all the years of dog racing and not having enough water available to him. His throat is so chronically dry, he can't even bark.

I switched the subject and began telling S&W about Maxwell and all his achievements.

Me: Maxwell used to turn the tap on with his hoof.
Sam: You've told us that before.
Will: Shame Ted couldn't have turned the tap on with his paw.
Pippa: (*irritable*) Ted Hughes was a racing dog and didn't have time to go round turning taps on.

Later at supper AB was asking about Pippa.

AB: Who's the woman with the dog?
Me: It's this friend of mine, Pippa. She used to be a nanny until there was a falling out.
AB: She's very nice hair.
Me: She gets it done.
AB: Lovely color.

Me: It's dyed.

AB: Dare I mention the dog?

Sam: It's called Ted Heath.

AB: Oh dear.

Me: Ted *Hughes*, not Heath.

AB: Well, that's better.

Nunney reckons the Wife of Bath is a dog lover (significantly). I must've missed that.

Hope all's well.

Love, Nina

⁓

Dear Vic,

MK never likes to be caught off-guard. She was saying this at supper.

Me: Such as?

MK: Asleep, for instance.

Sam: No one's ever seen her asleep.

Will: Apart from Father Christmas.

Me: I hate being seen yawning.

Will: What about picking your nose?

Sam: Or looking at your hands?

Me: You can't avoid being caught out sometimes.

MK: Unless you remain *on guard* at all times.

It reminded me of the photograph of Misty in the newspaper (at Cruft's dog show, looking at the bottom of her shoe). She (Misty) thought it was embarrassing, not the looking at the bottom of her shoe, but looking *worried* about it.

Told MK who said, "If you can't look worried at a dog show, where can you?"

MK had a load of people round. Including a bloke who bought her a bunch of roses even though it wasn't her birthday yet and she was only offering a pan of soup and M&S table wine (no pudding). They didn't look much (the roses), just buds and leaves, but were supposedly going to blossom gradually in the vase (jug).

The bloke handed them over and said something muffled. I think it was shyness. MK was nice and said thank you with her head on one side. Maybe something's going on. The bloke is nice. Arty and thoughtful.

The roses: MK didn't know, and neither did I (then) about the thing where you have to bash the stems or they die. So the next morning (yesterday), I was surprised to see all the little rosebud heads hanging, and so was MK (surprised).

Me: Oh no, look at the rosebuds.
MK: What's wrong with them?
Me: They're dead.
MK: They can't be already, they haven't blossomed.
Me: (*lying*) Maybe they'll perk up.
MK: (*resigned*) Or maybe that's that.

I said it was just like the camellia all over again, referring to the plant that a previous one gave her last year (that died even though I sprinkled acidic granules).

Later, AB arrived and I pointed out the sickly roses and he shouted, "Get the steak mallet," and I shouted, "The what?" and he shouted, "Get the rolling pin," and I riffled among the kitchen utensils and passed it to AB who grabbed it, bashed the rose stems and flung them under the cold tap. Within an hour they'd perked up.

Me: Look at the roses now.

MK: Ooh.

AB: You see—you have to bash the stems.

MK: Yes, thank you.

AB: Did you not know that?

MK: It rings a bell now.

Anyway, that's what you have to do with cut flowers, otherwise they can't take up the water and the heads flop.

Tonight. Roses were blooming, custardy petals already browning at the edges. I said in my opinion roses were overrated as a flower and AB agreed, saying *cut* roses generally have no smell to speak of, and the smell being the main thing (about a rose).

Mary-Kay said she wondered why we'd bothered with the emergency procedure the night before just to criticize everything about them now they'd made a good recovery. AB said it was the proper conduct—according to the Hippocratic oath (meaning, you save lives and question later).

Told MK what you said about buttercups. She had to agree.

Made an unsuccessful shepherd's pie. Unsuccessful due to the potato top being made out of new potatoes, as opposed to ordinary.

You're not meant to mash *new* potatoes, only old. It's a cookery rule that you'd never know until you've seen it for yourself (like bashing the rose stems). New potatoes go gluey if you mash them and aren't nice to eat. It was a shame because the bottom half (of pie) was v. nice with lots of celery, carrot, and onion and two Oxo cubes.

AB: You can't really mash new potatoes.

Me: How do you know if they're new?

Sam: They're small and muddy.

Me: So you can't mash them?

Will: No, never mash new potatoes.

125

Me: How come everyone knows so much about potatoes?
Sam: You just pick these things up.
Will: Yeah, you live and learn.

Love, Nina
PS Did you know about not mashing new potatoes?

∽

Dear Vic,

Good news. Mary-Kay has pranged the car at long last—a relief after all mine (prangs). She drove into a rope, which was "the same color as the road and sky." Plus it was roping off an area that isn't usually roped off.

Sam: It's mum's first time crashing.
Me: Yeah, but it's worse than any of mine—in terms of damage done.
MK: Hmm.
Me: Mine never required any action to be taken.
MK: Only the untangling of deception and denial.
Me: You dented the number plate—irreparably.
MK: True, but my credibility remains intact.

Told Misty that MK is unusual.

Me: She's just very unusual.
Misty: Is she a bit mad?
Me: God, no, she's 100 percent sane.
Misty: That's unusual.
Me: That's what I mean.

S&W talking about whether or not they're going to take up smoking.

Will: I'm going to have one after every meal.
Sam: So four per day, then?
Will: Three.
Sam: It's unhealthy.
Will: Yes, especially if you've got asthma.
Sam: I'm going to smoke one per day walking to the tube.
Will: What about walking back from the tube?
Sam: Two per day, then.
Will: What about after every meal?
Sam: Stop encouraging me, I'm just having one per day.

Love, Nina

⌒

Dear Vic,
Leaving the house for Great Ormond St. appointment.

Me: Do you need spare batteries for your Walkman?
Sam: (*thinking*) No, it's only a four-song trip.

Waiting at Great Ormond St.

Me: Are you famous?
Sam: Yes.
Me: Are you to do with sport?
Sam: No.
Me: Are you on telly?
Sam: Er, yes.
Etc. . . .

Me: OK, I give in, who are you?

Sam: Anne Kirkbridge.

Me: Anne Kirkbridge?

Sam: Yes.

Me: Who's Anne Kirkbridge?

Sam: She's on the telly.

Me: Doing what?

Sam: This and that.

Your garden sounds very nice now.

If you want to sit in the garden here, you just take a hard chair from the table and sit out there, bolt upright, alone, in a drainy area near the small blue shed. There's no lounging.

Me: (*about garden*) Maybe we should have a bench or something.

MK: What?

Me: I was thinking about garden chairs.

MK: We never go out there.

Will: Sam goes out there and acts weird.

Sam: I don't.

Will: He potters and looks over the wall.

Sam: I do not.

Will: What the hell do you do out there if you don't potter or look over the wall?

Sam: I just wander round.

MK: That's pottering.

Sam: OK. But I do not look over the wall.

Funny, because in France they're outside all day long with just their cozies on. They'd never do that here, even in a heat wave.

Love, Nina

Dear Vic,

The Saab was admitted due to the overheating thing. Good job Nunney came with me to the mechanics (to do the talking and listening).

Me: Good job you were with me.
Nunney: Why?
Me: I'm phobic about car garages.
Nunney: I thought it was butchers.
Me: It's car garages *and* butchers.
Nunney: How are you with abattoirs?

Have been using AB's Audi for essential trips. Don't think much to it. Poor vision at the back and a bit tinny.

Me: Can I borrow the car for a minute?
AB: Yes, where are you going?
Me: Just up to Jake's.
AB: Righto.

Thing is, there's no Jake, I just said Jake's like that because I wanted to nip up to Hampstead and I knew if I said I wanted to nip up to Hampstead he'd say, "Can't you get the bus?"
Later, at supper:

Sam: (*to AB*) I like your car.
Me: I'm not keen, you can't see out the back.
AB: I can see out of the back.
Me: You're taller.

AB: Put a cushion in.

Me: I won't need it again.

AB: Not to nip up to Jake's?

MK: Who's Jake?

Me: A friend.

AB: She borrowed the car to drive over there this afternoon.

MK: Jake? Jake who?

Me: (*frowning at MK*) Yes, Jake, you know.

MK: (*to AB*) There's no Jake, she was just joyriding.

Still on Chaucer. Reading the *Wife of Bath's Prologue* (translating). Nunney's getting on great with it (chuckling and making observations). I'm less so.

Nunney: We shouldn't assume the narrator's voice is Chaucer's.

Me: Whose is it, then?

N: The character's.

Me: The character doesn't exist.

N: For fuck's sake—suspend your disbelief.

Hope all else is well in the Midlands.

Love, Nina

∽

Dear Vic,

Got stopped by a policeman in the bus lane on Camden Road. It wasn't about driving in the bus lane; it was about not wearing a seat belt. The policeman leaned on the car and rambled on about safety and laws etc.

I thought he might notice my feet (bare) and start going on about the law of wearing shoes when driving. So, to prevent it, I looked him right in the eye so he couldn't look anywhere else. It was strange. He will have thought I was mad, but he didn't see my feet and that was the point. Sometimes you just have to appear mad to prevent a serious consequence. After some time, the PC asked if I was aware of the seat belt law. I said, "Yes, sorry, I forgot." And I put my seat belt on, but I kept looking straight at him while I did it and I even said, "Clunk-click, every trip" in Jimmy Savile's voice.

He said he *could* fine me, but he wouldn't on this occasion, as I seemed to have got the message. Then he said, "On you go, Miss," and patted the car.

Now Sam keeps saying, "Clunk-click, every trip" and "On you go, Miss." MK wanted to know why Sam kept saying those things and I said we'd had a talk about road safety.

Pippa has switched to black coffee. It's only for show. She used to always have tea two-sugars. But tea isn't cool enough anymore. She only has black coffee, no sugar. I can tell she doesn't like it as much as she used to like tea two-sugars—she gulps it down like a cowboy swallowing whiskey and coughs.

Told MK about Pippa's coffee switch.

MK: Maybe she just wants a change.
Me: No, it's totally for show.
MK: Why is coffee more impressive than tea?
Me: It's more sophisticated and European.
MK: Do you feel you're being left behind?
Me: A bit.
MK: You could switch too?
Me: I can't, not for a year at least; it'd look like I was influenced.
MK: Idiot.

MK doesn't get it. She might get Shakespeare and Chekhov and all

131

their complex characters but she misses things in real life, like people's true motivation for switching drinks.

Trying to drink more water. Friend of MK says you're supposed to drink at least one large glass every two hours. Tea and coffee don't count, nor Perrier, it has to be tap.

Love, Nina

∽

Dear Vic,

Cooked a chicken casserole. Celery, onion and garlic—fried, add chicken thighs, cook a while, and add a tin of mushroom soup (condensed). Cook for 30 mins (low bubble). Sprinkle with parsley.

MK: This is nice—I haven't had rabbit for ages.
Will: (*horrified*) What? Is this rabbit?
Me: No, it's chicken. I never cook rabbit.
Will: It smells like rabbit.
MK: It seems like rabbit.
Sam: I hate rabbit.
Me: It's not rabbit. I'd never cook a rabbit.
Sam: Why not?
Me: I just don't like the idea of it.
Will: Me neither, I'm not eating any more of it.

MK keeps buying Break-Ins (M&S version of Breakaways). S&W don't like them—mild coconut flavor. I don't like that M&S call them Break-Ins, trying to pass them off as real Breakaways. There are 3 packets of 6 in the pantry. Same at 57 (I've seen in their biscuit tin).

In fact, it's about the only thing Mary-Kay and Claire Tomalin have in common, apart from liking books.

Harriet was telling S&W about the foundling hospital near Great Ormond St:

H: It was very sad—people would leave little bundles on the steps.
Will: Bundles of what?
H: Babies. Babies that people couldn't look after.
Sam: I should be left there.
H: Why?
Sam: Because of my Riley-Day (*meaning his illness*).
Will: OK, we'll drop you there later.
H: Oh, you meanie.

Sam says things like that in front of Harriet and so does Will—because they both get the response they're looking for.

Love, Nina

～

Dear Vic,

Drinking more coffee. I like frothy coffee, but not black.

Mary-Kay likes the coffee (Continental roast) from the coffee man on Delancey Street. I like going there for the smell, but the bloke's overkeen to talk about the coffees and lifts the beans up in his fingers—you have to be careful not to give him the chance. Best to be already in a conversation with someone else when you go in (but not about coffee, or he'll just butt in).

In there waiting in a queue, with Will.

Will: The taste of coffee is disappointing because the smell is so nice.
Me: Don't talk about coffee at the mo.

Will: But we're in a coffee shop.

Me: Sssh, talk about something else.

Will: Why?

Me: Otherwise you'll start the bloke off.

Will: That's harsh, it's all he's got.

The other day I was making mini burgers for S&W when Stephen Frears called in (looking like a tramp). He picked up a raw burger and ate it. I was appalled but acted normal. Told MK later and she said it's a thing (eating raw beef).

Funny that Sam calls Stephen "3-5-9-1-8-1-5." It's his phone number.

Me: How come you call Stephen by his phone number?

Sam: It's the norm.

Me: It isn't the norm—you don't call me by my number.

Sam: But your number is my number, you fool.

They disliked the all-bran cookies by the way. But liked the flapjacks. Would like to try R Patel's Biriani recipe—can you scribble in next letter?

Love, Nina

PS Have you tried balsamic vinegar of Modena? It's a vinegar, but much nicer than Sarson's or red wine etc. It's dark brown. Looks horrible like medicine, but is nice. Nunney has a mate who drinks it off the spoon.

∽

Dear Vic,

Thanks for recipe. I didn't do it exact—too many ingredients. I've not done anything with more than five/six things in it so far. Plus we don't have the right attachments or a pestle. So I did my own version:

Cooked chicken, almond flakes, curry powder, and parsley, plus two packs Bachelor's savory rice.

AB: This is tasty.
MK: Do you have to say tasty?
AB: It *is* tasty.
MK: I'm not denying it, but there's no need to say tasty.

Questioned by AB about the ingredients (suspicious?).

AB: Have you put cardamoms in it?
Me: They were optional.
AB: Did you opt for them?
Me: No.

Using fresh herbs these days instead of dried. AB says you have to understand how they work. Which is tricky if you don't know.

MK likes: basil, tarragon, garlic, rosemary.
AB likes: dill, watercress, basil, tarragon, garlic, rosemary, cardamoms.

Here's my herb round-up:

Tarragon: the cookbook says tarragon is "misunderstood." Not by me. I understand it. It's horrible.
Rosemary: makes things taste like disinfectant.
Thyme: nice, but smells a bit lawny.
Parsley: nice, fresh, not dried.
Mint: the smell of mint leaves in hot water (aka peppermint tea) reminds me of a toilet in a particular café. But chopped up raw, just on things, I like it.

Basil: is nice all mushed up with cheese and garlic and olive oil (pesto). It has to be olive though. Misty did it with Mazola by accident and it wasn't all that nice.

Pippa's friend. (beautician) Mel almost poisoned herself by accidentally eating daffodil bulbs, thinking they were shallots. She nearly put them in a cheese and onion sandwich, but began to suspect there was something wrong with them (no onion smell).

MK: How come?
Me: She thought they were shallots.
MK: So, where were they?
Me: In her fridge, in the salad compartment.
MK: Sounds like one of your tricks.

Love, Nina
PS It wasn't me. I've never been to hers.

⤴

Dear Vic,
Thanks for the cutting. Tried to reminisce about it with MK but she wasn't very interested.

Me: Pears have discontinued the Three Wishes range.
MK: Is that a bad thing?
Me: I used to like the deodorant—the green one.
Sam: If you had three wishes, would one of them be to have the Three Wishes stuff again?
Me: Probably not, I've gone on to Mum roll-on.
Sam: If I had three wishes, I'd wish for a hundred wishes.
Will: You're not allowed to do that, you only get three.

Sam: Says who?
Will: The Genie.

The door buzzer. The thing is, when the doorbell goes it could be anyone (except when it's AB because of his short ring). So the doorbell goes and we buzz people in from the kitchen and wait a moment until they start coming down the stairs and we all look to see them coming into view (feet first). And that's when we know who it is.

Now, after the bloke incident, MK says (quite rightly) we should start speaking on the intercom thing when the doorbell goes and ask who it is.

MK: Can we find out who it is *before* we buzz them in.
Sam: Why?
MK: Because it's the sensible way to do it.
Will: It could be a murderer.
Sam: Or Frank Bough.

Later on, the doorbell went and Sam did the new procedure... of speaking into the machine.

Sam: Hullo, who is it, hullo, who is it? Hullo, hullo.
MK: Let them speak.
Sam: Bloody hell, who is it? Say something then (*buzzes them in*).
MK: Don't just say, "Who is it?" then buzz them in—you need to know who it is *before* you buzz them in (*someone comes in*).
Sam: (*shouting up the stairs*) You can't come in yet. Wait there. Go out again (*the door closes again*).

Then we all crowded round the intercom thing. And Will shouted "State your name, please" and Sam said "Hullo" lots more times.

But there was no response. Will ran upstairs to find the person who had come in and gone out again, but they'd gone.

Love, Nina

PS I've worked out that Sam and me are a tiny bit nicer if people are round for supper. Mary-Kay and Will are a tiny bit grumpier. Not counting AB in that.

∽

Dear Vic,

Mary-Kay has started wearing two shirts at once. I don't know where she's picked it up but it's a thing, apparently. Both shirts have to be very thin and fine, you couldn't do it with hard or thick type shirts. Still, even with silk ones it looks like you've forgotten you've already put your shirt on. Like Mr. B getting dressed twice by accident.

Reading a good book (not on syllabus) that Jez put me on to. It's about a bloke (called Josef K) who gets arrested even though he hasn't done anything and it goes on like that.

MK says she's had to buy three new pairs of little scissors since I came.

MK: I spend my life buying little scissors.
Me: What's that got to do with me?
MK: You lose them, or nick them.
Me: No, you take them up to the sitting room and don't bring them back. They'll be in your desk area.
MK: Feel free to search my desk.
Me: Desk *area*.

Went up to the sitting room, and immediately saw two pairs of little scissors in a dish with postcards in it. And two rolls of eye tape.

138

Me: Look here, two pairs straightaway and eye tape.

MK: You just put them there.

Me: No, I came up here empty-handed.

MK: Empty-pocketed?

Me: I feel like Josef K.

MK: *Very* good.

She hardly ever says *very*.

Ran out of milk. Had to nip out to Top Food & Wine late. Saw Rik Mayall in there buying Dairylea and Jacob's Cream Crackers. I said hello, he said hello. I've met him a couple of times (to do with Stephen) and once when him and Adrian Edmondson came to visit Sam at Great Ormond Street (and they were very funny and nice) but Rik didn't know who I was in the Top Food & Wine context.

I had no shoes on.

Love, Nina

∽

Dear Vic,

Yesterday the fridge started humming. It took me a while to work out where the noise was coming from. I thought it was Will. Will thought it was Sam. Sam thought it was me.

MK: What's that noise?

Me: It's the fridge.

MK: Why's it doing that?

Me: I don't know, maybe it means it's broken.

MK: Does it?

Me: I don't know. Elspeth's used to do that and she'd slap it with her palm really hard.

MK: Have you tried that?

Me: No, it never worked—Elspeth just kept slapping hers out of habit.

(*MK kicks the fridge. It stops humming.*)

MK: (*pleased*) There you go.

Pippa has been dogsitting Ted Hughes again (two weeks while grandma on Nile cruise). He's gone back now and Pippa is missing him. He didn't bark once the whole time she had him. She's actually never heard him bark. She puts it down to the dehydration during his racing years.

Ted Hughes's racing name was the Dingo but Pippa's grandma changed it to Ted when she got him from the trust (because of the connotations).

Me: Is she a fan of Ted Hughes's poetry?

Pippa: No, I added the "Hughes" on myself.

That is bloody typical of Pippa, trying to impress people saying it was Ted Hughes when it was just plain Ted. Like having black coffee when she doesn't like it and smoking all the time (but not inhaling). I couldn't be like that. I couldn't say a dog was called Ted Hughes when it was just called Ted.

Mary-Kay liked that Pippa had added Hughes herself. Saying it made life more interesting.

That sums writer types up. They're not bothered what happens in the world, they're never bothered or angry about stuff (like normal people), they're pleased when things happen and interested and then they write about it. One way or another.

I couldn't be like that either. I couldn't enjoy that someone said a dog was called Ted Hughes. I wouldn't be interested, I'd be annoyed. I'm not interested. I am annoyed.

Anyway Pippa is missing Ted and might get a kitten, but not sure because it would put a stop to dogsitting Ted in future (Ted doesn't like cats or kittens). Even so, she's seriously considering getting a kitten. I pointed out that landlords don't always agree to kittens and she said, "Landlords don't always have to know about kittens." She means you can hide the fact that you've got a kitten.

Tonight, at supper, the fridge started up its humming again. MK got up and kicked it again. It stopped for a bit but started up again later. AB said he didn't mind the humming (they all make some noise, they are a piece of machinery after all), but he didn't like MK kicking it. He hates aggression.

AB: Oh, don't do that.

MK: I don't like the hum.

AB: Kick it when I've gone. It's not doing it any good.

MK: It stops it.

(*Fridge starts humming again.*)

AB: Look, it's humming again already. (*Has a look inside the fridge.*) You've stuff freezing at the back here, look at all this frozen... (*holds up bag of frozen watercress*). You've got it on very low (*temperaturewise*).

MK: Oh, is that why it's humming?

AB: I expect so; it's trying to be a freezer.

(*AB adjusted it to a normal setting and it stopped humming straightaway.*)

Will: I'm going to miss that mellow hum.

MK: I'm going to miss kicking it.

Love, Nina

Dear Vic,

Great day.

Had my interview at Thames Polytechnic with a tutor called John Williams.

I slipped in about Hardy making me feel insignificant early on which turned out to be unnecessary because we had a proper chat. I said I was beginning to worry about actually passing the A level (because of not loving the syllabus and never doing exams before).

JW said it's not all about the grade but about *you* (me), and some of the best students ever come from non-traditional backgrounds. They get all sorts of losers there by the sound of it. Mature students etc. He asked what I'd read that I *had* liked and why etc. Mentioned the best stuff I could think of including my FBOAT (favorite book of all time), *My Side of the Mountain* by Jean George. He'd not heard of it. But overall, he made me really want to go to Thames Poly (just by being jolly and encouraging).

Had a good look around the campus and it seems OK. Apart from a row of polystyrene cups with fag burn holes in them in the refectory, it had a good feeling. Big library. It's across the square from the station and there's a market down the road.

Later, did your veggie chili but didn't put much chili in it. Pippa was staying and it makes her nervous in the night. But put a tin of those red beans in and served it on rice, so it looked the business.

Stephen's girlfriend Annie is a brilliant famous artist called Annie Rothenstein and has done a painting for MK, which MK likes. Nice shapes and colors. The sort of thing you could do yourself if you had the equipment.

Saw a second-hand easel in War on Want. Thought I might get it for S&W and mentioned it to MK.

Me: Do you think they'd like an easel?
MK: No.

Me: I thought they might want to do paintings.

MK: They haven't so far.

Me: Maybe if they had an easel.

MK: You think maybe it'll unleash something?

Back to Thames Poly interview: have almost decided on Thames Polytechnic (if I get to choose). The only thing is, it's a long way from NW1, which is a drawback. Don't want to live over there. I'd miss NW1 etc. and there's Sam's eye to think of—MK thinks it's OK when it's not and it's not OK when it is. Even Mr. Mackie says I'm the eye expert and he actually is (the eye expert).

I'd have to commute all that way. But that would be OK. I can dodge the fares on that line easily. Pink tickets. And I can read loads on the train.

Thanks for cuttings. Best was "Five Ways with Cabbage." I am getting to be an OK cook. They like strong flavors/herbs. MK not fussy (about food). Will likes burgery things (but not turkey) and complex sandwiches. Sam likes mushy things. Keep sending.

See you soon.

Love, Nina

PS I get a mandatory grant from Leicester County Council.

⁓

Dear Vic,

One of Mary-Kay's brainbox mates dropped by unexpectedly on Saturday for an impromptu coffee stop (his words). His friend or his wife was looking at something in Primrose Hill—it might have been property or crockery, none of us quite heard (he can't pronounce his Rs) and he couldn't face whatever it was and thought he'd pop in.

Brainbox: Hello, Mary-Kay!

MK: Oh, right.

BB: Can't stay long.

MK: Good.

S&W and me tried to impress him and sang "We're On Our Way"—the whole thing, all through, harmoniously. I was almost in tears when we finished, it sounded so good.

MK: (*very pleased*) Sing it again. (*To Brainbox*) Did you like that?

BB: Um, it's a bit "old hat."

MK: Better than *no* hat.

S&W and me: "We're on our way, we are Ron's 22. Hear the roar of the red, white and blue, this time, more than any other time, this time, we're going to find a way, find a way to get away, this time, bringing it all together, to bring it home."

MK: (*clapping*).

BB: (*looking at watch*) OK, thanks for the coffee, must run.

Later on, supper was ready at a slightly earlier time due to it being Mary-Kay's turn and her getting it done.

Sam: Shall I ring he-llo (*his name for AB*)?

MK: Yes.

Sam: (*on phone to AB*) He-llo, sup-per's ready—(*covers mouthpiece, speaks to MK*) he says it's a bit early.

MK: What the fuck?

Sam: (*to AB*) She says what the fuck?

At supper:

AB: How's the studying going?

Me: Fine.

MK: Except she hates everything.

Me: No, I don't. Only Hardy.

MK: And Shakespeare and Chaucer.

Me: No, I'm OK with Chaucer now.

AB: What's wrong with Hardy?

Me: It's this little picture you see everywhere of his round head.

AB: I don't think you should hold that against him.

Sam (*changing the subject*): I hate it when people climb trees.

Me: Why?

Sam: It just annoys me.

Me: I know what you mean.

MK: I like it.

Sam: Why?

Me: I suppose it's one less person on the ground.

MK: No. I like people in trees.

Love, Nina

PS MK has given (lent) me a book, *The English Novel from Dickens to Lawrence*, which has a bit about Hardy, including common misconceptions and people writing him off. The book actually belongs to M Neve. It says so inside.

∽

Dear Vic,

Have discovered that I can make my mouth into a perfect square. Showed Sam and Will. Sam said he knew someone else who could do it. Will spent ages trying to do it but couldn't.

Mary-Kay was just interested to know how I discovered I could do it. I said I'd just done it while blow-drying my hair and then she was interested in the fact that I've got a hair dryer.

Jez and me had a kebab. My first ever...not much to write home about. Except it's good watching the carving bit. Have you had?

Jez had had one (or two) before. Said he didn't think much to them, but not until we'd ordered and there was no going back.

Sam—bad eye and fed up.

Will—hates school—he doesn't like posh kids but goes to a posh school.

MK—grumpy.

Me—reading.

Love, Nina

༄

Dear Vic,

I love AB's house (inside). He's really put some thought into it. He's done a collage of faces (like the one I did when I was about twelve). And he's got a bowl full of dried-out lemons that looks like an old painting. I've re-created it at 55.

MK: Do we want all these old lemons?
Me: I'm drying them.
MK: For?
Me: They just look nice.
MK: Do they?
Me: Well, once they're dry, they will.
MK: If you say so.

Mary Hope is getting her house done bit by bit. She's had a dark brown shag-pile carpet in her bedroom. She says she's always fancied one. And the walls are dark brown too. It's all very brown.

The rest of the house is paler.

They've got various bits of African art dotted about. One (the main one) is a long piece of fabric (five feet long, like a length of wallpaper) and on it are long smudgy streaks of blue and green roughly painted on. It's meant to be a waterfall but it just looks like someone's wiped the paint off a few brushes down it. They love it.

Shirley Conran lives next door. Her alarm keeps going off and bugging the hell out of Mary. Disturbing her (in her brown bedroom).

MK: How's it living next door to Superwoman?
Mary: Her burglar alarm keeps going off.
MK: That's not so super.

In theory we could climb over the wall at the back of our garden and be in Mary Hope's garden. But in reality it's all shrubs and trellis and I can't see anyone actually making it through.

Lucas would've struggled. Even Superwoman would.

Sometimes we can see them going about their business, through the window.

Me: Look, I can see Mary (or Polly).
Sam: What are they doing?
Me: Going about their business.
Sam: (opens window, shouts) Oi, Mary, Poddo, JDF.
Me: They can't hear you.
Sam: I'll ring them.
MK: Why?
Sam: Just to say we can see them going about their business.
MK: Leave them be.

147

Hope all's going well with you.

Love, Nina

∽

Dear Vic,

Holborn library to return the LP of the bloke reading Chaucer's *Canterbury Tales* (excerpts) in the old English. Librarian took LP off me and looked impressed (did a little nod of approval).

Librarian: Did you enjoy the recording?
Me: Yes. I've made a cassette of it.
Librarian: (*suddenly angry*) You've done what?
Me: Made a cassette.
Librarian: That's illegal.
Me: Oh, sorry, I'll throw it away.
Librarian: (*looking at LP*) I'm afraid there's a fine on this—it was due back some time ago.

The annoying thing is, she was about to ignore the lateness when I mentioned the cassette and that angered her (in a possessive way). And she pressed charges.

It's not done my relationship with Chaucer any good at all.

Later, Sam and Will wanted to clear out the shed so they can have a yard sale. They've seen one on the telly where this kid makes a fortune.

The shed is the size of a wardrobe. Its only use is to be climbed on and jumped off (by Will and the Smiths next door). Found two fishing nets, can of floor polish, bike (small) and the Millers' saw (the one we borrowed last Xmas).

Took saw inside to show MK.

Me: Look!

MK: What? Are you off to do something awful in Holborn library?

Me: No, it's the Millers' saw. Someone should take it back.

MK: You borrowed it.

Me: You hid it.

MK: You found it.

Me: He's your friend.

MK: You care so much.

I took it back.

Me: This is your saw.

JM: Oh, thank you.

Me: We borrowed it last December.

JM: Yes, I remember. Well, thanks for bringing it back.

Me: Sorry it's taken so long.

JM: That's all right, I'm sure we'd have hollered if we'd needed it.

Back at 55:

MK: What did they say about the saw?

Me: Jonathan said to tell you never to ask to borrow anything off him again.

MK: Was there a fine?

Love, Nina

～

Dear Vic,

Sam and Will have had new, more extreme, basin-cuts. It's a

London thing, you see it a lot. I think it means "my kid is too cute to object to this fucked-up hair style."

S&W had a row yesterday afternoon. To annoy Will, Sam said he might switch to Manchester United. Will called Sam something mysterious in German, which he claimed to be extremely offensive, but turned out to be mother-in-law (according to AB).

At supper:

Will: (*to Sam*) By the way, it was "swiegermutter."
Sam: What was?
Will: What I called you—it's German for "motherfucker."
AB: "Swiegermutter"? Actually, I think that's German for "mother-*in-law.*"
Will: Oh. What's the German for "motherfucker," then?
MK: Probably "motherfucker."
AB: (*pondering*) It might be "mutter*ficken*"? Or perhaps "arschficken," "arshlock"? But *please* can't we discuss nicer things?
(*Pause.*)
Me: (*to assembly*) What's your favorite word?
Sam: Not this again.
Me: What's your favorite word *of the moment*?
Will: Not counting "swiegermutter," I like "antidote."
(*We all mutter, "Yeah."*)
Sam: I can't decide between "oblong" and "toad."
(*We all mutter, "Toad—yeah," "Oblong—yeah."*)
Me: I like "hoof."
(*We all mutter, "Yeah."*)
Will: I thought you liked "trousers."
Me: I used to.
AB: I like "Lvov."
(*No response.*)

Sam: What about "skull-fuck"?

Will: Only for special occasions.

MK: (*taken aback*) Glad to hear it.

Will: (*to MK*) Which do you like?

MK: They're all pretty good, except "lozenge."

AB: No one said "lozenge" — we've had "trousers," "skull-fuck" and "oblong" . . .

MK: (*to AB*) *You* did.

AB: I said "Lvov."

MK: You're not allowed place names.

That's what our evenings are like. Reading the dictionary and discussing words and arguing about whether brim is better than flank— wordwise. And how to offend—in German and English. It's good.

Love, Nina

༄

Dear Vic,

At supper, we discussed the old lady on *Jim'll Fix It* who scrubbed an elephant with a yard broom. Do you remember it? The old lady was tiny and the elephant as big as can be.

Me: The old lady had always dreamed of scrubbing an elephant.

AB: What a thing to dream of!

Me: She wrote to Jim and asked him to fix it.

AB: I might write to him.

Sam: What do you want him to fix for you?

AB: I'll have to think.

Sam: You could have tea with the chimpanzees.

AB: I do that anyway (*laughing*).

Will: You could take a rice pudding with you.

(*Pause.*)

Me: She really enjoyed scrubbing the elephant.

MK: Did the elephant like it?

Me: I think so.

Will: Elephants like being scrubbed.

Sam: How do you know?

Will: It's a known fact.

AB: Yes, I think they're known to like a scrub.

Will: They love it.

Me: Yeah, I think they do.

MK: Sounds like Jim killed two birds with one stone, then.

Sam: (*Jimmy Savile voice*) Now then, now then.

When Sam said he hated broccoli AB said (for some reason), "You are what you eat," which didn't help.

Sam: Are you what you eat?

AB: Well, in a sense, yes.

Will: Sam's a banana, then.

Sam: Yeah, and Will's a cornflake.

Will: And Stibbe's just nuts.

Love, Nina

⌣

Dear Vic,

Thames Polytechnic has sent me an offer. Unconditional.

It's good because it means I can go there and do my degree (whatever happens). But it also means I don't *have* to pass the A level (and that they're not bothered how clever/thick their students are).

Me: It means the whole A level thing has been pointless.

MK: How?

Me: I could've just applied and gone anyway.

MK: But this way you've learned how to study *before* you go.

Me: I suppose so.

Nunney is really pleased about the unconditional offer.

Me: At least I've learned to study *before* I go.

Nunney: Well, I wouldn't go that far.

Been doing some practice papers for the exams. It's not the same without the anxiety.

I'd left the Seamus Heaney (*Selected Poems 1965–1975*) till last because of Nunney not being keen. Now I look at it, it's the best thing—the only really good thing—on the syllabus. Mary-Kay said I'd like it and I'd regret leaving it till last. And I do.

Seamus Heaney

I've got to you at last
Your clotted water, and Irish air
Your dad and his dad
And your scruffy hair

But I'm on my own with you (no help)
Struggling in muddy lines
You in your duffel coat
Smiling with a field behind

You're not like Hardy
Tho some stuff's the same

But what d'you mean in *Summer Home*?
Why was the rhododendron to blame?

That's my poem for Seamus Heaney (I wrote it in five mins). What I'm saying is, I like you, but you're a challenge.

Love, Nina

∾

Dear Vic,

Professor Picton congratulated Sam on a "lovely job" cleaning his teeth. Sam and me both surprised.

At supper all talked about dentist things. MK hates going to the dentist and has to have an injection just to be inspected. I told them about making half-coffee/half-tea for my old boss, Mr. Johnson.

AB: What did Mr. Johnson *think* he was drinking?
Me: Coffee in the morning, tea in the afternoon.
MK: (*shaking head*) And what did he do to deserve that?
Me: Lots of annoying things.
MK: Such as?
Me: He was a snob.
MK: (*still shaking head*).
Me: How come you're so concerned about Mr. Johnson?
MK: It's you-being-a-psychopath that concerns me.

Told them about Nunney's trick. Makes *one* cup of tea, then he asks if anyone (at 57) wants one. They say no (politely) and he gets the credit for offering but doesn't have to make and gets to keep the tea. Added to which, he gets the thrill of the gamble (his words), meaning:

they might suddenly say yes (they do want one) and then he'll have to hand over his cup.

MK: Why doesn't he just make himself some tea?
Me: He likes the gamble.
MK: Crikey, he's living on the edge.

I haven't had a cup of tea made by MK for months. I avoid it. First, she doesn't pour water onto the bag soon enough after the boil. Second, she only fills the cup halfway. Third, she makes heavy weather of it.

She calls a cup of tea "a teabag." She offered Pippa a cup once.

MK: Would you like a teabag?
Pippa: Lovely—if you're making one.
MK: I'm not making one. But I will make one if you'd like one.
Pippa: Oh, well. No thanks, then.
MK: Suit yourself.

I don't offer to make her tea very often either. It's not worth it.

Me: Do you want a cup of tea?
MK: I don't know. Not in that cup.
Me: Is that no, then?
MK: No, it's yes but don't give me Derby County.

Prince Charles drove past Nunney and me in Trafalgar Square on Saturday in a Daimler and looked straight at me. Ordinary, brown hair. Looked a bit like Dad (parting too far back).

Nunney did a rant (because I'd been slightly excited) and sitting there in the Breadline Café he lectured me about the royals and their awfulness throughout history. He cleverly linked it to Chaucer to get my attention. It could have been a turning point Chaucer-wise, but I just haven't got the time.

Will's started another novel (writing one) about a wild dog lost in a hostile city. It was going to be called Fang, but there's already a lost literary dog called that, so he's switched to Scooby to be going on with. Scooby eats leftovers from outside Maxwell's and people are always shouting at him to clear off.

He was busy on the novel plan but had urgent homework to do (geometrical shapes), so I took over (the homework).

Nunney: What are you doing?

Me: Cutting out shapes, it's Will's homework.

Nunney: (*cross*) Why isn't Will doing it?

Me: He doesn't like paper craft and he's writing a novel.

Nunney: Cutting out paper to exact measurements is maths... Will should do it—it's a life skill.

Will: I'll never need to measure paper in real life; I'll buy it already measured.

Nunney: (*to Will*) Don't let her ruin your life.

Will: She's helping me with my novel.

Nunney: (*shakes head*) Fucking hell.

Me: Stop judging us, go and judge them at 57.

Nunney: They don't need judging, they self-judge.

Love, Nina

༄

Dear Vic,

Funny. Jez told Sam (who told Tom) that the FA Cup final was going to be a Subbuteo game, not a proper match.

Sam: Why?

Jez: Players' legs are too tired, but their fingers are OK.

Sam: So it's the same players, but doing Subbuteo?

Jez: Yeah.

Sam: Will it be on telly?

Jez: Yes, lots of close-ups of the fingers and action replays.

Sam: How will I know which finger plays for which team?

Jez: They'll wear colored rubber bands.

Love, Nina

∿

Dear Vic,

Dreading exams as I haven't got to grips with the Seamus Heaney. I like/love it, but not sure I *get* it and it's a bit late to get to know the man behind the pen. I don't even think he'd want anyone getting to know him behind his pen. In my opinion, his pen is an embarrassment to him for not being a spade (like his dad's and his dad's dad's).

And the rest of the syllabus is too unbearable to even think about. Why do people like Shakespeare? I wish I did. I've tried but I don't. Maybe you need a jokey teacher to bring it to life.

Nunney has kept saying I made a big mistake in focusing on the Hardy when I would've enjoyed the Heaney. MK has said exactly the same thing.

I reminded Nunney it was him who rejected the Heaney at the outset.

Me: You said you didn't fancy the Heaney.

N: Yes, but I'm me, and you're you.

Me: Not when it comes to the syllabus.

Nunney's off soon to hitch-hike round France/Spain (on his own) for a couple of weeks. He's going to take *The Hitch-Hiker's Guide to Europe* and Chaucer's *Canterbury Tales* (the whole thing) with him so we can thrash it out when he gets back. I don't want to thrash Chaucer out really. But mustn't look a gift horse in the mouth.

I must make sure I've read the Heaney by the time he's back, to make up for not reading the *Canterbury Tales,* which I won't have.

Love, Nina

∽

Dear Vic,

Trying to read the Chaucer so I can impress Nunney when he returns. I'm still not liking it that much.

Me: He's going to come home and be au fait with Chaucer's entire *Canterbury Tales.*
MK: He won't even have looked at it.
Me: Hope not.
MK: He'll be having far too good a time.
Me: God, that's worse.

MK says the secret is to *get* it (Chaucer)—you don't have to *like* it. And though I'm not 100% liking it, I am beginning to get it. Especially the *Wife of Bath*. She's unreliable—i.e. she says she's voracious (for sex), but also says she has sex for money (via strategic marriages). Anyone truly voracious would do it for free, or even pay to do it.

Knowing she's vice-ridden and unreliable, and that I don't *have* to like her, actually makes me like her (a bit).

Exams soonish. Here is a summing up.

R&J: Romeo and Juliet hardly know each other, but think they're in love and both kill themselves. The nurse is an irresponsible idiot. The Friar is a moron. It's a ludicrous story.

Return of the Native: Egdon Heath (a heath, not a person) is the main character. Eustacia is a slag. Clym is a wimp. Wildeve—landlord of the Quiet Woman—has got wandering-hand trouble.

Winter's Tale: King is mentally ill. Queen is a fool.

Chaucer: W of Bath is an unreliable old bag but not a hypocrite. Marries for money but likes shagging, thinks woman should be in charge.

Prioress. Dislikes and mistrusts Jews but feels sorry for trapped mice and weeps if someone hits a dog.

Seamus Heaney:

> He loves the land—its peaty features,
> and likes the sound of farmy things.
> Creel, he writes, and flax and furrow.
> But when effing winter brings
> a stubble-face with peaceful eyelids
> the whole thing starts him worrying.

Love, Nina

PS Brutus isn't in *R&J*, you might be thinking of Tybalt (Juliet's aggressive cousin, dies at the end).

∽

Dear Vic,

Kids at UCS (Will's school) are making homemade chewing gum with Blu-Tack and toothpaste. Will had a go but it wouldn't blend. I think you have to heat it, but didn't tell Will that.

Me: Has it worked?

Will: (*chewing*) It's not blended—I'm blending by chewing.

Me: Don't swallow it.

Will: I'm not going to (*coughs and looks shocked*).

Me: What?

Will: Nothing.

Me: Where's the Blu-Tack?

Will: I swallowed it.

Me: God, Will, do you feel OK?

Will: (*shudders*) Yes, minty fresh.

Rang Amanda for advice.

Me: Will's swallowed Blu-Tack.

A: So?

Me: Will he be all right?

A: I don't know.

Me: Should I induce him to vomit?

A: No, that's for poisons. Better to sluice it down, make him drink some warm milk.

Me: That'd make him vomit.

Discussed it with Will.

Me: Could you vomit it back up?

Will: No, it's gone down fine.

Me: How big was the Blu-Tack?

Will: About as big as a bean.

Me: What kind of bean?

Will: Baked.

Me: How do you feel now?

Will: Stupid.

Sam was down to two pairs of PJs. Reason: we've left a few pairs behind at Great Ormond Street. Plus one pair of bottoms got used in an emergency when "someone" forgot to put the petrol cap back on. They couldn't go back to being pajama bottoms after being the petrol cap, due to smell—even after three washes. Got him a new pack of two from Woolies, with a Man-in-the-Moon motif (it was either that or a teddy in a nightcap).

Sam: I don't really like these (*new pajamas*).
MK: Why?
Sam: I don't like the hard thing in the middle (*embroidered Man-in-the-Moon motif*).
MK: It's the Man in the Moon.
Sam: I hate space.
Me: Ignore it, then.
Sam: You can't ignore space.
Me: Would you have preferred a teddy in a nightcap?
Sam: Well, yes, I could've ignored it.

More bad news.

Washing machine was sticking on the main wash and not moving on. Therefore it was just washing and washing and washing (going round and round). And you had to nudge it on, via the dial, which doesn't do it any good in the long run.

Once neither of us nudged it and it went for hours and everything came out all matted. AB suggested it was something to do with the water not heating up to the target temperature and therefore not moving on to the next part of the cycle. It's amazing how much AB knows about appliances (when you consider he's a writer and pretty much just writes all day.)

Me: You're good with appliances.

AB: (*proud*) Well, I don't know about that.

Me: You sorted out the car, the fridge, the phone, bike tires and now the washing machine.

AB: I don't think I'm particularly good.

MK: But it's nice to know you've got something to fall back on.

Anyway, it's fixed now, a bloke came round and it was what AB said (temperature thing).

Love, Nina

∽

Dear Vic,

Something from ages ago. I asked Michael Neve if he or MK had ever been in one of Stephen Frears's films and he said, "Yes. Wilmers and I did star together in a long-running drama." Something along those lines.

And so I asked MK what thing of Stephen's she was in and she said she never was in a thing of Stephen's (unless I counted the marriage).

At the time I thought either Neve was lying to impress me (unlikely) or MK was being modest (likely) and didn't want me going on about it. But now I've got the hang of things, I know they never were in a film, it's just Neve's way.

The chicken thing was nice (thanks for recipe) but I overdid the tarragon a bit, which proves AB right on the subject (tarragon can overpower a chicken).

The reason I overdid it (the tarragon) was that the dish is called Tarragon Chicken. Why call it that if there's only a tiny bit of tarragon in it? You may as well call it Onion Chicken—there's loads of onion in it, which doesn't get a mention in the title. I don't even like tarragon.

They liked the banana loaf. I'll leave raisins out next time, Sam took his out and they went through the wash in his pocket. Will put Flora on his but scraped it off again.

Sam has raffle tickets from school to sell. Prizes (donated by parents and local businesses) include frozen pork (half a pig) and a meal for four at Beckett's fish bar and a dozen bottles of assorted wines and spirits to the value of £50. And many more.

Strange. A glass of fizzy water I've got by my bed (now) that's been there for an hour suddenly just bubbled up noisily.

Love, Nina
PS MK has now bought some tarragon vinegar (vinegar with a clump of tarragon in it).

∽

Hi, Vic,

Thanks for recipe. Not our cup of tea really but did your potato thing. Sam loved it. Also did the lentil dhal thing you got off R Patel. V good.

My version was: red lentils, onion, celery, water, tin toms, Patak's curry paste. Yoghurt and cucumber on top. Served with basmati rice.

Me: It's R Patel's recipe.
MK: It's very nice, tell R Patel.
Sam: It's too spicy.
AB: Strictly speaking, it's a side dish.
Me: R Patel serves it as a main.
MK: Nice rice.
Me: Watered by the snow-fed rivers of the Himalayas.
AB: Oh, very nice.

Misty has started a frog collection. Like your geese and Elspeth's pigs, G's giraffes, Nunney's mother's Afghans, AB's lemons and the penises in Rhodes.

Bought her a paper clip holder (made of two frogs, for her collection) but it turned out to have a sexual aspect. So donated it to the kitchen dresser.

Will: Why is she collecting frogs?
Me: It's a thing people do, they collect stuff in the shape of a thing.
Sam: It's instead of supporting a football club, for women.
Me: Yes, and they buy mini soaps and everyday items in the shape of their chosen thing.
Sam: What's yours?
Me: I don't have a chosen thing.
Sam: How about a sea horse?
Will: Or shark?

Misty gave me a money-saving device for collecting up little nub ends of soap. It squeezes them together and you have a new bar of soap (eventually). Showed MK.

Me: It's a money-saving thing.
MK: How much did it cost?
Me: £2.99.
MK: How much is a bar of soap?

The thing is we have Simple soap which forms deep cracks if it dries out, which it does if it doesn't get used. Which it doesn't. We never have nub ends, we have great big, dried-out old cracked bars of Simple. We discuss the nub end thing and soap in general.

Me: Maybe we should use a different soap, which stays nicer.

MK: Or maybe we could just *use* the Simple soap.

I want to go back to Imperial Leather which never cracks and just stays in a neat soap shape and wish I hadn't mentioned the cracks in the Simple.
Hope all's well with you.

Love, Nina

⁓

July 1984

Dear Vic,
Nunney home from his time hitch-hiking across France/Spain. He's had a very nice time and keeps going on about it. He told me about going to Pamplona and how a chubby woman (aroused by the charging bulls or tomatoes or whatever they have there) had very forcefully tried to have sex with him but he'd resisted her advances.

Nunney: She jumped me.
Me: Oh.
Nunney: But I resisted.
Me: Well, you didn't have to resist on my account.
Nunney: I had to resist on *my* account.

He also mentioned about a bloke and another couple of women making advances (in cars while he was hitch-hiking) and described how he skillfully and tactfully resisted *their* advances.
He seems to have spent his whole time tactfully resisting offers of sex from the population of France/Spain. I asked why he thought he

was so popular and desirable all of a sudden. He said it's the same wherever he is.

He's come back wearing espadrilles. Not sure about them (in general) or on him.

Love, Nina

PS He enjoyed Chaucer's *Canterbury Tales*. Apparently the book was very attractive to women, who often approached him to talk about the great English writer and ended up buying him a beer.

∽

Dear Vic,

Saturday: went to the zoo with Nunney. He climbed over, I thought I'd have a go, but in the end went through the entrance and paid. I wanted to see the camels first and foremost. But was also interested in the famous penguin pool and anything very big.

The camels were disappointing with patchy fur and poo clumps. The worst thing was that they seemed unhappy. Even the camel keeper said, "They have been known to nibble each other out of boredom."

He said nibble but he probably meant bite. Possibly even kill if left to their own devices. Poor things.

Nunney liked the wolves. I didn't much (yellow eyes). You can see them from the park side of the fence anyway, sloping around looking mean and furtive.

Sam's trying to make a ball out of elastic bands. He ran out (of elastic bands) so we went round 57 and found a few. Some were holding things together, bundles of letters and stuff. Also changed the letters on the key hooks from CLAIRES KEYS to SCARY SLEEKI.

I thought it was quite clever, but Nunney is a bit outraged. More so than usual, probably because he's no longer on the payroll and is now a "friend of the family."

Nunney: What did you do to the key hooks?

Me: I changed the letters.

N: You fucking psycho.

Me: It was clever, I made new words.

N: It was not clever. It was cuntish.

Me: Surely people are forever changing those letters around, they're removable.

N: No, no one does. Only you.

Love, Nina

⁓

Dear Vic,

MK's birthday (43, 44?).

S&W and me did tea. BLT sandwiches (triangles)—same as she had in New York. She thought it was funny and nice that we'd remembered her saying about them.

Sam kept calling them DLTs.

AB said we should've toasted the bread slightly to make them authentic New York style. He's right, it would've been better. The bread, untoasted, sticks to the roof of your mouth.

Thin sliced white bread (slightly toasted)
Bacon grilled crispy
Tomato slices
Lettuce leaves
Mayonnaise

Will made a tower of pancakes (5) with syrup. He wanted to set them alight but he was getting mixed up with crêpes suzette.

Mary Hope gave MK a nice thing that she'd knitted herself—

sweatery thing, speckled that she's got one the same as, only brown/orange. MK's was gray/blue.

AB gave her some soap you can only get in France.

Polly drew her a map of Africa with all the countries done in a different color. She's done the same for Granny Wilmers, only bigger and on card. She knows all the borders off by heart (Polly does).

We're getting a lot of little floaty black flies in the kitchen. AB says they're fruit flies.

Glad all good there (except for Brandy news).

Love, Nina

PS A friend of MK's gave her a chiming thing you hang in the garden that makes a tinkling noise and keeps away bad spirits. MK didn't want it—(a) she doesn't like tinkling noises and (b) she's not 100% anti bad spirits. I kept it (for you, if you want it).

꩜

Dear Vic,

To France next week to Mary-Kay's house.

Feels funny not having the syllabus to think about. Nunney says I must get straight on with the Thames Poly summer reading list and work my way through as much as I can over the summer to prepare for the course because many of the other students will have been to school and done all sorts of learning and exams.

The Thames reading list is not referred to as a syllabus, just a reading list. The list is very long with sections for different subjects. I've not read a single book on the list. Nunney said to pick something enjoyable and easy to start with, like *The Ragged Trousered Philanthropists*.

Showed Mary-Kay the reading list. She also thinks *Ragged Trousered Philanthropists* is a good place to start (social, political, economic and cultural).

So that's where I'll start.

I'll read it in France and on the journey. It's a big book. Sam has Sherlock Holmes cassettes to listen to on his Walkman, lucky Sam.

I'll ring when I'm back.

Love, Nina

෪

(Postcard)

Dear Vic,

France. Sam and me shared a tiny room on the train (bunk-beds). It was brilliant. Sam listened to Sherlock Holmes tape and I could tell it was exciting. I borrowed it as soon as he'd finished and wished I hadn't—really spooky. Couldn't sleep in my little bunk-bed—a bit scared—Sam got fed up with me trying to chat and ended up shouting at me to shut the fuck up and let him go to sleep. I felt quite proud of him.

Love, Nina

෪

August 1984

Dear Vic,

Nunney rang me in France with A level result. I was shocked. I knew I hadn't done very well, but an E is really bad. Nunney says it's a pass and that's fantastic (considering).

I didn't even think an E was a pass to start with, but it is, it says so on the sheet apparently. But it's the worst pass you can get except for a plain "pass" with no letter. There's also an F (but that's a fail).

169

Told Mary-Kay and co I got a C.

Sometimes you just have to lie. And I had to because the result came while I was at MK's house in France and loads of her mates were there, eating basil and speaking French. I couldn't say, "Oh, yes, I passed. I got an E."

Even saying a C sounded bad enough.

MK: So?
Me: What?
MK: Did you pass?
Me: Yes, I got a C.
MK: A C?
Me: Yes.
MK: Very good.
The others: (*mumbling*) Well done.

Apart from the E, France was great.

The house is lovely. Thick walls, stone floors and melons growing in the fields along the roads. Sam listening to his Walkman and singing along to *Scoop* by Pete Townshend—including "I Just Wanna Be Popular" which he does, and is.

Loads of fresh herbs. One day we only had green beans for lunch and another day just a salad and bread.

Love, Nina

∾

Dear Vic,

Back in London. AB was away and did not require supper.

Me: Where is AB?

Sam: He's gone to Coventry.

Me: Literally or metaphorically?

Sam: I hate it when you say things like that.

Me: Literally or metaphorically?

Will: He literally hates it!

For ages Mel the trainee beautician friend of Pippa has been saying I should have this, that and the other done, beautywise, and how great I'd look etc. This is how she gets business, saying how much better you'd look if you had a manicure. A bit like Mr. Mackie's plastic surgeon friend. They make you feel insecure so you'll fork out. Anyway I agreed to let Mel do an eyebrow and eyelash tint on me for £2.50.

We did it in her flat. While she did it she told me not to speak in case the eyelash tint seeped in (apparently your eyes flicker when you speak). So she did all the talking.

She told me about when thieves nicked her handbag in the Spread Eagle. They'd lifted the bag off the door peg while she was on the toilet. She couldn't chase after it because she had her dungarees down and they're quite complex to put back up. She thinks the thieves targeted the dungarees (with getaway time in mind). I just said "mmm" occasionally.

It reminded me of Mr. Johnson, who used to bore his patients to death while they were unable to talk back ("my lawn is like a hayfield, Mr. Dewick, I don't know about yours"/"I recently discovered that authentic lasagna has sausage in it, I didn't know that").

Afterward:

Beautician Mel: (*holding mirror right up to my face*) There you go, lovely black eyelashes for up to six weeks.

Me: They look very red.

Mel: You were sensitive to the ammonia.

171

Me: Isn't everyone?

Mel: Some tint must've seeped in while we chatted.

Me: I didn't chat.

At 55.

MK: That's better.

Me: What?

MK: Whatever you've done.

Me: To what?

MK: Yourself.

Me: I had a lash and brow tint from Mel.

MK: V. good.

Will likes a café called Garfunkel's. The waiters are unhappy and the food is rubbish/fancy. There's a pudding on the menu called Toffee-nose Sundae. Why not just Toffee Sundae? Said this to Will. He said, "I think you just hate the word 'nose.'" And ordered one. Will was impressed that the bread rolls were in nice shapes. Earlier in the week we'd made bread shapes after seeing people do it in Camden Lock. Sam did a football and Will did the letter A. I did a hedgehog. They all just came out like bread rolls.

Love, Nina

∽

Dear Vic,

I had to do the big shop today, due to MK being very busy at the paper.

I hate Sainsbury's. The fridgy smell and the coldness. I don't usually feel cold, but in Sainsbury's I feel chilly and I realize that's how most people (esp. women, i.e. MK) feel a lot of the time (cold and annoyed), which explains a lot. It's not a nice feeling and no wonder they're always snuggling up in cardigans and buying walnut whips to cheer themselves up.

MK has been given a notepad where every page is the shape of a strawberry (by a friend's daughter). MK uses the notepad now and we keep getting strawberry notes.

Strawberry note: pls get vegetables / salad whatever. And strawberries?

Remember I thought the O'Connells' painting of a flamenco dancer was a red pepper? The same thing happened to Sam.

Writer types are compelled to write. So in cafés, when they're supposed to be eating and making nice conversation, they write ideas on napkins in felt tip. MK does it a bit, but Neve does it the most. The other day he drew a heart on a napkin and wrote "mK Wilmers" in it.

Sam: (*scrutinizing napkin*) What's that?
Neve: That, my dear Sam, is my heart.
Sam: Is it?
Neve: Yes, with your mother's name etched on the pericardium.
Sam: Oh, it looks like a red pepper.
Neve: Thank you.

Neve is a very funny man.

Love, Nina

⁓

Dear Vic,

There's a woman who walks down the street every day with the biggest arse you've ever seen. The thing is, they don't like being mean

173

about people in that way (except Will) so I was keeping it to myself (apart from Will).

Then Will brought it up at supper.

Will: I think I've seen that woman.

Me: What woman?

Will: That one you mentioned with the huge arse.

MK: What woman?

Me: Oh, just this woman.

Will: It's huge.

MK: What's huge?

Will: Her arse.

AB: That's not very nice, Will.

Will: (*laughing*) You're right, it's horrible.

MK stayed quiet on the subject (unlike her).

Me: You've seen it, haven't you?

MK: I might have.

Will: You'd know.

MK: I have.

AB: Don't be so mean, all of you. Honestly!

MK: (*to AB*) It *is* huge.

AB: Stop it!

MK: But you've not seen it.

AB: I *have* actually, but I don't think you should make fun.

MK: He's not seen it.

Me: No.

Sam is back to school, but not Will yet. And MK is still interviewing nannies. Her favorite is this awful one with a high ponytail from Kent. Her second favorite is a very nice one from Somerset—too nice in my opinion.

Overdid the sunflower oil this morning and Sam was late for school.

MK: How much did you put in?
Me: A dash.
MK: It's meant to be a teaspoon. It's porridge, not a marinade.

Love, Nina

꩜

Dear Vic,

I'm moving into Mary Hope's spare room. It'll be my digs while I'm at Thames Poly. The house is great (as previously reported) and Mary and Polly and JDF are great. Plus the fact that Polly is not only brainy (literaturewise) but funny too.

MK isn't 100% happy about me going there but she isn't 100% unhappy either and that's the way it goes. She'll be pleased in the long run. Just needs time to get used to it.

Me: Mary has said I can live in their spare room.
MK: Oh.
Me: I thought you'd be pleased.
MK: That you'll be psyching out the new nanny and putting grenades in our supper—great, can't wait.
Me: And I'll be able to look at Sam's eye.
MK: There is that.

Anyway, all feels very strange and I haven't even gone yet. Nunney's gone to Sussex.

Love, Nina

~

Sep 1984

Dear Vic,

Watching England play (E. Germany?). My last telly football match at 55. I didn't mention this to anyone else, decided to just enjoy it.

Sam: (*speaking to Bobby Robson*) What do you go and pick two bloody Ipswich players for (*taps the screen*)?
MK: Stop tapping the screen.
Sam: (*to Bryan Robson*) Come on, Robbo.
MK: Stop putting your hands all over the screen.
Sam: Come on, England.
Sam: I can't watch. I hate football.
Will: It's only a friendly.
Sam: (*to Bobby Robson*) It's only a friendly, Bobby (*taps screen*).
MK: Sam, stop touching the screen.
Sam: I can't watch.
MK: Neither can we—all we can see is your hands.

I felt sad at the end. But didn't say anything.

I don't think Mary Hope & co watch much football whereas MK and S&W watch as much as possible. So I'll have to come round here for it. Not that I like it that much, but I like watching it with them. MK mentions if a player has nice hair and Sam puts the Vs up to the ref and Will covers his face at the tense bits. They're just themselves watching football only more so.

Love, Nina

II
MOVING ON
1984–1987

Dear Vic,

Moved into Mary Hope's house on Regent's Park Terrace. It's v. nice.

Started Thames Polytechnic.

First day was just getting to know stuff and sorting out options etc. Second day actually had a seminar. History of Western Thought.

We had to go (in pairs) and use the library and write a short paper to prove or disprove the existence of God. I looked round the room looking for someone to pair with and ruled out anyone (a) with spiky hair (b) over fifty (c) stupid-looking (d) posh. This left one person. A girl called Stella Heath (northern, perm, thin white belt). She said, "I'm Stella Heath," and then spelt it out for me (H-E-A-T-H).

She wasn't as brainy as I'd thought she was going to be. She hadn't read a single thing off the summer reading list and wasn't familiar with the Cogito ergo sum thing (Descartes: I think, therefore I am...etc.) and is only at Thames Poly due to getting unexpectedly bad grades.

She was a bit of a letdown, to be honest.

Me: I chose you because you seemed brainy.
SH: I'm not really.
Me: It might've helped if you'd read the summer reading list.
SH: I was working in a doughnut booth at Butlin's till last week (*defensive*).

Off we went to the library and looked up all the relevant bits of Modern Western Thought and Stella Heath kept putting a Vicks Sinex thing up her nose (summer cold).

We spoke a bit each of our argument (God Does Not Exist) and the bloke (Peter Widdowson) said we made a coherent argument via Descartes, and that that was what he was hoping for.

He did say that students more often proved the *existence,* rather than the *non*-existence, of God via Descartes, as that was what

Descartes would have wanted, but not to worry, we'd got the gist.

So I was pleased. Had a cup of tea in the refectory and Stella Heath told me her mother was an Alan Bennett fan. How funny. I didn't say anything (about AB) but it just shows how popular he is.

Then I came home, to here. And it's great and I'm lucky to be a student and have such a great home, but I'm missing S&W & MK and feel a bit strange about it all.

Keep seeing them going about their business across the gardens and want to go round and see them and to tell AB about Stella Heath's mum being a huge fan. But won't yet.

Love, Nina

PS I know how AB feels now.

$\backsim$

October 1984

Dear Vic,

Sam refuses to walk round to Regent's Park Terrace on his own now—since he got cornered by Yogi at the railings. Yogi's owner (next-door-but-one) did her best to smooth things out.

Woman: (*to Sam, through letter box*) Yogi was probably as scared as you were.

Sam: (*inside, talking through letter box*) I don't think he was.

Woman: He's very friendly really.

Sam: So am I.

Woman: (*to me*) Would he like to come out and shake paws?

Sam: No fucking way.

180

Don't know what type Yogi is, but he's very small and friendly. Mary Hope thinks he's a Pekinese, but he's too fluffy in my opinion. She's a bit anti small dogs (her dog, Chilly, is a Labrador).

Now I have to walk round to meet Sam outside Joan Thirkettle's (halfway), which is annoying. Sometimes one of us has to wait there for the other, usually me. What must she think (Joan Thirkettle)?

Wondering about getting a stepladder for the back wall. Two stepladders.

MK is not getting along with new nanny that well. I'm guessing she keeps asking her if she's had a nice weekend…and has she had her hair done etc., which gets on MK's nerves. But there's no stopping some people. I know because she does it to me. She's too nice. I knew she would be.

I remember once, in 1982, asking MK if she'd had a nice weekend and I could see it didn't go down well so never asked again. Still don't, even to other people. I don't like it myself now.

For instance, Nunney on the phone the other day.

Nunney: Did you have a nice weekend?
Me: What?
Nunney: I'm being platitudinous.
Me: What?
Nunney: The gulf gets wider by the day.

And I had that annoying thing where you understand perfectly what someone means, but not till half an hour later.

I'm giving *some* people a special code for the phone so I'll know if it's for me. Otherwise I'm running up and down taking calls from Heal's for Mary.

Remember this: Dial my number, let it ring three times and then hang up. Wait a moment and ring back. Then I'll pick up (if I'm at home). If you don't do the code I won't answer and Mary or Polly will say I'm out. It's designed to filter out people I don't want to talk to and to save time. It's called the "three-ring difference."

Sam knows the code but can slightly hear this phone ringing at 55 and it confuses him and he often goes to four rings before he hangs up. It still works though. Three or four rings are OK. Don't let it slip to five rings or it'll be picked up before you hang up.

Mary-Kay knows the code too, unfortunately. She rings now and again to ask if I've got things of hers.

MK: (*on phone*) Have you nicked the *Halliwell's*?
Me: No.
MK: The video card?
Me: No.
MK: What about the big stripy towel?
Me: No.
MK: The one with the green, blue, and red stripes.
Me: No.
MK: I can see it, in your room, right now, hanging on a chair.
Me: (*pause*) OK, I've got the towel but not the rest.
MK: How can I believe you? You lied about the towel.
Me: I wish I hadn't given you the code.
MK: Well, you did.

Mary-Kay likes the three-ring code and says she might adopt a similar phone-answering system for 55.

Me: It could get tricky for the people we have in common.
MK: We don't have people in common.
Me: There must be someone who rings us both.

MK: There *mustn't.*

Me: God, no, there isn't. I'm just an offshoot.

Love, Nina

PS Please come and stay soon.

∾

Dear Vic,

Thames Polytechnic is very good and I like being at college. Sometimes I see a reflection of myself walking along with my little bag of books (the texts) and I feel…thrilled is the only word I can think of. I can't believe I'm studying for a BA Hons Bachelor of Arts (don't know what the Hons bit means).

The lecturers know the stuff inside out and make it interesting and funny.

Lectures: You just scribble down everything the lecturer says (you have to be quick)—don't interrupt or put hand up, as it's strictly the lecturer talking.

Then go to the refectory for a coffee and talk about the lecture/ lecturer. I'm having coffee almost all the time now. Learnt that bad tea is a lot worse than bad coffee (bad coffee is only a bit worse than normal coffee, especially if you prefer tea).

Then other people (non-attendees of lecture) turn up and ask to see people's lecture notes and copy them down. To be honest, I'm not keen on this ritual and think it's like doing someone else's work for them, but I go along with it so as not to look a cunt.

I can always tell which students have stayed on at school and taken A levels and which ones didn't. The ones who went through sixth form don't take sugar. The ones who left school before exams (like me) always take two sugars. Except for me. I'm more like the traditional students (sugarwise).

Seminars: for each seminar you have to have read a certain book or play and a bit of connected theory. Then you have the seminar and discuss certain aspect(s) of the text(s) for an hour.

This is your chance to be noticed as brilliant or idiotic. You must contribute (intelligently) to the discussion, otherwise it looks as though you haven't read the text(s). The academic might say, "Who's actually read this?" and "What's the point of coming?" to those who haven't. Sometimes people who haven't read the text are told they may as well leave the seminar and that's the ultimate shame. It nearly happened to Stella. She hadn't read the Alfred Lord Tennyson (not one single poem) but got away with it due to me having said something about Darwin in the coffee bar beforehand.

Tutor: What do we assume Tennyson's referring to here?
Stella: Is it to do with Darwin?
Tutor: (*excited*) YES! Exactly. Tennyson and his cronies were reeling from the new theories, which questioned everything blah, blah.

I *always* read the texts plus extra stuff, but that's because I'm officially a mature student (20+) and we're the reliable ones. Plus I couldn't bear to not have read the text(s).

Stella says it shows a fear of authority. I say it shows I'm not an idiot.

One bad thing is I've had to pair up with this kid called Zig for a short project. We were paired by register proximity (I didn't choose him). Stella is paired with a posh kid with a fear of the marketplace (his words) called Henderson.

I don't know if mine (Zig) is a girl or a boy, which is awkward. All I know is s/he is reluctant to do any work and just keeps picking his/her nail varnish off and that s/he is disappointed there aren't as many punks as s/he was expecting in the Woolwich area. I know this because s/he's written a song called "Where have all the punks gone" about a lonely neo-punk. It reminded me of Will's lonely dog eating burger buns in Hampstead.

Round at 55. Moaning about Zig.

Me: I don't know if he's a girl or a boy.

MK: Does it make that much difference?

Me: Yes, we're doing slavery together.

MK: But why do you need to know?

Me: I just do.

MK: See him as a colleague, not a sperm donor.

(*AB arrives.*)

AB: How's it going at college?

Me: Really good.

MK: She's hanging around with Tootsie.

AB: And how about living with Mary and Polly?

Me: Great.

MK: She's taken half our stuff with her.

AB: No?

MK: Yes, she's a thief and a liar.

AB: No, don't say that.

MK: Yes.

Me: It was *one* towel.

MK: I'd have given you a towel if you'd asked.

Me: Yeah, but not that big stripy one.

MK: That's true.

Love, Nina

PS Tennyson (Alfred, Lord). Poems are good and a bit shocking. "Maud," about a woman called Maud whose brother basically stops the narrator from seeing Maud. Narrator then kills the brother in a fight and has to flee.

185

I'm noticing that blokes in poems (and plays) are always having to flee and leave women to die of broken hearts (Maud dies of one). So that's the story, but ignoring that, the actual poem is good and there's a bit that starts "I hate the dreadful hollow behind the little wood" that's quite breathtaking.

∽

Dear Vic,

Mary Hope held a belated little housewarming party at Regent's Park Terrace.

Jez and me and one of my friends from Thames Poly were the waiters. We just wandered about giving people glasses of champagne and little bits of bread and paste and it seemed to go well.

The morning after, the girl from Thames Poly came into my bedroom and said she'd had it off with X in Mary's basement flatlet.

Me: Oh God.
Girl: (*grinning*) Yeah, he was a real Brian Hooper.
Me: What do you mean?
Girl: He had an enormous lute.
Me: Oh.
Girl: (*giggling*) He nearly pole-vaulted out of the window.
Me: Oh no, are you serious?
Girl: Yes (*biting lower lip*).

It seems such a rude thing to have done in someone else's house (flatlet), with someone else's friend and after being paid by Mary Hope to take a tray round. She must've been flirting all evening instead of circulating properly and making sure no one had an empty glass (as instructed). Told Mary H (in case she'd got wind of it) and I wanted to distance myself from it.

Mary H didn't mind at all though, she thought it was "wonderful."

Went to 55 for supper later and told MK. She thought it was "fantastic" and when AB arrived (with a can of Skol and a bowl like a horse's hoof with an old pudding in it) she straightaway wanted me to tell him about it.

MK: Tell him about the thing.

Me: Oh, you tell him.

MK: I can't remember all the names and terms.

Me: OK. The names are X and X and Brian Hooper and the terms are "lute" and "pole-vault."

AB: Yes, enough, I get it.

MK: To caper nimbly in a lady's chamber to the lascivious pleasing of a lute.

Me: What?

MK: It comes from something or other.

AB: Say it again.

MK: (*quickly*) To caper nimbly in a lady's chamber to the lascivious pleasing of a lute.

AB: Anyway, there's not much left and it's a bit claggy, but would anyone like a spoonful of rice pudding?

I'm like AB now. I don't live at 55 but I go round all the time. And I think it's fine that I go round all the time. And they think it's fine. I'm halfway between a visitor and part of the household. When MK gets home from the office, she half expects me to be there and half the time I am there.

The nanny doesn't seem to mind, she's very welcoming, because she's nice.

I might have minded if, when I was the nanny, the Leeds United predecessor had kept popping in and cooking pancakes. But she didn't (keep popping in).

Love, Nina
PS Don't forget the three-ring difference if you phone.

⌒

Dear Vic,

Handbags: I'm going to say "thanks but no thanks" to the Handy Organizer—(a) I'm not that kind of person (unfortunately) and (b) I don't have to be organized in that kind of way.

I'll say no on MK's behalf too. MK uses a kind of basket thing. Like a shopping basket, but soft stuff, like hay, not straw, but straw-colored with muted stripes. Long leather straps over the shoulder and a pickpocket's dream.

I've gone on to a longish canvas bag like a plumber's bag. MK can't bear to look at it (not because of it looking like a plumber's bag—some other thing). Will says it's Pinteresque (which is good and bad). Sam quite likes it, it reminds him of a cricket bag.

College is awkward (bag and shoewise)—you can't be girly or you look like a slag, therefore it's easy to go the other way and be too blokey.

The other day I wore a long green cardigan that Mary Hope gave me from a shop called Hobbs where everything's smart (and good quality) and a bloke in my seminar said I looked "luxurious." And all the girls wanted to try it on. In other words: it was inappropriate.

But thanks for the bag offer anyway and good luck in shifting them.

Love, Nina
PS Doing Nunney's sister's Chicken Supreme tonight.

~

Dec 1984

Dear Vic,

Thanks for gift. I love it. Hadn't mentioned it here (b'day), but Sam (who always remembers stuff) remembered and alerted everyone.

MK gave me a book of short stories called *The Little Disturbances of Man*. Good, but not your cup of tea.

Mary Hope gave me a cardigan and said, "Change it," but I won't—lovely color (grayish green). Gave it me early (the one I mentioned that I wore for college and was inappropriate).

Will gave me a Curly Wurly and had a bite of it and all the chocolate fell off. And Sam gave me *Whittaker's Almanac* (not from Central Stationers).

Going out now. Movie and food.

Love, Nina

~

Regent's Park Terrace, Xmas 1984

Dear Vic,

Went round to 55.

Xmas tree up. Properly upright in an attractive bucket in the stair bend, where it always goes. Not wobbly or at an angle, but solid. The new nanny had erected it and was about to rush off (for Xmas).

Me: The tree looks good.
Nanny: I had to take a few inches off it.

189

Me: Did you use a saw?

Nanny: Borrowed Jonathan Miller's.

Me: Where is it now?

Nanny: I took it back.

Disappointed. I could've taken it back myself to make up for previous year...but no, she'd already done it.

Went round to 55 again later to decorate the Xmas tree. The boxes came out and we all held up things we like (or don't). I like a little bell with the word "Noel" on it. I like it because it tinkles when the tree shudders (which it won't do this year).

Me: The bell won't tinkle this year, the tree's too steady.

MK: Can't have everything.

Will likes a glass snowflake, which he used to call an icicle, and Sam likes a pinecone with snow on it (which MK dislikes for being big.)

MK: What do you like about it?

Sam: It's big, and it's real.

MK: Christmas isn't about big things or real things.

Sam: What about the tree?

MK: The tree's the only big, real thing allowed.

Will: What about baby Jesus?

MK: He's small.

MK likes an old M-E-R-R-Y-C-H-R-I-S-T-M-A-S bunting thing in multicolored metallic letters. This is strung up along the top of the dresser. It's a bit ripped on the second M and fixed with eye tape. She also likes an angel that Sam made with a doily skirt who goes on top and falls off a lot. And a purple anemone.

Baubleswise, MK doesn't like big or tasteful things. Only shiny, small, pretty, tatty and all mixed up. And therefore hated my idea of a theme—a thing I'd heard about that Americans do, where they choose one image-of-Xmas and one color and stick to those. So you might choose the color Red and Robins (you're allowed silver or gold as well) and that would be what you'd have on the tree and dotted around. And you'd do something different the next year.

I saw a shop where they'd decorated all in pale blue and sandy (Bethlehem colors) and even homemade potato-prints of camels. I didn't suggest it.

AB not around. In Yorkshire or New York. I prefer him being around...God knows what he does in NY (if it is NY), can't imagine him there, being shouted at by taxi drivers and prostitutes. Though his coat would work.

Love, Nina

⌒

Dear Vic,

Mary-Kay has been having a builder round to plan some renovations and to make a new room in the loft and general improvements to various rooms.

I think Carter (the builder) fancies MK.

Carter: Tell you something, I hold that lady in very high esteem.
Me: Who?
Carter: Mary-Kay.
Me: Why?
Carter: She's a rare breed.

I like "a rare breed." I'll try to say it from now on. Told MK that Carter said she was a rare breed.

Me: I think Carter fancies you.
MK: I doubt it.
Me: He thinks you're a rare breed.
MK: (*shrugs*).

MK's got him in to do various work. Including the nanny's quarters. Carter was telling her about this plastic wood—a floor covering that's the image of wood but is actually plastic and therefore washable, even with bleach.

Carter: (*holding a sample*) It looks like the real thing, you'd swear it was wood.
MK: I wouldn't.
Carter: It's bloody tough this is (*jabs at it with screwdriver*), but, to look at, you wouldn't know the diff.
MK: I would.
Carter: You're barmy—this stuff is the business (*jabbing*).
MK: (*looks at him*).
Carter: OK.

That's why Carter likes her. He can't get one over on her. And there's no way she'd have plastic wood however convenient or tough, she'd always want wood, however limited and useless.

I'm pretty sure now the new nanny hasn't worked out. Maybe, psychologically, that's why MK wants the house renovations. Improving the things she can improve (the rooms) to help her accept the things that can't be improved (the nanny).

I think she (the nanny) is good/bad in all the wrong places, which isn't her fault. It's OK to be bad, but it has to be in the right way(s).

Which I just happened to be (on this occasion). You have to be a quick learner and not use too many platitudes. And, most importantly, you have to be nice without seeming to be or overdoing it.

Love, Nina

∽

Dear Vic,

Babysat S&W at 55.

Wore new shoes that I hate but wanted to give them a chance. MK didn't like them either. So that's it. They're too much shoe for her tastes. She likes very little actual shoe and no buckles or flaps (slim feet).

MK: (*frowning*).
Me: What?
MK: Shoes.
Me: I know they're bad, don't look.
MK: I can't stop; I'm trying to work them out.
Will: Me too.
Sam: They're a bit clippy cloppy.
MK: I don't mind the clippy cloppy, it's all the stuff.
Me: I know.

I made very early supper (leek and potato soup) and put too much pepper in.

MK: Nice but peppery.
Me: If you think this is peppery, you should try Mary's pepper, it's not ground up, it's in chunks, you're chewing it.
Sam: Mine's too peppery.

AB: Some soups call for a lot of pepper.

Me: Yes, this soup called for it.

MK: My soup didn't call for quite this much.

Will: Mine did.

Sam: Mine didn't.

Me: Can't please everyone.

MK: Perhaps if you'd responded to individual calls.

MK was going out after the soup (hence me babysitting) and she looked just like a boy (floppy white shirt all scrunched up and hanging out. Gray jacket with pointy lapels and three-quarter-length sleeves).

Me: You look like the Artful Dodger.

MK: You *behave* like the Artful Dodger.

Love, Nina

PS Soup would have been OK if I hadn't overdone the pepper. Leeks, potatoes, onions, stock cube, water, and cream (and pepper). Serve with toast and cheese.

∽

Dear Vic,

Just realized I love American drama. Thames Poly has literally hundreds of plays on video and we get to watch them. Which is fantastic. Albeit all crowded round a little telly.

Also, drama tutor Vicki got us all tickets to see an Arthur Miller thing in the West End. Stella isn't used to going to plays and said she felt uncomfortable at the actual "live" theater (as opposed to watching the telly).

SH: I just feel uncomfortable at the theater.

Me: Me too. It's the anxiety that something embarrassing is going to happen.

SH: No, I mean the seats.

Anyway, the Arthur Miller play was good but Stella fell asleep because she'd had a couple of pints of beer in the pub beforehand and snored.

Tutor Vicki: Was someone snoring in Act Two?

SH: No.

Me: Yes, someone was, but it wasn't any of us.

Told Stella later that the knee-jerk denial wasn't believable and made her look guilty (which she was). She's so immature.

Remember the girl from Thames Poly ("he nearly pole-vaulted out of the window")? She's in my theater studies tutor group. She's chirpy and very much models herself on Rita from *Educating Rita*.

Tutor Vicki: How can Chekhov show us it's winter and yet hint that spring's just around the corner?

Girl: Frozen bird shit at the junction.

She might even have got that line from *Educating Rita* (it was so funny).

Told Will about it. He loves hearing stuff about college, especially when people are funny like that. Will's way ahead of himself literature/dramawise and has already seen two hard-hitting things about salesmen and reads Dickens.

Sam's still on *Wind in the Willows*.

Love, Nina

Dear Vic,

Stella Heath definitely keen to be friends. She'd arranged for a bloke from the council to go round to her house to look at her roof (a flock of birds are nesting in there and bothering her). And she asked if I'd go back with her when he was due (for moral support).

Me: Won't your boyfriend be at home?
Stella: He'll be asleep.
Me: At three in the afternoon?
Stella: He's a postman.

We went back to hers on the day in question (after a seminar about religion conning poor people into believing that an acceptance of an unfair/dreadful life on earth will earn them a place in heaven). The council birdman was waiting outside in a van. He said he was from pest control but specialized in birds.

Stella broke the first rule of dealing with people by failing to offer him a hot beverage. And that set the tone. As soon as he realized she wasn't going to offer, he was grumpy.

SH: There seem to be birds under there (*points to roof*).
Birdman: (*grumpy*) What makes you think that?
SH: Bird noises and flapping.
Birdman: What kind of noise?
SH: Bird type noise.
(*Birdman looks up at roof and there's a long pause.*)
Birdman: Is it a coo or more of a tweet?
SH: I think it's a coo, but it might be a tweet.
Birdman: Cooing and tweeting mean different things. Is it like this (*coo*) or this (*tweet*)?

SH: I think it's a coo. What does cooing mean?

Birdman: It's pigeons (*looking hopeful, smiles*).

SH: It's cooing.

Birdman: (*satisfied smile*) It's pigeons!

Me: (*aside*) Did you say it was cooing just to please him?

SH: No, of course not. Why?

Me: It seemed like you did.

SH: I didn't. It is cooing.

Me: You didn't seem that certain.

SH: I am.

The birdman went up a ladder. Stella and me went into her house (bizarre) and she had a hazelnut Ski, then a fag and put the telly on for *Countdown* and put the fag out in the yoghurt pot. After a while, when we'd forgotten all about the birdman, he suddenly tapped on the French window. Stella screamed because she thought it was the landlord (she's got outstanding bills and they've drunk his homebrew).

Birdman: I've sealed the place where they were getting in.

SH: OK.

Birdman: Be vigilant.

SH: OK.

Birdman: If you hear cooing, ring the council.

SH: What if I hear tweeting?

Birdman: Ring the council. Ditto squeaking.

After the man had gone we heard definite tweetings.

Me: Is that tweeting?

SH: Shit.

Me: I knew it.

I went home then and felt that although I always read the set text(s) I'm somehow less of a student than the likes of Stella with her birds and landlord worries.

Went round to 55 to tell about my day. They'd had supper but not pudding. Was telling them about Stella and the birdman and that I love US drama when Mary Hope arrived. Which was funny (fancy seeing you here, etc.).

MK: Such as?

Me: Tennessee Williams, Arthur Miller, Edward Albee (the best), Sam Shepard (second best), David Mamet (third).

MK: What about Sam Shepard?

Me: I said him.

MK: So what about the birdman, then?

Me: Oh God, that was weird.

MK: So what happened?

Me: The most significant thing was when he knocked on the window and she screamed.

MK: Why did she scream?

Me: She owes rent and she thought it was the landlord.

Mary H: (*frowning*) Is this Sam Shepard?

Me: No, it's Stella Heath.

See. Two worlds colliding. We had hot apple pie (lattice) and cream. Then Mary H and me came back here and Polly told us off for being noisy.

Love, Nina

∽

Dear Vic,

Called in at 55 and MK told me to go away because they were going to Mr. Mackie's. I asked if I could go with them. They said OK.

Walking on Harley Street, late for the appointment with Mr. Mackie. MK mardy, in court shoes, me and Sam in plimmies.

MK: We're late—can't you two walk any faster?
Me: Yes, but can *you?*
MK: I'm holding back for you two.
(*Sam and me speed up and overtake.*)
MK: That's running.

At Mr. Mackie's.

Mrs. Boyce (receptionist): Hullo, Sammy.
Sam: Hullo.
Mrs. B: Sorry, but his twelve o'clock has gone in before you—you're a bit late.
MK: Fair enough.
Mrs. B: And if his twelve thirty arrives on time I'm afraid he'll go in before you too. So it might be a bit of a wait. You might have to be patient. You might want to rebook.
MK: We'll see how it goes.
Mrs. B: Or you could rebook.
MK: We'll take our chances.

Thirty seconds later Mr. Mackie calls us in.

MK: (*to Mrs. B*) Our patience seems to have paid off.
Mrs. B: Indeed.
Mr. Mackie: How have you been, Sam?

Sam: What, me in general, or my conjunctiva?

Mr. Mackie: (*laughs*) You've a good memory.

Sam: The nanny's always saying it.

(*Mr. Mackie smiles and looks at me.*)

Sam: She's not the nanny anymore.

Mr. M: Well, it's nice that she still comes along.

Sam: She misses seeing you.

Mr. Mackie seemed pleased, but not as pleased as Sam.

Love, Nina

∽

Dear Vic,

Hair cut.

New hairdresser Melinda. Her real name's Melissa but there was already a stylist called Melissa at the salon (real name Donna) and they can't have two Melissas for obvious reasons. Anyway, Melinda (Melissa) says a wedge would *not* suit, due to high maintenance, so I've had a scruffy bob, but shorter.

Melinda gave me some blow-dry tips (for our type of hair) which I'm going to pass on to you:

Dry the hair the exact opposite of the way you want it. So if you have a left side parting, blow-dry it to the right and so on.

Smooth: if you want it smooth/straight, blow-dry it upside down.

Wavy: if you want it wavy, blow-dry it straight, make it 100% dry. Do not touch or brush it till 10 mins after it's cooled down. Spray with water mist.

Get a decent hair dryer.

I'm going to get a decent hair dryer and a headhog brush. Mary-Kay's got a Krups, but I don't ever hear it going.

MK has a new boyfriend. He's quite scruffy but it might be deliberate. Slightly wonky face that looks good on a man (but not a woman). Nice nose. Navy trousers and brown shoes (combination preferred by writers). Nice in a careful way.

I can tell MK likes him. Not in a handholding way but she's cheerful and having herbal tea.

Me: You're having herbal tea.
MK: I know.
Me: How come?
MK: I'm in a good mood.

And she's got a new coat—tweedy black/white/gray. Big and big collar. She looks tiny inside the coat—wears it with the collar up and her hands in the pockets. Saw her in Inverness Street yesterday. I noticed the coat—it looked like it was moving along by itself.

AB has a new coat too. Neutral. Good fit. He likes coats.

MK had a hem coming down on a skirt. In a rush, she stuck it up with a piece of eye tape. The eye tape's not very sticky so the hem was down again (worse) before she'd left the house.

Me: The eye tape hasn't worked.
MK: (annoyed) Have we got any Sellotape?
Will: I've got Blu-Tack.
MK: Where's the stapler?
Me: You can't staple it. Wear a different skirt.
MK: I don't have a different skirt.
Me: You might snag your leg.
MK: I'll cope.
Me: Don't come running to us with a lacerated leg.
MK: I'll try not to.

She stapled it up (four staples) and it looked fine actually.

Love, Nina

∽

Dear Vic,

Mary-Kay seems serious about the new bloke (in love with?). Anything could happen (holiday/marriage/new bathroom). She's had a sloping bob.

Neve is bothered about the new boyfriend (compared with how unbothered he seemed about the last serious one—Floppy). Probably because though Floppy was nice (and clever), this one is more MK's cup of tea.

Neve came over on Saturday. To take Sam and me for lunch, but mainly to talk about the new bloke.

Neve: (*at the door*) Where is he (*meaning the new bloke*)?
Me: Not here.
Neve: Good, I don't have to punch his fucking lights out.

In the café:

Neve: What does she see in him?
Me: I don't know.
Neve: Yeah, too fucking right, you don't know. (*To Sam*) Is he that fucking great?
Sam: Yeah, he's a nice guy.
Neve: Stibbe's got the measure of him—what shall I do, Stibbe?
Me: Probably nothing.
Neve: So that's it? This guy's in there—is that what you're saying?

Me: I think so.

Neve: Fuck. It's over, it's finished. I'm fucking finished.

Waitress: Are you ready to order?

Sam came back to RPT with me because of the dust at 55 (due to building work) and we watched a video. We had to pause after fifteen minutes while Sam rang Mary-Kay.

Sam: I'm just going to ring Mary-Kay.

Me: What for?

Sam: To see how the dust is. (*On phone to MK*) Hello, mother, how's the dust? (*To me*) She says it's settling.

Me: Tell her not to move around too much, then.

Sam: Stibbe says don't move around too much. (*To me*) She says she's keeping as still...as...the...the what? who? The, the virtuous...Queen of...the Sicily...

Me: The what?

Sam: She says...Hermione.

Me: Who?

Sam: From *The Winter Tale,* or something...(*handing me the phone*)

Me: (*on phone*) Very funny.

Love, Nina

∽

Dear Vic,

College is marvelous. There's always something going on. Today Stella found out that a girl in our philosophy group was caught stealing in Superdrug. We were all keen to know what she'd stolen. Another girl from same course (the student from Luton) told us in confidence that the girl had slipped a bottle of Nizoral into a secret pocket in her waistband. Head & Shoulders not being tough enough for her stubborn dandruff and Nizoral being expensive due to being a "treatment" as opposed to a shampoo.

The student from Luton suggested we had a whip-round to get her a bottle (of Nizoral), seeing as she obviously really wanted it. The rest of us felt that she might not appreciate the gesture as it would signal that we all knew about the shoplifting (and the stubborn dandruff). I can't wait to see her now (the thief). She's gone right up in my estimation (the secret pocket).

Stella says she (Stella) uses Head & Shoulders and Timotei alternately. Apparently your hair and scalp get used to whatever you're using and get strong enough to fight the effects, hence you should switch and alternate.

Also, good news: Remember I had to pair up with that girl / boy "Zig" for the short slavery course? Well, I'm not with Zig anymore. I've had to go into a three with Stella and Henderson (fear of the marketplace). Reason being that Zig got "clipped by a lorry" in Deptford making a dash for it across a multilane junction.

Anyway Zig's had mild concussion. And though s/he's not in danger, s/he won't be able to do the short project in the small amount of time allotted...hence me tripling up with Stella and Henderson.

I'm thinking that Zig's probably a boy (crossing a complex road in a stupid place to get to Spud-u-like—would a girl do that?).

Love, Nina

∽

Dear Vic,

Went all the way to Thames Poly but didn't need to. Time-tabling error (mine). But it was worth it because one of my tutors (Peter Widdowson, my favorite) asked how everything was going.

PW: How's everything going?

Me: Great.

PW: Great.

Me: I don't know if you remember my essay on Mrs. Gaskell.

PW: Of course I do, it's indelibly printed on my mind.

Me: (*pleased*) Thanks.

Realized later that he'd meant "Of course I don't remember your essay." And, to be fair, he must read a hundred essays per week, so that's fine. I really think Peter Widdowson is the BMITW, not in a "Want to marry him" kind of way. He's just great in an everyday kind of way and in a making literature bearable kind of way.

Back in NW1, Smarts dry cleaner on Parkway (the one at the top) had a rail of uncollected items for sale on the pavement outside the shop (a year's worth of forgotten stuff). The woman from the other dry cleaner's (bottom of Parkway, where MK goes) was looking through it.

Me: Do you have sales like this at your shop?

Woman: No, our stuff always gets collected...apart from one rug last year.

I mentioned this to MK and AB (the sale). I didn't mention the rug because I had a feeling the rug was ours. Anyway, we started grappling with the mystery of things being forgotten at one dry cleaner but never forgotten (apart from one rug) at another.

AB: Perhaps people don't make it up the hill to collect.

MK: Maybe the top one has a higher turnover.

Me: Maybe the bottom one is lying.

MK: Why lie?

AB: Maybe there *is* forgotten stuff at the bottom one but it's not identified as such.

Me: Maybe the bottom one just keeps the left stuff.

Will: Because it's nicer than stuff left at the top one.

MK: Can we move on?

As well as the two dry cleaners on Parkway, there's a laundrette that offers a dry cleaning service. And there's one on Camden Road. Plus another on Camden High St. In other words, a lot of people in the Camden Town area have their clothes dry-cleaned a lot. Unnecessarily in my opinion.

Me: Why don't you just hand-wash with Stergene?

MK: (*irritable*) The stuff I take is dry clean only.

Me: How do you know?

MK: (*more so*) I read the instructions.

Me: Labels say "dry clean only" to be extra, *extra* careful and so you don't return the item saying it's shrunk or ruined or whatever.

MK: Yes. The label and I want the same thing.

Love, Nina

PS Remember if you ring me always do the ring three times and hang up thing.

꙳

Dear Vic,

MK is an art lover and has a wide variety of pictures (some v. good, some rubbish). She's got a picture of an emu just standing there (side view) and one of a big vase of daisies (unrealistic yellow) on a green background, also a cricket match on a green background.

206

In fact, quite a few of her art things have a green background. Not bluey-green, which would be more obviously MK, but bright plasticky green.

And that's just some of it. There are pictures in every room.

Bought a new camera. Better than old one, more features but I'm still in control. New one is equivalent of Olympus Trip, but half the price.

Had a cup of tea with S&W. Will had a Mars bar and cut it into lots of thin slices. It was nice like that, all cut up. Then we tore the wrapper into squares and did that thing where it looks like you've got a tooth missing.

Tried to take pictures with new camera. Will acted unnatural, Sam screwed his face up trying to smile, Mary-Kay pulled her sweater over her head, AB shielded himself with coffee filters. Took some pictures out of the window instead, including one of Claire Tomalin with a pen in her mouth stroking a cat (to put on Nunney's windscreen).

Homemade fizzy orange gave Will the hiccups. He tried the usual methods to stop them. They didn't stop. Sam got anxious—he'd read in the *Mirror* about someone who had hiccups for two years and tried to commit suicide because of it.

We all reassured Sam that it was normal to get hiccups and that they'd stop soon etc. The hiccups stopped while we were reassuring Sam (that Will would be fine) but no one noticed.

Love, Nina

Dear Vic,

They all went mad here for this tea loaf from the hippie shop on Inverness Street. And because I'm not 9–5, they were all putting in orders for it. And I'm supposed to get it.

Example conversation:

AB: Could you fetch me a loaf of that tea bread?
Me: I'd rather not commit.
AB: You're passing, aren't you?
Me: Yes, but what if you're not in when I've fetched it?
AB: You can leave it on the step.
Me: Won't that encourage pests?
AB: I'll be in all day, so don't worry.
Me: Why can't you fetch the tea bread, then?
AB: I'm on and off the phone all day.

That's how it's been for a while since MK discovered the loaf. I don't really like going into the hippie shop partly because it smells spicy/herby and also because the Bagwan Shree Rajneesh woman always looks at me as if she wants me to convert to the Bagwan, which I would never do.

Then today I went in for AB's and MK's loaf (Mary H away and didn't require any) and it's been superseded by a less good-looking cinnamon bread with currants.

Me: Do you have the tea loaf?
Bagwan Shree woman: (*calmly*) The tea loaf has been stopped.
Me: Oh no.
BS woman: (*calmly*) Another sweet loaf has taken its place in our bakery selection.
Me: What sweet loaf?
BS woman: A cinnamon loaf with currants.

So. Back at 55 I broke the news:

MK: What, no more tea loaf?

208

Me: No.

MK: Are you sure?

Me: As sure as I can be.

MK: No more tea loaf?

Me: They've stopped it.

MK: Did you get the recipe?

Me: (*lying on the spot, to soften blow*) Yes.

MK: Oh good, you can bake it.

Later:

MK: (*to AB*) Did she tell you about the loaf?

AB: What?

MK: (*to me*) Haven't you told him?

Me: Not yet.

AB: Told me what?

Me: The tea loaf has been superseded by a cinnamon bread.

AB: What a shame, I liked that loaf.

MK: She got the recipe.

So now I have to go back to the shop and ask what was in it and try to bake the damn thing. It's taken over my life and I don't even like it that much. I'd rather have a Rich Tea.

Hope all's well with you. Let's make a plan soon.

Love, Nina

◊

Dear Vic,

Zig came into college to tell us *he's leaving* and to get his chest-expander back. London hasn't worked out very well for him.

I'm glad I assumed he was a boy. He is (a boy)—we all saw his ribs when he showed his injuries.

It's not just London that's been a disappointment: he's just split up with his girlfriend of three months. He was very candid and talkative (unusual for him and probably a side effect of the recent mild concussion). He told us the exact reason for the split, which was to do with something his ex-girlfriend liked that he didn't like (in the bedroom dept). The thing (that he didn't like) sounded very odd and I think the girlfriend must've been a punk.

But Stella and I both said we felt a bit warmer toward him now he's had a road accident and he's leaving.

Train back to NW1 very late. Read a short play called *The Zoo Story* by Edward Albee. The introduction calls it an "early dramatic venture" (i.e. not quite a play). It's not as good as two other things I've read/seen by the same bloke. Dated and a bit biblical, and not nearly so funny.

From train window I saw graffiti, "I fuck my couzin," in long white letters (very neat) and I thought of Charles Darwin and felt quite impressed with myself.

Hope you're well. Funny about X and the caravan.

Love, Nina

⁓

Dear Vic,

I tried to tell Mary-Kay about Zig being clipped by the lorry, him going to hospital with mild concussion and calling his mother a witch and so forth... but MK zoned out after a while because of its complexity and her supper preparations. She's not very good at getting on with supper if there's something else going on. So she has to concentrate.

She managed to pick up on the candid chit-chat aspect though (Zig saying what his girlfriend liked/he didn't like—in the bedroom). I'd meant to stay vague about that bit, but you know how it is when someone's onions start burning and they lose interest in your story. So I mentioned *that* bit and then AB arrived and MK brought him up to speed straightaway.

MK: Another one of her college pals has got a sex thing.

AB: Good grief—it all goes on there.

Me: It doesn't. We're reading Hegel most of the time.

MK: So what is it that he doesn't like doing?

Me: I can't say.

MK: OK.

Me: OK, the girlfriend likes to have her hair tugged.

MK: What hair?

AB: Upstairs or downstairs?

Me: Down.

MK: Tugged—golly!

Me: I know.

MK: Is tugging just pulling but harder?

Mary Hope's visitor friends are worse than MK's—they stay for days on end, just doing their own thing and use the house like a hotel. At least MK's houseguests have to do the cooking etc. One's staying (here) at the moment and using my bathroom. I regret using her vitamin-rich night cream—it's got a depressing smell. The friend before this one used "fragrance-free" Clinique. Preferable.

See you soon.

Love, Nina

PS Made a tea loaf. You make it with actual tea. Supposed to use yeast but couldn't find any so used baking powder. It was OK. Like a hard, square scone.

Dear Vic,

Went to see Sam in Great Ormond Street. Karel Reisz was there. Sam was asleep. Karel said he'd dropped off while they'd been chatting. Karel and I spoke about Harold Pinter—whose play *The Birthday Party* I saw at college earlier in the week (I loved it even though it's not American).

Dandy Nichols from *Till Death Do Us Part* and the bloke from *Jaws* in it. Menacing and brilliant. Said that to Karel and he agreed with my description.

Sam's area was a mess. *Daily Mirror* all strewn about, around and under his bed. I was starting to pick it up when Sam woke up.

Me: What's all this mess?
Sam: Frank Bruno did it.
Me: What?
Sam: The boxer.
Me: Frank Bruno?
Sam: (*weary*) Yes, Frank Bruno. He came in and asked me how I was. I told him to fuck off and he chucked my *Daily Mirror* around.
MK: (*arrives with food*) Hullo, what's all this mess?
Me: It's something to do with Frank Bruno.
MK: I should've guessed. (*To Sam*) How are you?
Sam: Better for seeing you (*hugs*).
Me: You didn't say that to me.
Sam: You didn't ask how I was.
MK: You didn't ask how he was?
Me: I didn't think I was allowed. Look at what happened when Frank Bruno asked.
MK: (*looks curious*).
Sam: I told him to fuck off.

Me: And Frank threw the *Mirror* around.

MK: What a day you've had.

Love, Nina

PS Frank Bruno didn't. Sam did. The nurse wasn't even aware that Frank Bruno had been in the hospital that day. Sam was just trying to blame someone else. As per.

∾

Dear Vic,

I'm hardly doing any cooking nowadays. Mary and JDF have soups and healthy stuff or ready-made and I'm not usually there for meals and if I go to 55 I can't really cook because I don't live there. But I do sometimes, but only what's in the fridge already. I don't plan any 55 meals.

I did cook a chicken there yesterday, but only by accident.

Mary-Kay said I could stuff it with bulgur wheat and spinach—if I wanted to. So I did, but forgot the all-important tarragon and garlic, so made an oily thing to drip on instead. It was nice apparently. I didn't have any, it looked odd.

Mary-Kay has bought toilet paper with pink rosebuds on it. Looks nice until you use it.

Me: I don't like the rosebud toilet paper.

MK: I know, I know.

Me: It's worrying.

MK: I know, I didn't think it through.

Stella is beginning to make a bit of an effort in seminars. She's gone mad on poetry and this has caught the eye of Peter M, the poetry lecturer. I didn't choose that course because he seemed such a mardy-arse. But Stella loves it and now I think maybe I should have taken it. Not that I like poetry much.

Love, Nina

PS I know how it must seem...but you have to understand that Sam telling people to "fuck off" is the same as anyone else saying "no thanks" or at worst "you must be joking."

⌒

Dear Vic,

Not having 100% success with the three-ring code. Some people just won't play ball. S&W do it fine. They like stuff like that (procedures, secrets). Others, control freaks like Nunney, just ring up in the old-fashioned way and wonder why I'm never at home.

Also, Mary Hope is getting a bit annoyed with it.

Mary: People keep hanging up on me.
Me: Oh, do they?
Mary: Yes, just as I pick up.
Me: It might be my phone code thing.
Mary: Oh well, it's rather irritating.
Me: Don't answer till after at least four rings.
Mary: I thought it was *three* rings.
Me: It sometimes goes to four. If it's four rings, it'll be Sam.
Mary: I can't keep up.

Also, Mary-Kay caused havoc this week. She did the three-ring code, I answered and she asked to speak to Mary Hope. And Mary Hope was there, in the next room grinding seeds by hand. Listening.

MK: Is Mary there?

Me: Is that you?

MK: Yes.

Me: You did the code.

MK: Well, whatever, is Mary there?

Me: Yes, but she'll be confused, you did the three rings.

MK: Just get Mary and stop messing about.

Me: Speak to me for a moment to legitimize it.

MK: Fuck (*hangs up*).

I told Mary H to ring MK.

Mary: (*ringing MK*) She's not there.

Me: Did you do the code?

Mary: For heaven's sake, do *I* have to do the code to her now?

I rang 55 (*using the code*).

MK: Hello.

Me: Mary wants to speak to you.

MK: Put her on, then.

Don't know what MK wanted Mary for but I heard Mary say "bladder in jeopardy."

Love, Nina

∽

Dear Vic,

Stella and me have opted to take a course called *Autobiography & Fiction*. So far it has been my absolute best thing and Stella's worst nightmare.

Had a seminar earlier this week in which we all spoke briefly, autobiographically, just to get the hang of it. Tutor Peter H said we should try to say something revealing or even difficult.

Here are some of the things we said:

A: My sister, aged fifteen, is podgy and can't spell house. I'm ashamed of her and ashamed of being ashamed (three ashameds).

B: I often dream I'm eating shit and can actually taste it (everyone horrified).

C: I'm frightened of insects and if I see one or think of one when I'm eating, I almost throw up. If a thing flew in here now, I'd find it difficult to remain in the room (everyone bored).

D: I don't connect with my parents, grandparents, siblings or anyone I know in Luton. Since my father laughed at my bra when I was twelve (everyone amused).

E (mature student): When I was twenty-one I married my husband. Two weeks later he moved back in with his mother and never spoke to me again. I never got over it (everyone sad).

Stella: I used to be prejudiced against people with scratches, cuts or grazes on their hands and plasters, bandages or any wounds (everyone a bit cross).

I said: When I went to Greece last year I saw Germans for the first time and I couldn't imagine what it must feel like to be German. I feel bad enough being English (mixed reaction).

Tutor Peter H seemed pleased.

When we came out of the seminar, some students, inc. Stella, were all wrung out and we went to the 5th floor coffee bar to discuss things further. All except the insect girl.

Next we have to read some stuff, then *write* some stuff.

Hope all's well with you.

Love, Nina

Dear Vic,

Went to University of Sussex near Brighton to stay weekend with Nunney. He's living in the Halls of Residence on campus. It's very green and hilly and not at all like Thames. It's full of students, but they seem a different type to the Thames type. More studious and longer hair.

I weed in the basin when Nunney was in the shower and felt guilty enough to run the tap and squirt fairy liquid down the drain (it's a small room).

Went for a walk on the Downs and a meal at the Ship Hotel where Elspeth and Paul had their honeymoon in 1960. Had fish pie and threw up (me, not Elspeth and Paul).

Also went to Rottingdean where Rudyard Kipling lived and a few other places of interest.

I stripped right off on a beach in Eastbourne. It was funny and like old times seeing Nunney outraged and shocked, but quite pleased really.

Strange being with him. Strange being with him *there*. Strange going away again. Got the feeling it was all over. Or something.

Brighton seemed pleased with itself again.

Love, Nina

1985

Dear Vic,

Thought you might like to see some photographs.

(photo 1) Tall building with orange curtains is Churchill House

217

(Humanities and Arts, 3rd floor). The woman emerging is Valerie Stead, a Thames Poly bigwig.

(photo 2) A homeless man sleeps in the porch—same man every night. For ages I thought he was an engineering student.

Used a special technique which I might have told you about before (Nunney taught me). You do *not* hold the camera up to your face, therefore it doesn't appear that you're actually taking a photograph— good for getting natural shots in public scenarios. It's a bit hit and miss. Used the technique to try and take a picture in a seminar but ended up with photo of a dusty ledge.

A group of us are starting a new student magazine (for students' work—art, stories, poems, photographs). Not sure Thames Poly needs or wants another magazine but that doesn't affect our plan. The existing magazine is an official thing connected to the library. I think it's called the *Thames Poly Magazine* or similar. We want to have a good look at it as our magazine will compete with it but we can't find a copy. Not even in the library. There's one bloke, a materials science PhD student, who says he once saw a copy, so we asked him what it was like, what was in it and so on. He could only remember a recipe for minestrone soup and a picture of Desperate Dan and that was it. So at least we know to avoid those two items.

Discussion about what to call our new magazine ended in a secret vote.

The name *Blurt!* was chosen (with exclamation mark)—four votes to three. Other options included: *You Say. We Say. Your Say. I Say. Thames Gems* (mine).

I've done lino prints for the first front cover (see photo 3) and for the "call for submissions" and I've submitted the accidental dusty ledge photo for inclusion in the first edition. It might be monthly or less often.

Will has started saying "scenario"; I've picked it up and keep saying it all the time. Sam has too.

218

MK: Why's everything "a scenario"?

Will: That's just life.

MK: I mean, why's everyone saying "scenario" all the time?

Sam: Cliff Richard's got one.

Will: What?

Sam: Cliff Richard's got a five-seater Scenario. He keeps it in Spain.

Me: You mean his Renault (I'd read the same article in the *Mirror*) — he has it in Portugal. It's half car, half minibus. It's not called a Scenario, it's a Renault, but I'm sure it's not a Scenario.

Sam: What is a scenario then?

Me: A situation.

Sam: Well, when I say it I mean Cliff Richard's five-seater car thing in Spain.

Will: When I say it, I mean a *complicated* situation.

MK: Sounds like you're both right.

Later I thought we should've called the magazine *Scenario* — so much better than *Blurt!*

Love, Nina

∽

Dear Vic,

Will's homework was about the weather (rain, sun etc.). I showed him Hardy's poem "Weathers" — it's one of his few good ones (Hardy's) and this started us talking about weather. Weather we like, weather we don't like.

MK — Likes: dry days, preferably hot. Dislikes: drizzle and rain, especially sideways rain.

219

Sam — Likes: blizzard conditions (if he's at home). Dislikes: hot, muggy days.

Me — Likes: hot, sunny. Dislikes: windy (chaos, things being blown around).

AB — Likes: warm spring day (April or May). Dislikes: too hot, too cold, too windy.

Will — Likes: hot, but only if you're not at school ("any weather but not a school day"). Dislikes: any weather on the way to school.

I've taught Will how to draw a tattoo (Death Before Dishonor) with a dagger going through the skin and the skin being where you can have a name written. He drew one on paper (it being a weekday) and wrote his own name and I said that wasn't advisable. Better to have a girl's name.

Sam: I'm going to get a West Ham tattoo.
Will: You'll get beaten up.
Sam: What are you going to have?
Will: A dagger.
Sam: *You'll* get beaten up.
Will: With a dagger? I doubt it.

Will showed us that if you draw a face on the pad of your thumb it will always look like someone you know. It's uncanny. Will's looked like Brian Clough. Mine: Willie Thorne. Sam's looked like Paddington Bear and MK said she doesn't draw on herself. Will said hers would probably look like Elvis.

Will: You've got something on your hand now.
MK: (*looks*) Oh, that was a thing.
Sam: What is it?
Will: A dagger.

It said "bank."

These are some of the things I've picked up so far at Thames Polytechnic.

English Literature ignores most of its subject.

It's not important for a thing to *be* true, but to *ring* true.

Women have been ignored but have been their own worst enemy.

You should give Thomas Hardy a chance (P. Widdowson).

They don't *tell* you this stuff; you work it out for yourself. I've learned lots more than that, but I'm just mentioning those for now.

Michael Z, tutor (American, nice, clever), lives in Camden and we sometimes take the same train home from Woolwich Arsenal. The other day he saw my much-used train ticket and said, "Jeez, how long've you had that old ticket?"

So I told him I'd had the same ticket for months and that was the end of our chat. The Americans can be a bit black and white (when it comes to crime).

Stella has got a crush on a lecturer called PB and has been scratching at her teeth with a pin to get the nicotine off the margins. She wants to look her best. I said I wouldn't worry about your teeth, read the texts, that's all he'll care about.

Apparently, according to AB, girl students often develop harmless crushes on male lecturers—it's a thing—and they're used to it (lecturers are) and they just ignore it and get on with the job in hand.

I was honest with Stella: one, you don't really notice her teeth—stained or not—you barely notice them, even when she smiles. And two, lecturers are used to girl students having crushes etc. and just ignore them.

I have to say though, Stella's crush on PB—although harmless/pointless—is a good thing because she's actually doing some work at long last. It's good for me because her laziness was beginning to

annoy me and I was on the verge of moving on to this other friend—
the one from Luton with the bra (and the laughing father)—an idiot
but at least she reads the texts.

Love, Nina

⌒

Dear Vic,

The renovations at 55 are almost complete. It looks great. S&W
have got my old rooms and the bathroom has been made smaller
but better. S&W's old rooms are now the nanny's quarters, smaller
but better with wood floors and new kitchen stuff and a nice dresser
thing, new blinds and sweet table. Sam and Will were yabbering about
what they're going to have in their rooms and how they're going to
nick stuff out of the new nanny's fridge etc. and I felt a great feeling of
wishing I could be that nanny.

Not that I'm *not* loving Thames—I *am* loving Thames v. much.

Anyway, I was just thinking that when suddenly Mary-Kay
mentioned me moving in.

Me: (*looking around*) It's great.
MK: So do you want to move in, then?
Me: OK.
MK: Do you mean, "Yes, please"?
Me: Yes.

I was a bit astonished after last week's ding-dong. But very pleased.

Sam has found out that he shares his birthday with Les Dawson
and Will shares his with Mae West. Will disappointed.

Love, Nina

Dear Vic,

Had another *Autobiography & Fiction* seminar and we spoke autobiographically again. Quite a few students didn't turn up, so those who *were* there felt exposed. I didn't (feel exposed).

The girl from Luton spoke up again and talked about her father laughing at her bra again. This time she added that she'd stuffed it with "copious amounts" of toilet paper and could quite understand why her father might have laughed. I think she was going for laughs this time whereas last week she was presenting it as a tragedy that's affected her whole life.

PH was pleased with her for speaking up and said that was the thing about autobiography—we're forever adjusting our angles and degrees of truth. I think you need to make your mind up and stick to it.

We're all working on "essays" for the course. These aren't like other essays, where you just read a text(s) and write about what you've read, say what you think and what a few others have thought. This is your own story.

My plan is to hand in a bit of my ongoing semiautobiographical novel. I have asked tutor PH if I'm allowed to use a "real ongoing thing" and the answer from tutor PH was "Yes, that would be terrific."

So, I've been reading it through to myself—a complex domestic situation with moments of high drama—and decided to get a second opinion, so I asked Stella to read the opening paragraphs. I just wanted to see her first impression.

SH: I don't think you should hand that in.
Me: Why?
SH: It's so revealing.
Me: Yes, it's meant to be revealing—remember the seminars.
SH: I wouldn't want to reveal that much at this juncture.

223

Stella is saying things like "juncture," "caliber" and "apropos" at the moment. It's all part of her being literary. However, I took on board what she said and will make it slightly less revealing.

Stella's plan is to present a (true, but not very revealing) story about going to the cinema and having a pair of gloves nicked. Then, walking home with cold hands and having to hold hands with a bloke and secretly being pleased about the theft of the gloves.

SH: So that's the basic plot. I don't know how to flesh it out.
Me: Could you say the thief was sitting behind you and cut your plaits off and you leave the cinema with short hair whereas before you had long (childlike) hair and you have a sexual awakening?
SH: (*laughing*) Like the opposite of Samson?
Me: Well, it's more dramatic than the gloves.
SH: It *was* gloves though, in real-life, that's what happened.
Me: It's not much of a story, that's all.
SH: But it's how it was.

Then, I noticed something strange on her shoes.

Me: What's that stuff on your shoes?
SH: Oh, it's muffin paint.

Then a story worth telling came out:
On her way to college someone had dropped a tub of paint (color: muffin) and it had spilled over the pavement. A plank of wood had been laid down for people to walk across but Stella still managed to get paint on the soles of her moccasins. Walking to the bus, she saw she was leaving muffin footprints and it seemed as though the muffin footprints were following her (chasing her). So she ran to get away from them but couldn't obviously (get away from them) and it was

like a bad dream. On the bus (top deck), she looked down at the fading footprints on the pavement and felt strange.

I told Stella that it made a better story than the stolen gloves. Stella didn't agree. She just said she was annoyed about the paint on her shoes. So gloves it is.

Back at 55 telling MK about the gloves versus the muffin footprints.

Me: Which do you think is best?
MK: It depends how you tell them.
Me: Well, like I've just told them.
MK: Well, the footprints, because you told it better. The gloves could've been good too, but you made it sound as dull as possible.

So it's the same old "it's how you communicate" thing. You have to wonder why authors even bother trying to make up a good story (chasing whales or living in a hollowed-out old tree) when just losing your gloves is good enough, if you tell it right.

Hope you are well and things are going well.

Love, Nina

⌒

Dear Vic,

MK went away for w/e (c. Sussex or Suffolk). She's not good at going away unless it's somewhere decent and not at all cold or miserable. This was someone's holiday cottage in a country village. I had a bad feeling about it as soon as I heard the word (village). You just wouldn't put MK in a village. She's better off in a town or city. God knows why she went. Sometimes she does things she knows she'll hate.

MK: It was good and bad.

AB: Tell us the bad.

MK: The winding lanes weren't great and a trying sweater didn't help.

Me: Trying?

MK: Dotty.

Me: How was the village?

MK: I didn't ask.

AB: And the good?

MK: There's more bad yet.

AB: Go on, then.

MK: It was cold.

AB: And the good?

MK: X made a nice meat loaf.

AB: Is that all?

MK: It was quite peaceful.

AB: Well, that's nice.

MK: Up to a point.

Will: Did you sit by a roaring log fire?

MK: Eventually.

Later in the week, MK re-created the meat loaf they'd had in the Suffolk/Sussex village with minced pork and bread. It reminded me of the meats we used to see at Brooks's—I looked at it and remembered Mrs. Brooks using the machine, and the slices collapsing into her open hand and being laid on paper. And sometimes people just buying one slice and it seeming so sad. I might include that image in my *Auto &
Fiction* essay.

I didn't have any (meat loaf).

MK won't hold it against the couple; she'll probably bear a grudge against the county (Suffolk or Sussex, whichever) but stay friends with the couple. And if the couple ask her to go and stay again, MK might say "maybe in the summer" and hope they forget all about it.

Great about Mr. B. We all love to know what other people have for tea. Mary-Kay and me both love to look into other people's trolleys in Sainsbury's. Me, just seeing what they've got. MK to copy their ideas (hence the stuff she buys).

MK has taken on a new nanny who won't live here but will come as and when. MK's really pleased with her because she's very bright and has all the good points of me and the last nanny and none of the bad points. So MK said.

Love, Nina

∽

Dear Vic,

Mary-Kay had made a plan to have people over and had been to West London to fetch a tub of crab pâté to give them as a starter (with a bit of greenery and discs of bread).

Then, on the morning of the actual day, she rang home and I answered. It was the three rings, so it had to be MK (no one else does it now I'm back at 55). I shouldn't have picked up (knowing this supper was looming).

MK: Good, you're there.
Me: (*realizing*) What?
MK: Can you check on the crab pâté?
Me: In what way?
MK: Smell it and see if it's OK. Ring me back.

I smelled it and it smelled OK. A bit crabby, but not rancid or anything. I rang back.

227

Me: Could I speak to Mary-Kay please?

LRB person: Who is it?

Me: Nina.

LRB person: Hang on (*muffled noises*). She's busy at the moment, can you leave a message?

Me: Um, yes, could you tell her "Yes, it's OK."

LRB person: So the message is "Yes, it's OK"?

Me: Yes, that's it.

LRB person: OK. Yes, it's OK.

Me: Yes, that's the message.

LRB person: OK.

Me: Tell her re the thing she rang about, it's OK.

LRB person: Re the thing she rang about, it's OK.

Me: Well, you should say "the thing YOU rang *Nina* about is OK."

LRB person: OK. The thing you rang Nina about is OK.

Me: Yes, the thing she rang me about earlier, just now, is OK.

LRB person: OK. I think I've got it. Bye.

Later, when MK got home:

Me: Did you get my message about the crab being OK?

MK: Yes, loud and clear.

Me: I didn't want to be too explicit, just in case.

MK: Very considerate.

Anyway. It was a nice supper and everyone liked the crab pâté and the next course, which was chicken pieces cooked with garlic cloves. No potatoes. Horrible little khaki beans out of tins and one of AB's salads (dressed). Overall, though, very nice and a gooseberry pie that came with a guest (plus one of AB's uninvited milky things).

Someone mentioned Beatrix Potter so I told about the

philosophy student with the squirrel in his pocket and MK said, "tell them about the horseshoe," and "tell them about the Appleseed girl."

MK: (*to all*) She has the most amazing time.
Writer Woman: Which college is this?
Me: Thames Poly.
Writer Woman: I don't know that one—where is it?
Me: The Greenwich area.
MK: I always think of it as Dartford.
Me: Well, from now on think of it as Greenwich.
MK: OK, but where is it?
Me: Woolwich.
MK: Right. Now tell about the Appleseed girl.

Ring me soon.

Love, Nina
PS Re P, I'd say no. But I'm not 100% against.

∽

Dear Vic,
Don't think I ever said I didn't *like* the name Peter. Might've been MK and her penis-names thing. Peter's fine. Though it does sound a bit penisy. But then, so many do.

When you read American fiction you get to accept all sorts of names that were unthinkable before. Dick, Frank, Milo, Chuck, Micky, Dick, Biff, Willie, Gullie, Happy, Augie, Fritz, Artie, Woody, Rocky, Bill.

A character in one of Nunney's favorite books is called Dick Diver.

Sam was given a bag of marbles by a friend of MK's (Will got a compass). Sam was unimpressed and ignored the marbles until the friend had left.

Sam: How do you play marbles?
Me: I don't actually know.
Sam: Is it to do with rolling them?
Me: I think so, but I'm not sure how exactly.
Sam: Didn't you play marbles in your day?
Will: She lost them at a young age.

Here's a thing. Whenever Misty has sex (with boyfriend) she thinks of St. Thomas's church opposite the Esso garage. She's wondering if it's a message from above. She's confused because she's never been inside the church. She did walk past once, years ago, and soon after passing it a dog (that looked like a pig) leapt over a low wall and chased her (growling) all the way to the park... where she was able to run in and shut the gate against the drooling dog.

And that whole episode plays through her head while they do it.

She asked my opinion. I said it sounded as though the dog-that-looked-like-a-pig is significant, *not* the church. The church is just a landmark. The church doesn't do anything whereas the dog leaps and chases and looks like a pig.

Misty: So it's not a message?
Me: It *is* a message, but from your subconscious.
Misty: What's it saying?
Me: It's reminding you to shut the gate.
Misty: Wow!

Also, she's had her ears pierced and is wearing tiny gold moons. Pretty.

Love, Nina

PS It's a shame Misty isn't at Thames Poly and in our *Autobiography & Fiction* seminar group.

Incidents full of revealing symbolism always happen to her and she doesn't even realize. She's at Roehampton doing science.

∽

Dear Vic,

Nunney came to visit the Crescent (i.e. Tom and S&W). He had his friend "the Dog" with him. The Dog doesn't smoke or drink tea so they all played a type of cricket in the car park while I had a cup of tea.

Nunney having the Dog with him reminded me about Misty imagining being chased by a dog-that-looked-like-a-pig during sex with her boyfriend.

I mentioned it to Nunney later. I didn't say who it was because Misty and Nunney know each other a bit and she'd be mortified to think he knew her intimate sexual imaginings. It wasn't a gossiping thing—I just thought it might be a bit Freudian and therefore of (academic) interest to Nunney.

Me: And then, running, she reaches a park and shuts the pig-faced dog out.
Nunney: (*thinking*) What's the boyfriend like?
Me: A bit piggy—why? Do you assume the dog/pig represents the boyfriend?

Nunney said the dog-that-looked-like-a-pig probably represents the boyfriend's thing. And Misty's imagined reaction to it suggests that she doesn't want it anywhere near her.

Honestly, sometimes I'm so relieved not to be studying Freud and

Jung etc. at college. Imagine having to go into all that in seminars and say things represented things etc.

Suppose you got it wrong and thought something represented a thing and it didn't... It'd be like being in a Woody Allen film.

Love, Nina

⌇

Dear Vic,

I'm so sorry about you having to sell Molly O. I know it's the right thing to do but it's still very sad.

I have written a five-minute poem for her. I know it's no consolation but it's the kind of thing people do when they're studying literature.

Let's promise we'll go riding somewhere nice on a beach soon or in Spain or somewhere exciting and new.

Beginning to love poetry courses. I avoided to start with because tutor seemed mardy and difficult to please. But: (a) Romanticism course was rumored to be running with a different tutor (the marvelous John Williams), and (b) the mardy-seeming tutor cheered up a bit anyway (due to private life improvements?).

Having said all that, I'm stuck on an essay (Romanticism).

I'd have loved to study Yeats, MacNeice, T. S. Eliot—I know them from them hanging around at 55 (the books, not the poets). Especially loved *The Secret Rose,* which I found underneath an old cup of tea (with a skin on it) in MK's sitting room when I'd gone in to nick a fag.

I am going to suggest you start reading poetry. I know it's the last thing you ever thought you'd hear me say but I mean it. The thing is, Vic, poetry can be beautiful and amazing even if it's quite old. And if you set yourself to read some, you might love it. And though you can't have a horse anymore, you'll have these poems in your life. And if you read a good one a few times and learn it, it can spring to mind at unexpected times and make you feel better, or at least clever.

But, when I say old, I don't mean *really* old—don't go earlier than 1900 (for now).

Told MK I'd picked the wrong poetry course.

Me: Not all that keen on the Romantic poets.
MK: Oh dear.
Me: Everyone else loves them, but I don't that much.
MK: It's sounding like Shakespeare all over again.
Me: It's not that bad, I just prefer later stuff.
MK: Such as?
Me: Stuff you have lying around—Eliot, Yeats and co.
MK: Mm, good and bad.
Me: Why?
MK: Good you like it. Bad you'll nick my copies.

I'm *typing* the essay (Romanticism) because someone's told us you get good marks if you type, even if it's total rubbish—lecturers being so grateful not having to read scrawl and scribble. The thing is, typing gives me an ache in my collarbone (left side, the one I broke) and I hate typing the word Wordsworth.

Always think of that shop (Worth's Gifts & Toys) where I bought the ashtray for Elspeth with sixteen squares of different-colored glass. And poor Mr. Worth claiming their name was actually Wordsworth but they'd shortened it for the shop-front sign so they could fit in the word "toys."

Love, Nina
PS Here's my poem for Molly O:

Horse For Sale

Dark and dappled Connemara mare,
Soft mouth, responsive, sixteen hands high.
Genuine, heart-breaking reason for sale,
Sound in heart and wind and eye.
I can't have a horse anymore,
Shan't live by pasture nor down a lane.
Got my eye on a blue Fiat Panda
But I'll never own a horse again.
Easy to catch, shoe, box and hunt,
Nice action, four legs, good pace.
Hardy, out to grass all year,
Maybelline lashes and a blaze on her face.
Quiet in traffic, runs on cinder or sand,
A perfect hack for someone's wife.
Molly O, I'm letting you go,
I need the three hundred to start my life.

❧

Dear Vic,

Been working on my *Autobiography & Fiction* essay. I have considered every word. It's very autobiographical with a touch of fictionalization. You're in it, obviously. I'll send you a copy (if you want). It's a few words over the limit. Our max is 3,000 words (unusually long, but PH said it's hard to keep autobiographical writing short) but he did ask us to keep it "very much shorter than that—if at all possible."

Unforeseen consequence: Before I began (essay) I thought Elspeth had been a bit of a menace as a parent. But now I see her as a bit of a hero (MK/Thames effect) and realize that if she'd been a bloke, people would not have treated her like a menace. And that would have been nicer all round. People treating her like a menace was the worst aspect (in my opinion).

But writing truthfully is very hard—i.e. I wrote about when we took the ponies upstairs and had to blindfold them to get them down again. At the time it seemed like a funny emergency but written, it seems cruel and mad.

I didn't mean it to seem cruel or mad (in the writing). I meant it to seem funny, but whatever way I wrote it, the ponies seem terrified and we seem insane. In the end the writing wins and you have to assume it was the way it seems in the writing of it.

Which is why you might be less than truthful. It's sort of: to tell the truth, you have to lie a bit.

That's what this course (*Auto & Fiction*) is trying to show us. I now feel a bit sorry for the student from Luton with the bra story that kept changing.

Stella is struggling for the opposite reason. Her upbringing has been very normal and quiet and, apart from a few foreign visitors (including Japanese and South American and Communists), it's been totally normal (you might say boring). Which might sound great to us, but when it comes to writing autobiography, it's the last thing you want.

Plus, she's not the show-off type and always likes to do the right thing, so even her recent life has been quite dull. Highlights so far: becoming a certified Clark's fitter and one summer season in a doughnut booth at Butlin's—where she met new people and, for the first time in her life, didn't have a fixed food schedule and could eat chips on Tuesday instead of Friday.

Anyway, all this means she's finding it difficult to write her autobiographical essay.

I said maybe she should really exaggerate the normality/boredom aspect and write a list of things in a monotonous way. She didn't like that idea and is considering doing it in a "stream-of-consciousness" style like Virginia Woolf. This has reared its ugly head because she's doing a modernism course.

SH: I'm thinking of doing it in a stream-of-consciousness, like Virginia Woolf.
Me: (*thinking "Fuck!"*) Yeah, s'pose you could.
SH: I thought I'd just sit down and let it all stream out.
Me: Yeah.
SH: It might turn out boring.
Me: But you could add interesting nuggets after, like the thief cutting your hair off and you having a sexual awakening.
SH: I don't want a sexual awakening.
Me: I wish you would.
SH: Why?
Me: It would be hilarious.
SH: Well, you have one.
Me: I can't, it wouldn't fit with my themes.
SH: Anyway, stream-of-consciousness means you present whatever comes streaming out, you don't tweak or add funny bits or sexual awakenings.
Me: I bet Virginia Woolf added bits.
SH: (*shocked*) No, she didn't, she invented the concept, and she wouldn't cheat her own system.

Hope you're all well. Bad about the toilet seat. Ours at 55 was like that (before the replacement). Nunney used to call it "the pincher."

Love, Nina
PS Anyway, about to hand essay in (eek!), tell me if you want to see a copy. You're in it!

Dear Vic,

Will's been on about how swear words that we use today have actually been around for centuries and were invented by clever and funny writers of old (Chaucer and Shakespeare for instance). Sam and me decided we wanted a new swear word for the modern world. It had to be annoying but not too rude, so that if we said it in front of anyone proper (Ras's mum) it wouldn't matter. Our main objective was to drive MK and Will mad.

We came up with the fantastic "flip-flop." We kept saying it, instead of fuck, shit or damn. Soon it began to get on Will's nerves.

Will: Can you stop saying flip-flop?
Sam: I got it off her (*me*).
Will: Yes, you both say it all the time and it's really annoying.
Me: We're saying it instead of F-U-C-K.
Sam: (*pots the white ball*) Flip-flop!
Will: I'm finding flip-flop more offensive than fuck.
Sam: Yeah, and we invented it.

Later:

Sam: (*to MK*) Will can't stand flip-flop.
MK: What?
Will: It's their pathetic new swear word, instead of fuck.
MK: I hadn't noticed.
Will: It's annoying.
MK: Yes, I prefer fuck.

Pippa phoned and asked if she and boyfriend could stay Saturday night (last) so they could attend various events at a jazz festival (MK & S&W were going to be away).
Asked MK:

Me: They just want to sleep here.

MK: Is this the one who masturbates all the time?

Me: Well, once a day.

MK: Yes, but *where* will he be having his once-a-day?

Me: (*realizing*) Oh, yeah.

MK: As long as he's safely in your quarters.

When they arrived, Pippa said they'd go in S&W's beds. I said no. Pippa insisted. Again I said no.

Pippa: Why not?

Me: Because of the (*quietly*) wanking.

Pippa: Oh, that! (*laughs*) He has an evening bath if we're away.

I daren't tell MK that—she uses our bathroom sometimes and she'll have thoughts and visions. I've already had visions. Also, the plughole sometimes regurgitates.

College is great. The girl (Appleseed) who kept showing off about her grandfather being a Swedenborgian and her grandmother being a suffragette has been cautioned over plagiarism. Whereas I got a B+ for my Romanticism essay and a note at the bottom saying, "You might consider this area for your extended essay."

Proves the theory that you get good marks if you type. The essay was awful and nonsensical.

Hope all's well with you and the Fiat Panda.

Love, Nina

∽

Dear Vic,

Here's a copy of my *Autobiography & Fiction* essay.

PH liked it so much I got an almost unheard of A+. I've never had one before and I told him that.

Me: I've never had an A+ before.
PH: It's a fine piece of writing.
Me: Thank you.
PH: I don't suppose you'll ever get another A+.
Me: How do you know?
PH: You don't write A+ essays.
Me: I just did.
PH: That wasn't an essay.

Anyway. I'm just pleased to have got an A at last. Noticed tutor PH had a slice of lemon in his tea. I kept staring at it thinking it was a biscuit he'd dropped in. Then I caught a whiff.

I'm sending it to you (the essay) because you're very much in it.

Hope you like it.

Love, Nina

∽

Dear Vic,

I don't mind that you didn't like the *Autobiography & Fiction* essay.

I will send you the next excerpt if you really want to see it, but don't blame me if you hate it. And remember, it'll cost a pound to photocopy, so you'd better like it — or at least not complain about it.

Remember what I said. There's always a lot of autobiography in fiction and fiction in autobiography. It has to be that way otherwise they'd be unreadable (except by the author).

Love, Nina

Dear Vic,

Stella is hanging around with a hippie called Ruth. She's got red gums. Stella says it's because she takes speed to stay alert in nightclubs and lectures. Apparently she's burning the candle at both ends.

Me: Her gums are bright red.
SH: (*proud*) That's because she takes a bit of speed.
Me: Rubbish, it's because she doesn't brush her teeth, or floss.
SH: How do you know?
Me: I see plaque build-up.
SH: She's busy in the mornings, early lectures etc.
Me: Not too busy to put parrot earrings on.

Anyway, this hippie Ruth is clever. In an essay that I read, she wrote the following: "Lenin was a man of narrow dogma... (such and such a thing) threw his ruthlessness *into sharp relief.*" I don't even know what that means. And I think that's why Stella likes her (clever). Not only that, she talks like a lecturer:

Hippie Ruth: You say he didn't like his mother but he didn't write another word after her death.
SH: Maybe he was driven by the hatred.
Hippie Ruth: That's way too simplistic.
SH: Right.

See, like a lecturer.

There's a rumor about her, which may or may not be true. If true, it makes me like her a bit. People say she hangs around the refectory looking out for people leaving, and then she swoops in for their leftovers. Apparently she never has to buy a single meal but dines out on pizza crusts and discarded salad garnishes and so on.

One time she finished off Stella's ham torpedo before she'd actually finished, but Stella didn't say anything.

Me: That's the thing about hippies.
SH: What is?
Me: It's all love and peace, then they're nicking your lunch.
SH: She can't stand waste when so many are starving.

She's got it down to a fine art. I have to admit it's impressive, the determination and the timing.

Love, Nina

∽

June 1985

Dear Vic,

Very worried about our end of year exams (you fail, you leave). I shouldn't fail and I've done lots of work and got good grades up to now, but I'm not good at exams as last year's E demonstrated.

Stella and the hippie and some others have been revising together at Stella's house and having coffee and biscuits etc. I have opted out of this because that kind of thing annoys me. But I have the feeling I should go. I said no thanks the first two times because I can't stand the hippie. Now they've planned a third event and Stella hasn't asked me.

Back at 55.

Me: I'm worried about the exams.
MK: You did OK with the A level and all you did was moan.

Me: I didn't do *that* well.

MK: You did OK.

Me: I didn't do OK. I got an E.

MK: I thought you got an A.

Me: No. I said I got a C, but I actually got an E.

MK: (*exasperated*) How can we ever believe a word you say?

Me: You're talking as if everyone else in the world tells the truth the whole time. They don't...it's only you who's clinically honest.

Sam: It's true, people sometimes lie.

MK: Well, you two certainly do.

Will: She told *me* she got an E.

MK: You told Will the truth but lied to everyone else?

Me: Yes, because he'd done badly in a test.

Will: And I can take the truth.

Love, Nina

∽

Autumn term 1985

Dear Vic,

Thanks for great time.

Crime & Punishment on the train. By the time we reached Kettering he'd confessed (and been overheard). I was annoyed (why speak so loud about committing murder?) and switched to Stendhal (same course), then ate some KP nuts.

Thanks for a great time. Still laughing about the dog show — having to lift Belle up onto the hay bale for the judge, and him looking her in the eyes. It was comical. You don't find it funny because you do it a lot (dog showing) whereas I don't and seeing an old bloke inspecting a dog like that seems funny.

Back at 55, the house smells of butterscotch because a mystery person spilt sugar on the cooker top (and didn't bother cleaning it up).

And MK's got a new jacket she doesn't like. Silky, but hard. Silver-gray (borderline shiny). She says it's noisy.

MK: (*walks*) Listen.
Me: I can't hear anything.
MK: Well, *listen*.
Me: (*listening*) What? The faint sliding?
MK: That's it.
Me: You're swinging your arms.
MK: That's how I walk.
Me: I've never seen you swing your arms like that.
MK: I move my arms—everyone does.
Will: A zombie doesn't.
Sam: Stephen doesn't.

Later, same subject.

AB: It rustles, *very* slightly.
MK: (*marching around, listening*).
AB: No one'll hear it, it's not offensive.
MK: I'm offended.

She can't return it because she's worn it and ripped the pocket (with all the marching around). I can't have it—too shiny for college and a bit small (she's a stick).

Discussed Will's holiday homework project—to produce one edition of a newspaper. Will is considering doing a *Camden Review of Books* but not sure it fills the brief.

Will: I'm not sure.

AB: What will satisfy the teacher?
Will: Just ruining the school holiday will satisfy her.

Glad you loved *Red Hanrahan*. I'll also give you J. M. Synge's *The Aran Islands*. No forcing a story around a big idea. He goes to the islands and looks around and listens to the tales of the islanders and writes it all down.

Here's a bit for you:

An old Aran man is telling J. M. Synge about a man who killed his drunken father with a blow of his loy (spade) in a passionate row, fled to the Aran islands and threw himself on the mercy of some Aran folk. They hid him and even when the police came over and offered a cash reward, the islanders wouldn't give him up. "After all," says the old man, "would anyone kill his father if he was able to help it?"

Simple. Just telling what people are doing and saying. No moral. No symbolism.

Love, Nina

∽

Dear Vic,

Will's fussy school having a crackdown on scruffy handwriting.

Will: You can't change it (*handwriting*) at my age, it's fixed.
Me: You can—I had scruffy writing, then I copied someone's nicer writing and it's been nice ever since.
Will: Whose?
Me: I don't know, but s/he didn't like school dinners.
Will: How do you know?
Me: S/he had written about it on a desk.
Will: What?

Me: "Eat school dinner & puke ya fucking guts up"—it was just a few zigzags and loops (I demonstrate).

Later:

Will: (to MK) I've improved my handwriting.
MK: Let's see.
Will: (shows her a page full of lines: "Eat school dinner & puke ya fucking guts up.")
MK: Golly, it is better. But what are you writing about?
Will: Something Stibbe told me. Apparently it helped her at my age.
MK: Very good (glances at me. I carry on shredding cabbage).

In Will's novel Scooby the Lost Dog, a kind-hearted tramp whistles at Scooby to alert him to a loose burger bun ("swit-Swoo!").

Me: What's this "swit-Swoo"?
Will: That's the tramp whistling.
Me: It sounds like a wolf-whistle, not an alert.
Will: Well, he is whistling to a dog.
Me: If he's whistling to get Scooby's attention, it should be "swoo-Swit."
Will: Should it?
Me: "Swit-Swoo" is more when a pretty girl walks past a building site.
Sam: How would you know?

Love, Nina

Dear Vic,

The second year is going to be much harder work than the first. I can already tell. I *haven't* chosen women's this and women's that (like Stella has) because I can't stand hearing the other students (women) rambling on about how unfair everything is/was. So I'm stuck with difficult stuff like The Novel. Which is probably going to be all about novels—the history, the early novels, the anti-novel, the nouveau novel, the neo-novel—basically, everything to make you sick to the back teeth of novels.

Told Will never to take a course like that if he's still determined to write a novel. He said he might go on to movies.

A boy at Will's school has told him about the Mile High Club.

Will: X's uncle is in the Mile High Club.
Sam: Yeah, 3-5-9-18-1-5 is in that club.
Will: I think not.
Sam: He is.
Will: What is the Mile High, then?
Sam: It's a club.
Will: Yes, but what sort of club?
Sam: (*on phone*) Dad, hi, it's Sam. Are you in the Mile High Club? (*Listening*) Oh, OK (*hangs up*).
Will: So, is he?
Sam: Not that he remembers.
Will: No one you know is in the Mile High Club.
Sam: Mum might be.
Will: Doubt it—she never goes on a plane, much.

Love, Nina

PS Mile High Club reminds me: terrible rumor at college. A bloke from politics options has broken his thing. It got bent "too far the wrong way." I didn't know that could happen. Do you know if it can?

~

Dear Vic,

November: a horrible month. "Cloud for most, rain for many" was the poetic weather forecast. I'd have added "so both for quite a few" since it's clearly not an either/or situation.

J. M. Synge has introduced me to the Irish word (for November) Samhain (pronounced *sawshain*) which suits it better.

Me: I hate November.
Will: Why?
Me: Dark, cold and a whole winter to get through.
MK: January seems worse.
Will: I hate February.
Sam: Oi! I was born in February.
MK: February *was* very nice in 1972.
Will: Well, for one day.
Sam: The 2nd (his birthday)?
Will: No, the 1st.

It's cold and dark and I have to wear shoes and socks and I hate that warm feet feeling.

Love, Nina

PS Thanks for info on broken things. God, that's awful. How come I never knew? Do they bandage, or leave to mend (like my collarbone)?

~

Dear Vic,

Hard work at Poly, but good.

Reading James Joyce (I *love* him, especially *Portrait of the Artist as a Young Man*).

Me: (*to MK*) I love James Joyce.
MK: You do?
Me: Yes, it's amazing.
MK: What is?
Me: I'm reading *Portrait of the Artist*...
MK: (*tuts*) Read *Ulysses*.

She means "and *then* see how much you love him." Probably meaning I'll love him more (though possibly less, I suppose). I'm not going to though, at the moment (read *Ulysses*)—it's too long and I haven't got time.

Stella keeps on about *Ulysses* too.

SH: You should read *Ulysses*.
Me: To be honest, I'm sick of hearing about *Ulysses*.
SH: Joyce employs different narrative styles including the stream-of-consciousness.
Me: I'm not fussed about the stream-of-consciousness.
SH: In *Ulysses*, he hardly ever uses the same word twice.
Me: I like the same words being used.
SH: I prefer a wide lexicon.

This is the new Stella. No more mornings in bed with the Goblin Teasmade making cups of Mellow Bird's. Instead she's filling in inter-library loan forms and going to extra seminars. She tried to explain the meaning of the term "hegemony" the other day and tied herself in knots. I steered her off by pointing to a woman (on a market stall called Pat's Hat's—two apostrophes) with red tips in her hair.

Me: Look at those red tips.

SH: Oh, yes, I'd love red tips like that.

Me: I knew you would.

SH: Could you do them if I got the dye?

Me: I don't have any dyeing experience.

SH: I thought you knew about hair.

Me: Only brushing and drying.

SH: Not dyeing?

Me: No.

Anyway, Stella had a birthday party in the cellar bar (dressed up like Mrs. Dalloway in a three-quarter length dress and a floppy hat). Three lecturers came to the party, which is unheard of, and one of them gave her a book titled *The Handmaid's Tale* (hardback).

At the end of the night Stella snogged a student who always has his shirt sleeves rolled up too high and his arms folded. I call him Popeye (because of the sleeves / arms).

Then on the way home Stella was a bit despairing about her crush on lecturer PB.

Me: He's a lecturer.

SH: I think that's why I like him.

Me: Nothing is ever going to come of it.

SH: I know, I don't mind that.

Me: What's the problem, then?

SH: I bet he thinks I'm thick.

Me: Just keep reading the texts and he'll never know.

Love, Nina

∾

Dear Vic,

On Monday Stella was wondering (out loud) why all the boys fancy these particular girls.

SH: Why do all the boys fancy those three posh blondes?
Me: The answer's in the question.
SH: What's so great about them?
Me: Their hair, first and foremost.
SH: But it's thin and blond.
Me: It smells nice.
SH: How do you know?
Me: It looks as though it smells nice.
SH: My hair smells of Timotei.
Me: Yours doesn't look as if it smells as nice as theirs.
SH: Thanks.

It's been a bad week for many.

MK—left shopping in car park and a two-day headache.
Misty—jury service.
Misty's mum—ran her own dog over, not fatal.
Dorothy the Mature Student—lost wedding ring and a silk scarf with horse bits on.
Mary H—locked herself out.
AB—broke mirror.
SH—has dyed her hair whitish blonde (she sees it as a good thing).
Sam—paper cut.
Will—not allowed to go canoeing (with scumbag-type dad of a friend).
Me—fed up.

Love, Nina

PS Will keeps saying "pubic." Also, I think Stella has gone whitey blond to compete with the posh blondes and in preparation for red tips, which she seems to think I can do.

Dear Vic,

On Monday I attempted the red tips in Stella's hair. I told her I'd had zero experience with dye but she begged me.

Had to mix up powders and ammonia wearing surgical gloves and a protective apron. The mixture melted the spoon, which was a bit unnerving. Stella got into the empty bath and started drinking gin and lemonade. I had to paint the dye mixture onto the last half-inch of each section of hair.

It sounds easy but the dye was difficult to work with (grainy) and so was Stella (drunk). In the end (hours later) her hair was 100% pinky-orange (tip to root).

SH: Oh God, I look like an Easter chick.
Me: Easter chicks are OK.
SH: If it's Easter and you're a chick. I won't dare go into college tomorrow.
Me: No one will even notice.
SH: (*staring into mirror*) Fuck!

I came home to NW1 feeling I'd let her down. I hadn't though. She'd wriggled and been uncooperative due to all the gin and lemonade and I was 100% open about my lack of experience.

At college next day, even I was shocked by it. She'd tried to hide it with a thin scarfy thing around her head but the bits sticking through looked startlingly pinky-orange and very chicklike.

251

In a quiet moment at the start of our seminar we heard someone say "crazy apricot" and Stella went into a defensive ramble—the girl said she was only referring to a lip balm flavor.

At 55 later, played a board game called Trivial Pursuit. You move around the board and answer questions on certain subjects and if you land on a certain place you can win a little wedge like a slice of cake. Mary-Kay got bored because she got three slices of cake before anyone else had got even one, and it looked like she was going to romp home. She didn't like being *that* ahead.

Then Harriet had a run of easy questions and MK had a bad run (and kept saying the cards were wrong) and Harriet caught up and MK didn't like being *that* equal. Then we noticed that Sam (who was asking MK's questions) was picking up two cards at once and therefore the answers were for the wrong questions (if you follow). Harriet insisted on going back over the questions that MK had apparently got wrong. MK said not to bother, but Harriet insisted again…and the game was over then because MK had basically won.

H: Well, that's it then, we're playing for runner-up.
MK: I knew it was Jane Fonda.

Love, Nina

∽

Dear Vic,
A new development re Misty.

Me: You're always hungry.
Misty: It's because I've gone on the Pill.
Me: What for?

Misty: (*sarcastic tone*) In case I have sex.

Me: Who with?

Misty: Anyone.

Me: Weren't you on it before?

Misty: No, we used the rhythm method.

Later, I asked MK what the rhythm method actually *is*. Is it just what I think it is? Or is there more to it?

MK: It's for people who don't do it enough to make other methods worth the fag.

Me: Oh.

MK: It works by not doing it most of the time.

Me: Right.

MK: It has a high failure rate.

Me: Oh?

MK: If you *do* do it.

Me: (*getting on with something else*).

MK: So, unless you pretty much don't do it, you shouldn't use it.

I've honestly never heard MK talk so much about a thing, she was practically rambling (for her). Normally it's everyone else yakking and being boring and pointless and her piping up with a defining two words.

Realized later she must've thought it was *me* using the rhythm method. But it's Misty. She's still going out with the same bloke (and when they have sex she still imagines the dog chasing her near St. Thomas's church). Going on the Pill seems a big step.

Anyway, thanks for our aprons. Gave MK the Ritz Cracker one and I had the other. MK has used hers but not gone the whole hog (didn't have the loop over head, except to try it on). She's not a sloppy cook but might (theoretically) wipe hands on skirt, so it was fine like that. Plus she likes Ritz Crackers (theoretically).

MK: It's very nice, tell Victoria. I don't usually wear orange.

Sam: It suits you.

MK: There you go, it suits me.

I don't do that cook-twice-as-much-as-you-need and freeze the other half thing. Partly because we don't have a freezer as such and partly because it goes against the grain.

Made my version of your Victoria cake but had to do it using an apple on the weighing scales (we've lost the weights) and it came out fine. I worked out that 1 large apple = roughly 5oz (you get 3 apples in 1lb).

Jam (blackcurrant) in the middle like you say, but also (by popular request) peanut butter. Everyone liked it except AB, who said the peanut butter should have been served on the side for those who don't partake.

MK does the big shopping—a mixed blessing—she buys stuff without a plan (I think she copies other people who know what they're doing). This is the kind of stuff that comes back:

quark (German style liquid cheese)
mustard with seeds
rye bread with seeds
balsamic vinegar of Modena (black vinegar)
fresh lichees
turkey mince
oatmeal crackers with seeds
figs, fig rolls
bourbons
spinach
bulgur wheat
Persil
Simple soap
seeds, sesame seed sweets
olives

break-ins
tiny oranges (bitter, you eat the skin)
herbal tea
honey

And other mysterious things that add up to nothing much when it comes to making meals. It's like living in another country.

Love, Nina
PS Thanks for gifts. Gave Will the juggling balls and Sam the fake ice cube with a fly in it—neither has mastered either yet.

∽

Dear Vic,
Saw Pippa for the first time in ages. Same as ever.
She's moved into a new flat near Richmond with beautician Mel who's got a job in a new shopping center there. The new flat is very nice apparently, except the kitchen cupboards all smell of semen.
I still can't take to Mel. I'm suspicious of anyone who eats an apple with a knife and can't forgive her for my six weeks with red eyelids.
Anyway, Pippa didn't want to hear anything about my Poly life and when I started an anecdote about *Blurt!* magazine she said, "Sorry, I'm not really interested."
Told Mary-Kay.

Me: She just put her hand up and said, "I'm not interested."
MK: Oh.
Me: Don't you think it's rude?
MK: It saves time.
Me: Yeah, but I listened patiently about her kitchen cupboards smelling of semen.

MK: That *is* quite interesting.

Me: More so than my magazine?

MK: Afraid so.

Also, the boyfriend that Mel the beautician was advertising as "a musician" turns out to be a busking one-man-band. Pippa was scathing.

Pippa: He was standing there in Long Acre playing a mouthorgan with a drum on his back and cymbals between his knees.

Me: Was he any good?

Pippa: He was a one-man-fucking-band.

Me: Maybe he's good.

Pippa: It's tantamount to being a clown.

Hope short letters mean you're otherwise occupied, not that you've got nothing to report.

Love, Nina

∽

Dear Vic,

Sam's getting on my nerves with *Chas "N" Dave's Knees Up.* It's gone beyond a joke. I'm struggling with *The Marriage of Heaven and Hell* and all I can hear is "Rabbit."

Which reminds me... Stella has managed to embarrass herself via a note to the beloved lecturer (PB). The note read as follows: "sorry essay is one day late. I had a bit of a struggle with Rhinoceros."

She was referring to a play called *Rhinoceros* that we'd looked at in a little course on the theater of the absurd (some v. good & funny plays, some really strange).

In a seminar today PB shared the note with the class. "This note,

clipped on to a student's work, made my day yesterday... (*reads note*)
I couldn't help imagining the struggle."

Everyone chuckled. He didn't say who'd written it, but Stella gave
herself away by dropping her lighter under a desk and staying down
for too long.

After the class:

SH: God—that was so embarrassing.
Me: No, it was funny.
SH: I felt humiliated.
Me: Don't be silly, it made his day, he said so. I'd have loved it if
he'd read my note out.
SH: Yes, but you're not in love with him.
Me: I'd have loved it even more if I were in love with him.

That's the difference between us. One of the many.

Love, Nina

༄

Dear Vic,

Yes, Stella has a perfectly nice boyfriend (live-in). He's clever, funny
and from Lincoln but Stella can't see any of that anymore (except
there's no ignoring he's from Lincoln). They bicker a lot and have
pretty much stopped liking each other. She thinks he's moved on to
pastures new—he is a postman after all and they have pastures new
on offer all the time apparently (especially in Plumstead, according to
Stella).

Her crush on lecturer PB continues. Still, at least now she's
bothering to read the text(s) and turning up for lectures (and
scratching her teeth).

PB was planning to run the first of his popular culture days with videos of popular gems such as the early *Carry Ons* (which were as full of symbolism and meaning as Pinter—only a lot more watchable) and chit-chat.

Stella was worried she'd be late (9 a.m. start). I said I'd ring her just as I left NW1 to wake her and give her plenty of time to get in. Which I did.

She turned up, looking flustered, ten minutes into it—we were discussing "Why comedy matters" unfortunately.

Me: How come you're late? I gave you an alarm call.
Stella: My kimono sleeve caught fire on the grill pan.
Me: What were you cooking?
Stella: I was lighting a fag.

Stella was a bit put out because we all laughed—she hadn't got into the comedy mood yet.

She did cheer up when the *Educating Rita* type girl turned up (also late) with a Wimpy breakfast bap but no bra on. Stella couldn't help mentioning it to her (her bra-less-ness). Rita seemed surprised and even checked by looking down her own shirt.

Rita said she gets this "phantom bra" thing where it feels like she's wearing a bra, even when she isn't. Stella, who knows about bra fittings (apparently), said the phantom-bra feeling is a sign of wearing a too-tight bra and it leaving an imprint. Stella's advice: get a looser-fitting bra.

Told MK about this later at supper.

Me: So it felt like she'd got a bra on and she hadn't.
MK: Oh dear.
Me: She looked terrible.
MK: Oh.

Me: Have you ever had phantom bra?

MK: Bra, no. Socks, yes.

Love, Nina

⌐

Dear Vic,

Your strawberry thief reminds me of Stella's garden robber.

In 5th floor coffee bar:

SH: He leapt over the hedge.

Hippie Ruth: Did you *see* him?

SH: No, we were watching *Bob's Full House*.

Me: Did he take anything?

SH: Three items off the washing line.

Hippie: The bastard. What did he take?

SH: One item was my silk kimono (*sad face*).

Me: I thought that caught fire.

SH: Yeah, it did a bit, that's why I'd put it through the wash.

Me: What were the other items?

SH: Delicate items.

Me: Pants?

SH: Yes, if you must know.

Hippie: Sick bastard.

Me: Did you call the police?

Hippie: Huh, more sick bastards.

The police advised Stella against hanging intimate garments on the line in full view of the street (corner plot). They also said that dogs are a good deterrent as are gravel moats (give-away crunching sound when a thief walks on it). She's going to put her smalls on the storage heater from now on, even though there's a sticker saying not to.

Stella wasn't bothered about the pants but was upset about the kimono—it coming from an exotic aunt who also gave her a box of illegal cigars that she won't let the boyfriend smoke (nice box).

Told them about it (knicker theft) at supper at 55 (which they enjoyed)... but it led to me recalling the "Coleman's fouling incident" of 1981. I thought they'd like it, but they didn't much.

Me: But—this is the thing—he pegged them onto the line again, after.
MK: After what?
Me: Soiling them.
MK: Eew!
AB: (*aghast*) Oh no!
Me: *No!* Not like *that,* only with mustard.
Both: *Eew!*

It put a bit of a downer on supper really. So I changed the subject to Mary Hope's disappointment with her new Zanussi (temperamental on the spin). I think she might be overloading. She washes *all* the bedding *every* week.

I mentioned MH washing all the bedding every week and somehow it seemed to bring us back to the subject of soiling, so I didn't say anything else.

Then AB said Zanussi is just Electrolux in disguise and things improved a bit.

Love, Nina

Dear Vic,

Misty talked me into going shopping with her (John Lewis). Then, in spite of saying she was "extremely depressed," bought vitamins, fingernail buffing things and tons of cosmetics and makeup and special shoelaces to match her shoes. Her basket didn't seem like the shopping of someone on the brink of suicide, it looked like the basket of someone keen to live life to the full.

Told this to MK.

Me: She bought tablets to make her eyes brighter, yet claims to have lost the will to live.
MK: Virginia Woolf had just had her hair done.
Me: When?
MK: When she drowned herself.
Me: God!
MK: (*shrugs*).
Me: So, making an effort doesn't mean…
MK: Not necessarily.
Me: Maybe it's all part of the run-up.
MK: Maybe.
Will: Enid Blyton had just opened a can of ginger beer.
Sam: (*suddenly interested*) Enid's not dead, is she?

Anyway, Misty seems better now her shoelaces are the right color and she's got tidy fingernails. But I suppose, with what I know now, that could be a cry for help.

Love, Nina

Dear Vic,

Took Stella to Camden to meet S&W and MK.

Sam: Who do you support?

SH: The Owls!

MK: Are the Owls Sheffield *Wednesday*?

SH: I think so.

MK: You *think* so?

On the way out:

SH: Mary-Kay's really nice, isn't she?

Me: I wouldn't go that far.

SH: Thought you liked her?

Me: I do.

Back inside, Stella gone:

Me: Well?

Sam: She supports the Owls.

MK: Well, hardly.

Me: She's nice at college.

MK: Thought she didn't do any work.

Me: She does now.

MK: Why all of a sudden?

Me: She's got a crush on a lecturer.

MK: I thought she had a chap at home.

Me: She does, but she's having a harmless crush as well.

Will: Her eyebrows were funny.

Me: She plucked them.

MK is doing a new food thing: roasted peppers. Put whole red

262

peppers under the grill and cook them (turning) until black all over. Then place them in a plastic bag and leave to cool. Then peel them and chop them up and sprinkle with a bit of balsamic vinegar of Modena and olive oil. They're a faff but nice.

Will made a Mother's Day card at school for Mary-Kay. It's a swirly pattern with a poem inside.

> Mum is playful, Mum is fun.
> Mum always gets things done.

Me: That's lovely.
Will: I know.
Me: She'll love it.
Will: Yes.
Sam: He didn't write that himself.
Will: (*smiling*) No, I copied it from the kid next to me.
Me: Why didn't you make up your own?
Will: That one did the job.

Sam bought her a card from the paper shop. It said: "Mum you're COOL!"

And had a picture of a woman apparently trapped inside a deep freeze.

Love, Nina

 ∽

Dear Vic,

Acorn Club sounds v. good. S&W and me talked about it for ages.

Me: He found it where he'd hung it two years earlier and a tiny oak shoot was growing from an acorn he'd left in his pocket.

Sam: When?

Me: When he returned from the war.

Sam: An oak tree?

Me: Well, a tiny shoot, from the acorn.

Sam: Did it mess the coat up?

Will: (*tuts*) It's just symbolic.

Sam: OK, but did it ruin the coat?

Will: You're ruining the story.

Me: The next day another old man told his story—an apple was left in his pocket.

Sam: (*bored*) Did an oak tree grow?

Me: Not an *oak*.

Sam: What, then?

Me: A tiny apple-tree shoot.

Sam: He copied the first man's story.

Me: It's a story lots of people claim as their own.

Sam: Once I left some raisins in my pocket.

Will: Did you find a tiny grape vine?

Sam: I did actually.

Will: Liar!

I'm going to tell PH about it. He'll love it. It's pure *Autobiography & Fiction*. He might use it with the next bunch of students.

Love, Nina

⌇

Dear Vic,

Sam and Will are chalk and cheese. Sam's perceptive whereas Will's inventive.

Example. Pippa wanted to meet for lunch and insisted I bring

264

Sam and Will, but then spoke in code the whole time about new boyfriend.

Pippa: He's better at exercising in the mornings, so we often have to get up early—if you get my meaning—for a jog.
Me: Oh.
Pippa: If I badger him to *exercise* in the evenings, he goes along with it, but it never comes to much.
Me: Right.
Pippa: I'm more of a night owl, so we'll see how it goes.
Me: Mmm.
Pippa: I'm not a morning person, especially, you know, for *exercise*.

Later, at supper:

AB: So, where were you lot all off to this lunchtime?
Will: We met Pippa for lunch.
MK: What is she doing these days?
Sam: (*laughing*) Her new boyfriend likes riding the hobbyhorse in the morning.
MK: *Riding the hobbyhorse?*
Sam: Y'know, doing the dirty stuff.
Will: No, she was talking about jogging, you pervert.
MK: (*to me*) Which?
Me: Sam's right. She was trying to talk in code.
Will: Oh, was she? I'm just too straightforward.
Me: She kept nicking Sam's chips and even dunked into his egg.
MK: Is that code too?
Me: No, she *literally* dunked a chip into Sam's egg.
AB: What a liberty.

Love, Nina

Dear Vic,

Stella invited me to supper (at her house). Went back with her after lit theory seminar (my worst, her best). I just sit there thinking what's everyone on about while she's joining in with the nonsense.

It's a nice walk up to her house and a bus sometimes comes and will stop even between stops so it's worth starting to walk. But Stella jumped into a taxi saying she was treating herself due to having a supper guest (me) and needing to prepare the meal. I felt sick in the taxi due to the air freshener (coconut with sunglasses on dangling from mirror) and Stella rambling on about Terry Eagleton. Then, ages before we got to her house, she asked the taxi to drop us and we walked the rest of the way. This was because she didn't want the boyfriend to know about the taxi.

The boyfriend is very observant apparently (recognizes the *sound* of a taxi two streets away). They're on an economy drive and he likes to catch her out wasting money (ditto she him).

Where Stella lives doesn't smell like London. Although it technically is. It smells of privet and Right Guard. London-proper smells of the bricks round a fireplace. And, at Gloucester Crescent, coffee and floor polish and overripe melons.

Stella's house isn't that nice. It's all carpety and cupboardy and there's no window in the kitchen because of unfinished renovations. The worktop is a door on its side and the fridge is in a hot little cupboard and smells of rice.

Stella went to make some tea and I talked to the boyfriend. He's funny and made clever comments. He was watching the horse racing in his boxer shorts. He told me he'd got an accumulator on (but not to tell Stella).

Boyfriend: So, Nina-from-Leicester, why are you here?
Me: I don't know.

Boyfriend: So, you're not taking the existentialism course, then?

Me: No.

Boyfriend: Who paid for the taxi?

Me: What taxi?

Boyfriend: The one that dropped you outside the fire station ten minutes ago.

Stella came in with three teas (no milk available). We watched the racing for a bit and the two of them bickered until Stella revealed supper plan: Bird's Eye Steakhouse Grill Dinners. The boyfriend jigged his legs about and said, "Bird's Eye Steakhouse Grill Dinners, yabadabadoo."

I don't know if he was serious, but they both seemed brighter at the prospect of the Grill dinners. We went to the corner shop, which was called Cleanthus Stores, and bought the Bird's Eye Steakhouse Grill Dinners (frozen) and a pint of semi-skimmed milk. She put them in the oven at gas mark 6 for 30 mins. They were ready at 5 o'clock. They had a cup of tea with it.

Ginger cake for pudding.

Then the boyfriend went to play snooker in Plumstead and Stella showed me the garden—forgetting that I'd seen it before when the council birdman came round. I didn't bring all that up again. She particularly wanted me to see the washing line (crime scene). Easy target (corner plot). I could see a low area of hedging where the thief apparently entered and exited again with Stella's kimono.

I walked back down to Woolwich Arsenal. No bus, no taxi. It took ten mins max.

Back at 55. Told MK the bare bones. She liked about the accumulator and the Bird's Eye Grills best.

MK: How was supper with Darby & Joan?

Me: You mean Stella & Boyfriend?

MK: Yes.

Me: Stella is funny.

MK: She didn't seem very funny when she was here.

Me: That's because she was trying to be serious and polite.

MK: She needn't have.

Me: People *do* that.

MK: That's their lookout.

MK has high expectations of everyone, even polytechnic students. She expects as much from Stella as she does from her Salman Rushdie mates. Unrealistic. Like Nunney, who expects the same high standards (though not the same exact things).

Love, Nina

⌒

Dear Vic,

All choosing our dissertation (extended essay) subjects. Five thousand words on the subject of our choice (pretty much).

I have decided to do Carson McCullers, author of *The Heart Is a Lonely Hunter* (which I absolutely loved when I read it a couple of years ago). The Student from Luton is doing The Plays of Samuel Beckett. The Hippie is doing Images of the Female in telly advertising from 1955 to 1985. Popeye is doing *Moby Dick*. Stella had trouble deciding between Althusser (Marxist bloke) and Philip Larkin.

SH: I can't decide.

Me: Which do you like most?

SH: It's not about liking, it's about the likelihood of writing something interesting and engaging.

Me: OK, which is easiest?

SH: Larkin.

She's pretty much decided on Larkin. It'll be a doddle. She'll just rehash some essays from her A-level and say how much she likes him.

It's a long time till we have to hand them in but the important thing is NOT to just leave them and get ourselves in a mad panic come the summer (PB's words). We should plan and read and write a draft, then go and see our supervisors for a progress check and work steadily.

Stella has done a rough plan. The plan includes interviewing AB for extra kudos. I stupidly mentioned that AB had met Philip Larkin and might have exaggerated it a bit.

Annoying. AB will show me up by playing down the relationship (which is already quite nothingy) and Stella will show me up by demonstrating she knows fuck all about Larkin or the true meanings of his poems (which in my opinion are the mardy ramblings of an oddball). And she'll say things like juncture, apropos or caliber or her other words. And AB will say, "Your friend Stella kept saying 'caliber.'"

She pronounces it cal-eye-ber.

For a while I couldn't decide between J. M. Synge and Carson McCullers. I like both. Nunney was no help, only saying I probably shouldn't choose something I really like. He said, "I don't think you should do something you really like, knowing you, you'll end up hating it." He's referring to the old notion of familiarity breeding contempt. I'm not worried though. I'm bound to hate whatever I choose and I'd rather hate something I started out liking.

J. M. Synge: I went out into the wet lanes in my pampooties and caught the influence.

Carson McCullers: they found Mrs. Langdon unconscious, she had cut off her nipples with garden shears.

I discussed it at 55. And Sam said I should do a West Ham player called Frank McAvennie.

Me: I can't decide between McCullers and Synge.

MK: McCullers, I should think.

Me: I was thinking Synge.

MK: So you've decided.

Me: No, not really.

MK: (*shrugs*) Synge, then?

Me: Why not McCullers?

MK: Because you had decided Synge.

Sam: You should do Frank McAvennie.

I took that as a sign that I should do McCullers (the names McAvennie and McCullers being so similar).

So that's who I'll do (probably).

Love, Nina

⌒

Dear Vic,

Just got back from Rochester, Kent.

Went in a hired minibus with visiting lecturer from San Diego State University called Nick Nichols (American). He wanted to see the five little graves in St. James's churchyard that inspired the opening of *Great Expectations* and other Dickensian stuff. Nick took a few photographs (of the graves) and said how incredible it was to finally see "Pip's graves."

A mature student called Dorothy (wasn't on the minibus, just turned up) lost a contact lens in a coughing fit by the graves. But Nick Nichols didn't let that spoil the mood for him. He said that's the thing about these bleak spots, the sea mist rolls in and has you at its mercy. Dorothy said it wasn't that, it was a mint imperial gone down the wrong way.

270

She didn't find the contact lens and had to go carefully after that because she was seeing double due to only having one lens in. Stella suggested she take the other one out but Dorothy explained that wouldn't be a very good solution. In the end she kept one eye closed and I couldn't look at her after that.

Went to a tearoom. Stella said afterward it was called Peggotty's Parlour (I hope it was called that, but I think she's gilding the lily) and our American tutor ordered a BLT. The Americans love that kind of sandwich (BLT, club and steak) that bit more than an actual sandwich.

NN: Could I get a BLT on white?
Tearoom woman: BLT? What's that when it's at home?
NN: BLT—bacon, lettuce, and to-may-doe—sandwich?
Woman: You can have bacon and egg bap, or bacon salad sandwich.
NN: What's in the bacon salad?
Woman: Bacon, lettuce, tomato, and cucumber.
NN: That sounds good. Can you hold the cucumber?
Woman: What for (*holding cucumber*)?

Nick Nichols thought the woman was being humorous. She wasn't. He also loved that she'd said, "What's that *when it's at home?*"

We went home via some murals Nick wanted to see in South London, but he scraped the minibus badly (both sides) squeezing it between two posts, which were there to prevent vehicular access. So we didn't pay much attention to the murals and drove quickly on.

Nick Nichols adores London and wants to see absolutely everything Londony and Dickensian. His wife (Lee) and son (Scott) are here too. They're staying in my tutor's house (my tutor is staying at their house in San Diego).

A group of us in Nick's tutor group went round to the Nichols's for pizza and to watch a video of *Great Expectations* (in prep for the

271

Rochester grave visit). They put us onto folded pizza. A sort of pizza pasty.

Stella got drunk on the Valpolicella on offer and made a show of herself—interrupting the movie to ask to borrow their lawn mower.

Me: What did you ask to borrow their lawn mower for?
Stella: The garden needs mowing.
Me: I need new shoes, but I didn't bring that up.
Stella: I saw their neat lawn and felt a pang.
Me: Can't your boyfriend do your lawn?
Stella: He's a postman.

Everyone knows he's a postman. Some of us have met him. Stella uses his postman status as an excuse. Brings it up to explain everything. I said she should stop using her boyfriend's postman status as a crutch. I meant to say excuse, but I said "crutch" and it sounded appropriate.

Anyway. It's very nice having Nick Nichols from SDU around. Just when you think everything's shit, he says how great everything is in his American accent and it's convincing.

Love, Nina
PS Didn't think much to Kent.

༄

Dear Vic,

Picked up my photographs from Edwards on Parkway. Funny little man. Misty will not take her films to him. One, he's expensive compared with Boots, and two, she always imagines he looks at her photos and wanks. I said she has a high opinion of her photos if she imagines people wanking over them.

Me: He must be sick to the back teeth of looking at photos of unknown people and dogs. I bet he doesn't even look.

Misty: Of course he does. You would.

Me: Not in a wanking way.

Misty: He must get bored in there all day and that's when they do it.

Got home, looked at my photos. A few nice ones of Pip's graves and Nick Nichols's BLT and a blurred one of MK's hoover (from an attempt at the secret photography thing, where you don't hold the camera up). Tried to imagine what Edwards of Parkway might have thought of them (esp. the hoover).

Showed MK.

Me: Look, another accidental photograph.

MK: What is it?

Me: It was meant to be you and Russell Harty but I got the hoover.

MK: I didn't know you two were acquainted.

Meaning me and the hoover.

By the way, you shouldn't use anti-dandruff shampoo unless you actually have dandruff. If you use it and don't have dandruff already, you will get dandruff. That's how it works. It removes dandruff unless you don't have it. In which case it causes it.

Told MK about Pippa wearing a headband (or "bandana").

Me: Pippa has started wearing a headband.

MK: Alice or Rambo?

Me: Halfway between the two.

MK: Nice.

Skipped breakfast. Not that I'm skipping breakfast but because I didn't have any. Told Misty I was hungry because I'd skipped breakfast.

Me: I forgot to have breakfast (*I put it like that*).
Misty: That's dangerous.
Me: How?
Misty: Your metabolism will slow right down.
Will: She means your body clock will go wrong.
Sam: What's your body clock?
Will: It's the clock inside you that makes you do things.
Sam: Like what?
Will: Get up, shit, eat crisps.

Love, Nina

∽

Dear Vic,

Mary-Kay has a good memory for certain things—things you wish she'd forget such as the first things you did/said on Day One etc. (saying, "I love books, especially the classics such as Dickens and Heriot").

You can't get away with anything. You can't change your mind about a thing, otherwise it's "I thought you said you hated daffodils" type thing.

She's always very careful about what she says and never just blurts things out without thinking apart from the time she blurted out that she thought Jez was handsome. But to be fair she only blurted it out because Mary Hope had said Tom was (handsome) and it was a comparative thing.

Me: Tom's gone home.

MK: Tom who?

Me: Tom Stibbe.

MK: Oh.

Me: Mary says he's handsome.

MK: (*quicker than usual response*) Who?

Me: Tom.

MK: Jez is more so.

MK remembers stuff I tell her about you and the others. She always says, "How are the others?" because she's picked up that I call you lot "the others."

She's quick to pick up quirky things, but not the key things about a person (or doesn't notice). Or, her key things are different to my key things. Maybe the quirky things are the key things (for her).

A woman came round to 55 the other day (to do with Sam) and I noticed that the woman said "prer-haps" (instead of perhaps) and she kept saying it. Prer-haps.

MK noticed she kept saying "to be honest with you." I didn't notice that (I think I say "to be honest with you" sometimes, hence my not noticing it).

MK noticed (and liked) that she sat cross-legged, even in a dining chair, and I noticed (and disliked) that her bangle kept hitting the table with a thud.

Stella's friend Ruth (the clever hippie with periodontal gum disease) says that bangles are symbolic of slavery and, more recently, of women being "owned" by men. She wears an ironic fake handcuff.

Hope all's well with you.

Love, Nina

PS Stella has sold her flute for £50.

Dear Vic,

Loved the story of Mr. Benson. How funny. You should write a novel about all the goings-on there. In fact, you really should (I'm not just saying that). I thought the other day that AJA should write a novel about his early life. He's got such a way with words and so many funny rural memories—it'd be like *All Creatures Great and Small*, only not a vet, a kid.

The dissertation subjects are all decided now and my plan is submitted to PH. My plan is to show, via my wide reading, that Carson McCullers was a brave young writer who had the guts to illuminate a less glossy side of USA life in her stories about deaf people, poor people, kids who can't write and isolated people.

I'll say that although the critics were unkind and the public was resentful, she continued to write about an underrepresented type of people. Her motivation being that she herself was isolated and reclusive due to having suffered strokes at a young age and accidentally marrying a homosexual who gallivanted with other isolated intellectuals in the Deep South.

I will show how her determination to write about isolated/not-very-attractive people, even though the critics were angry at her portrayals, influenced a whole new breed of writers (those who wanted to write about not-very-nice things) and that she ultimately deserves her place in the great Southern tradition. Blah, blah.

God. I wish I'd done J. M. Synge.

Changing the subject, Stella wants someone to work one of her evenings at Plumstead snooker club and I've said I might try it out.

You just turn up at 6 and serve drinks and frozen microwaveable snacks to the snooker-playing punters.

There are major perks. You can drink as many non-alcoholic

beverages and eat as many microwaveable snacks as you want. You can read texts while on duty. Apparently the punters like the staff to be ensconced in a book and just let them get on with playing snooker— they find it relaxing and it means they can make cash bets.

Stella says the only drawback is the toilets and the fact that the microwaveable snacks smell like sweat.

It's generous pay considering you don't actually do anything useful, except for looking away and microwaving.

Love, Nina

PS I meant it about you writing a novel or a diary or something. It would be very popular.

~

Dear Vic,

Mary-Kay went out to supper. Mysterious. Then, the next morning, there was a tiny bunch of violets in a tiny cup by the kitchen sink. I had a close look at the violets and they were really beautiful (five petals and little yellow blobs and heart-shaped leaves on a curved stem).

Just before they went over, I pressed some of them (between pages of heavy books). Asked MK if she was interested in having the pressed violets when they were done and she said not really.

Just when the violets were ready (for Amanda's birthday card/ picture) Amanda said, "I hate dried flowers." So I stuck them in the margins of a letter to Nunney, so as not to waste them.

Then when Nunney was over this w/e:

N: What were the dead things in the letter?
Me: Violets. I pressed them.
N: Oh.

Me: Didn't you like them?

N: Well, not really, they were dead.

Then later, had a sword fight with pool cues at the Edinburgh Castle (me and Nunney). I started it out of boredom, and we got chucked out. N was absolutely furious.

Went back to 55 mardy and told MK.

MK: So you attacked him because he hated the violets.

Me: It was a poke, not an attack.

MK: OK, but were the violets and the poke linked?

Me: A bit, maybe, but I regret both now.

MK: Especially the violets, I should think.

Me: Yes.

MK: Harder to live down than the poke.

Me: God, yes.

MK: Not that poking is a good thing.

Me: No. Anyway, now he's gone back to Sussex.

MK: Where the girls are less liable to poke him.

Too annoyed to write about anything else. But hope all's well with you.

Love, Nina

⌒

Dear Vic,

The Owner's outdoor shower sounds brilliant. It's a shame about you having to have the occasional glimpse of him in it (couldn't you just not look?) but other details (outside, bamboo and cold) are good—like something in the wild.

Mary-Kay's bath is a different kettle of fish—but still amazing. It's in her bedroom, right in the window. Of course she'd never go in it (the bath) with the shutters open (unlike your Owner), but if she ever lost her mind, it would be an obvious option.

It's got a great big mahogany cover over it with brass handles. It must be a right faff to get it off (the lid), especially as it has stuff on top. Books and things. That's why she uses ours so much.

I've upset Misty with a thoughtless (pointless) comment.

Me: If I ever get married I'll consider myself to have failed in life (*that was the thoughtless comment*).
Misty: Thanks a lot (*stomps off*).
Me: What did I say wrong?
Pippa: She was jilted, remember?
Me: Jilted? She's only twenty-three.
Pippa: It was when she was in the first year.
Me: Jilted on the *actual* wedding day?
Pippa: No, a few weeks before.
Me: That's not jilting.

I didn't say anything (else) but it started me thinking that jilting is one of the few things available in the modern world (to the total cunt). I mean you can no longer deflower, kill or rob people on the highway or steal their sheep, but you can jilt them at the altar.

I can imagine how annoying it would be (to be jilted) because of the time Nunney canceled our camping weekend at short notice (it felt like being mildly jilted). I hadn't even wanted to go particularly, but felt I should make the effort and then he suddenly "postponed" at the eleventh hour when I'd announced to everyone that we were going camping in the New Forest and people had said "how romantic" etc.

Me: So you're canceling the camping?

Nunney: I'm *postponing* it.

Me: I never wanted to go anyway.

N: You should have said.

Me: I was being nice.

N: Oh, was that you trying to be nice? That's what put me off.

Love, Nina

∾

Dear Vic,

5th floor coffee bar. Talking about parents. Funny to hear how odd they all are, not just straightforward odd, but funny habits and peculiar life-styles. It's great to hear because it makes you feel so much better.

The Student from Luton revealed that her parents have slept "apart" for years due to her dad's "night strolling" syndrome (like sleepwalking, only the person doesn't actually get up and walk, they just move their legs while still in bed). They now have twin beds and touch hands across the gap every night before going to sleep (which seems nice and romantic). But the Student from Luton says her mother won't splash out on a new single duvet cover for him, so he's stuck with Star Wars.

Then we started discussing our own sleep positions and it came out that I slept in the fetal position, which I demonstrated on the floor.

Student from Luton: You shouldn't sleep like that.

Me: Like what?

SL: With one leg on top of the other.

Me: Why?

SL: The pressure of the top leg will bring on varicose veins.

So, since then I've gone into a new sleep position, it's pretty much "the recovery position"—according to the Student from Luton (who's St. John's trained)—and will not cause veins or choking or anything untoward. I told her that it's not that comfy and she suggested placing a "leg pillow" under the knee of the bent leg (like a pregnant woman). It seems a lot of faff just to avoid possible future varicose veins.

Later at 55.

Me: I've gone into a new sleep position.
Will: What is it?
Me: It's like the recovery position (*I demonstrate*).
Will: So, are you still like that when you wake up?
Me: Um (*thinking*), no, I'm not, I think I go back into my old position.
Sam: What was your old position like?
Me: The fetal position.
Sam: What, with your feet up?
Me: No, *fetal*, like a baby in the mother's tummy (*I demonstrate*).
Sam: Why have you changed?
Will: She was born.

Surprised about Gordon Banks. He's very distinctive (looking). Send a photo if you can.

Love, Nina

⟡

Dear Vic,

Gordon Banks is much more famous than George Melly. Banks played for England for almost ten years and (according to Sam) is the best goalie England ever had.

I don't think your Gordon can be the *actual* Gordon Banks. Unless he looks like my sketch (a bit Spocky), it's not him.

I can't see the real Gordon Banks in a swanky bar. It just doesn't sound like him. Sorry.

Love, Nina
PS Has anyone asked him (if he's the real Gordon Banks)?

~

Dear Vic,

I knew it couldn't be the actual Gordon Banks.

And strictly speaking, being "distantly related to the human cannonball by marriage" is not related to the human cannonball at all, it just means that someone to whom she's distantly related *married* the human cannonball.

Anyway, what actually is a human cannonball? It's not like they're a brilliant pianist or a marvelous writer. They're just an attention-seeker. Like the birdseed bloke of Mornington Crescent.

Have gone on to Earl Grey. Trying to develop my tastes.

MK always has Earl Grey unless on a train. Has chamomile if

in very good or very bad mood. She got really grumpy the other day when the kettle had gone missing and accused me of "doing something weird" with it. Then she found it in her room. She'd taken it up to water her plant and got sidetracked.

She was about to make a chamomile, but switched to regular tea out of mardiness.

I found a wedge of Edam cheese with a bite taken from it. Right in the middle. Presented it to Sam & Will. Both denied taking the bite. I could tell it was Sam (by his gazing around the room). He denied it, but as he protested, I saw he had that red wax all over his teeth.

Me: You're such a bad liar.
Sam: You only knew because of the red stuff.
Me: No, I knew before that.
Will: He's rubbish at lying.
Me: Yeah, for someone who tells so many.
Sam: You can't talk.
Me: I can lie perfectly well if I've planned it.
MK: What do you mean "if you've planned it"?
Me: Not on the spur of the moment.
Will: I'm happy to lie, if necessary, but not on the spot.
Sam: Mum couldn't lie on the spot.
MK: I *could,* but I don't.
Me: It's best not to.
MK: (*raises eyebrows*).

Will's friend is a vegetarian but will eat anything that's died of old age. Apparently the kid's mum gets hold of chickens from a chicken rescue that have died of natural causes.

Reminded me of Helen who will eat anything that's had a nice life except for lamb, frogs, and snails—which she doesn't eat however nice a life they've had (because she dislikes them).

Love, Nina

∽

Dear Vic,

Woolwich is full of people with red tips in their hair nowadays. Even this quiet girl on our course (Fiona, calls herself "Fee") has had red tips done. Fee's red tips are really good, neat little tips, very bright red. Effective. She must have had it done at a professional hair salon.

Stella spotted them in the refectory and was envious. She went and spoke to her (Fee) about the red tips. You could see the girl (Fee) edging away (egg & bacon flan on her tray).

Stella thinks she and Fee have got something in common now Fee's had the tips done. Stella seems to have forgotten that her red tips didn't work out (only she and I know that her pinky-orange hair is the red tips gone wrong). Stella's acting as though they both have the tips and it's freaking the girl (Fee) out.

Fee was in the Director General later drinking a pint of lime cordial, looking shy but crunching ice cubes and deliberately making everyone cringe. There's something annoying about that kind of shy person. I mean, why should they get away with it when the rest of us have to speak? If you're shy, fine, but you shouldn't be allowed to have red tips in your hair. I mean you're either shy or you're not.

Said something along those lines to Stella, who thought I was being intolerant and said that Fee's red tips are a non-verbal way of expressing herself. Ditto the ice cube chewing. Stella only stuck up for her because she's got the red tips and in Stella's mind they're in the same team.

Love, Nina

Dear Vic,

Very windy in North London last night. This morning found a wind-mangled umbrella had been thrown over our wall. Went to chuck it in the dustbin shelter and saw one of our bin lids had blown away. Hunted about for the bin lid and saw a pile of soil and a broken terracotta planter (with Greek meander pattern) in next door's front yard.

On the plus side, a sex-card from the phone box had blown into 57. It said, "If You Like Pain, Ring Sarah Jane" and featured a line-drawing of a woman with a whip being pulled along in a chariot by a decrepit naked man. I propped it up on their bin for them all to see.

Agree about Dickens—hence taking the Dickens course. Unfortunately the novels on the course are the gloomy ones (course is called *Dickens the Great Reformer,* so to be expected really). Just read *Hard Times.* Awful (but short).

I agree with you 100% about *Great Expectations.* It made me think about people who have done good deeds...so much nicer than grudging the people who've done you wrong. I always think of Joanne O'Connor's mum who gave me a bottle of Asti Spumante on my 18th and made a big fuss of me. I was slightly embarrassed at the time, but looking back it was one of the nicest things anyone's ever done. Not the wine, the bothering.

Also MK who, when J—died, had the guts to talk about it and said, "Borrow the car, go on," and then later, when I was dwelling on it, said, "Don't do that thing of making it an excuse to do less. Do more."

Anyway. Agree about Charles Dickens in general. Everyone likes Charles Dickens.

Me: Everyone likes Charles Dickens.
Will: Dickens is my second best Charles.
Me: Who's your first best?

Sam: Is it Charles?

Will: Charles who?

Sam: Charles at school.

Will: No way! I hate him.

Me: Who, then?

Will: Charles Darwin, he was crucial.

Sam: What about Prince Charles?

Will: No way, he's worse than Charles.

Love, Nina

∽

Dear Vic,

Will reads a lot. In various places. He looks serious (even worried) when he reads.

Me: Is the book OK?

Will: It's hilarious.

Me: But you look so serious.

Will: I'm laughing on the inside.

Sam: I hate it when people laugh out loud when they read.

Will: Me too, that's why I hide it.

Sam: They're showing off about reading a funny book.

Will: About *finding* it funny.

AB: (*from kitchen table*) I think you're allowed to laugh if something amuses you.

Sam: Not a book.

AB: I think one's allowed an involuntary snort... or two.

MK: One.

Moldy banana in a rucksack in Sam's bedroom.

Sam: I haven't used that bag since I was eleven.

Me: So that banana's over a year old.

Sam: Do you think we missed its birthday?

Me: Yes. Put it in the kitchen bin.

Sam: What a pointless life it's had.

Me: What?

Will: Forgotten fruit always upsets him.

Sam looks at his hands. It's a habit.

Will: Why do you do that?

Sam: I like it—that's all.

Will: Are you looking, or thinking?

Sam: Looking...I think. I don't know, no, thinking (*looks at hands*).

Will: It looks weird.

Sam: You should try it, it's very sympathetic.

Will: (*looking at hands*).

I looked at my hands and it was comforting. And I thought this: I know these hands very well. They're not perfect and a bit rough, but I like them. I have to admit the thumbs are nicer than the fingers and look nice with polish.

I expect this is what it's like having children.

Told MK about the hands/children thing. She ignored me and said she was going back to her mother's salad dressing recipe (it's less intrusive than the balsamic). She does that sometimes (ignores a philosophical thing in favor of a practical thing).

Love, Nina

Dear Vic,

Went to Will's sports day which was held at a sports ground miles away from his school, practically up the M1. Not knowing its location, I got there a bit late and lurked on the edges for a while thinking I might be at the sports day for the wrong school (kids looked different not in stripy blazers).

Then I wandered into a no-access area and got yelled at by a teacher. Later, Will said it looked as if I'd had nit lotion in my hair— which I had, but denied (it needs 24 hours for effectiveness).

Later, at supper, talking about Will's individual events, running, jumping and javelin.

Me: Sports day was fun!
Will: It looked like you still had nit lotion in your hair.
Me: Will! Do you really think I'd go to your school sports day with nit lotion on my hair?
Will: No, s'pose not, but you did stand in a corner on your own for ages and then suddenly march across the cricket pitch in the middle of a match.
Me: Did I?

Sam then remembered he'd volunteered for the tug of war at his (sports day) next week. AB said the trick is to wear non-slip shoes and gloves and to have a proper stance from the outset.

AB: (*to Sam*) You really need to get a good grip.
Will: That's true.
AB: Tug of war is all about the grip.
Will: Whereas the javelin is all about the letting go.

I bought MK a bread knife from Camden Market. A crafty kind of thing, wooden handle. She liked it, "very nice, very handy." Later AB said it was actually a cake knife, not a bread knife (you can tell by the rounded end). I pointed out the wheat sheaf (ancient symbol meaning "bread") and the word "Bread" carved into the handle, but he wouldn't have it and said, "It's a cake knife, it'll not cut bread well at all."

MK used it to cut the bread next morning and it was rubbish— cut at an angle. MK said it might do better with cake. The thing is, it might've been MK, not the knife. The poor performance of the knife might have been a self-fulfilling prophecy. A concept Nunney has told me about where you make something happen because you think it might (happen). He says just because something happens doesn't mean it was definitely going to happen (type thing). Nunney's interested in all that human behavior stuff. Hence him always commenting on things people say / do. Annoyingly.

Agree about the Euthymol tooth powder. I think people who like it are either old, old-fashioned or anti mint flavor (possibly because of it making orange juice taste horrible).

Will found his toothbrush bobbing about down the toilet.

MK: (*to Sam*) Do you know how Will's toothbrush got into the toilet?
Sam: Why's it always left to me to explain these things?
MK: Do you mean, "Why do I always get the blame?"
Sam: Am I getting the blame?
MK: Yes!

Later, discussions about toothbrushes.

Me: Sensodyne Searcher is the best brush in my opinion.
Will: What's so good about it?
Me: Small head.
Will: Why is a small head good?
Me: It reaches the teeth, even the grooves.

AB: Let's not talk about bacteria again.

MK: I thought bristle was best.

Me: Bristle?

MK: Yes, real bristle.

Me: Who told you that?

MK: I read it.

Me: Where, in Samuel Pepys's diaries?

AB: I read about a rinsing device that *rinses* the teeth clean.

Me: I've never heard of it.

AB: Bubbles implode on the teeth.

MK: I heard about that.

AB: Yes, apparently rinsing's the thing.

Me: I've never heard of it.

MK: You're out of the loop.

Saw Pippa today. She said I shouldn't wear red and that I should "stick to blues and greens." Also, her Gran is going to the fjords for two weeks but hasn't asked her to dog-sit. She's offended.

Pippa wants to do a pottery course at Haverstock. Wants me to as well. Not sure. I might have agreed if she hadn't said I should "stick to blues and greens." So I'm quite glad she did.

When people say you suit blues and greens, it means they think you're pale.

By the way, am going to try out the Plumstead snooker club job. Stella says I have first refusal and if I don't accept, Ruth the hippie has next try. Apparently the hippie has a part-time job already, but is being cagey about what it is. It must be something she's ashamed of—like a prostitute or in a deli.

I'll let you know how snooker club goes.

Love, Nina

Dear Vic,

For your supper night I suggest the following: grilled cheese (Greek stuff) with Greek salad, then pumpkin ravioli (buy it fresh and boil it for 4 mins) with butter and herbs (sage), and some sort of lemony thing.

Don't do meat and you can't go wrong.

Egg mayonnaise doesn't really count—it isn't a recipe, it's just boiled eggs with mayonnaise on top. If you insist on serving egg mayonnaise, sprinkle red paprika on top and at least make it look as though you've made an effort. Which you haven't.

Annoying that R Patel doesn't like potatoes. It might be the calories thing, but more likely it's because they're not fashionable at the moment.

It's all pasta and couscous nowadays, in London anyway.

Good luck with it.

Love, Nina

Dear Vic,

Gossiping with the Student from Luton about a new bloke that Stella's hanging around with.

Me: (*to S from L*) Stella says he's perfect, apart from a bad walk.
S from L: (*winces*) A bad walk can mean bad feet and that can be indicative.
Me: Of what?
S from L: Problems further up.
Me: How high?

Later, investigating:

Me: (*to SH*) What's the walk like?
SH: Awful, off-putting.
Me: How?
SH: Like a cow.
Me: A cow's walk is OK—isn't it?
SH: The hind legs?
Me: Ooh.

The bloke's name is Gunter, which seemed unusual (to me).

Me: Gunter?
SH: Stop saying it.
Me: Gunter.
SH: Haven't you heard of Gunter Grass?
Me: No.
SH: He wrote *The Tin Drum*.
Me: You're going out with the bloke who wrote *The Tin Drum*?

Stella's Gunter didn't write *The Tin Drum*. She was just pointing out how common the name is. He's doing a science doctorate focusing on horse semen and its ability to travel (outside of the horse) for breeding purposes.

Anyway, saw Gunter at the Poly BBQ thing but he was sitting down in a chair most of the time and I missed the walk.

Spoke to him though and found out he's got a canary called Sandy that lives in a cage in his flat. Stella played it down.

Me: I hear Gunter's got a canary.
SH: Oh, he's exaggerating.
Me: He either has or hasn't got a canary.

SH: Well, he has, but he was given it.

Me: He could've refused it.

SH: He didn't like to.

Me: So he's got a canary.

Told MK and S&W about Gunter and his canary and they all thought I was being judgmental. They never slag people off (except me, for slagging other people off).

MK: What's so bad about having a canary?

Me: It's strange.

Sam: You're being horrible.

Me: No, I'm just saying it's strange to own a canary—at his age.

MK: She's being horrible.

Me: Why are you pretending it's normal to own a canary?

MK: To see what happens.

Will: How old *should* you be to own a canary?

Me: Young, or very old.

Sam: He could have got it when he was a kid.

Me: That would mean the canary is in its teens.

Will: Could it be?

Me: I've never met it but I'll ask.

Love, Nina

∽

Dear Vic,

Shadowed Stella in the so-called café at Plumstead snooker club. I watched her speak to some punters and prepare a microwaveable snack sandwich, wipe a table and help herself to a gin and lemonade. Then it was my go.

I didn't mind heating up the snacks or opening the bottles but I really hated going out into the dark space and calling, "Ron, could you come forward?"

Apparently a few punters have been self-conscious about food items being named and have asked staff to be less specific. The snooker club manager came up with "Ron, could you come forward?" (if their name is Ron) and the punters are happy with it.

Stella said if I couldn't face calling blokes to come forward for their microwaveable snacks, then I might ask myself the question: Am I temperamentally suitable for this job?

Walking home I admitted to Stella that I really couldn't face asking men to come forward for their snacks—I blamed it on being brought up by a single mother and not being used to seeing that kind of thing—and that therefore I must decline the job offer.

Stella was really disappointed. She said she'd been looking forward to swapping stories of our evenings and maybe even having a "Who sold the most steak sizzlers" competition. But even that didn't make the job any more appealing. Less so, actually.

Hope all's well with you.

Love, Nina

⌒

Dear Vic,

Love the picture. Have you had a perm or just let it go curly?

MK (fully straight hair, not even a kink) has started using an Afro comb (purple).

Me: What's that?
MK: A comb.
Me: Yes, why're you using it?

MK: It's less pully than the other sort.

Me: It's for people with perms or curly hair.

MK: Is it?

Me: It won't work on you. The teeth are too wide apart.

MK: What? You even know about comb teeth.

Light bulbs are a big deal because MK likes lamps and the lamps get through light bulbs like wildfire (ditto the ceiling lights), especially the 100-watt bulbs which are bright enough. 60-watt ones last a bit longer, but even I admit they're a bit gloomy. Anyway, MK used to change the bulbs when necessary. But now she seems to hate doing it. So I do it.

MK: I don't *hate* it. I just don't *do* it.

Sam: She doesn't enjoy it.

Me: No one *enjoys* it.

MK: You seem to.

Me: It's just that I'm eager to help.

Sam: She just likes getting up on a chair.

Will: Like some people like directing the traffic.

Sam had tea at a friend's house.

Sam: The pudding was nice.

Me: What was it?

Sam: Don't know its name, you just add milk.

Will: Angel Delight.

Sam: Yes! How did you know?

Will: I've seen it around. You just add milk.

Pippa looked after Ted Hughes again (after all) while Gran was in Norway. Ted was "off his food" and only nibbled at some boil-in-the-bag cod. Pippa has stopped calling him Ted Hughes and just calls him

Ted now. She says he responds to Ted better than Ted Hughes. He prefers a single syllable. She's found out that all dogs do—a single syllable mimicking a bark.

Pippa says she's not going to have Ted to stay again.

Will: Why not?

Pippa: It was like looking after a poorly actress, he's gone too needy.

Me: So, if you're not having Ted Hughes again, you can get a kitten.

Pippa: I've gone off the idea of a kitten.

Will: How come?

Pippa: Too aloof.

Me: You want something between needy Ted Hughes and an aloof kitten.

Will: Try Sam.

Love, Nina

༄

Dear Vic,

Did you know GM and Auntie X have been to stay at 55?

They came to see the comedy play *Noises Off,* and decided *not* to stay in Le Meridien Piccadilly as usual, but *here.*

It was a nightmare. The minute they arrived, they asked if I could introduce them to AB. I tried my best to put them off, not that AB would mind, just that I couldn't face the embarrassment of it.

Luckily, Michael Frayn (the actual writer of *Noises Off*) spends half his life at 57 (unofficially Claire Tomalin's boyfriend) and I thought I could get him to say hello instead of having to ask AB. Much less embarrassing because I hardly know him (M Frayn) and he wouldn't be at all interested in them. I thought I'd be able to take them round to 57 and M Frayn could just say hello and then we'd leave (I'd be in 100% control).

Me: I've got a better idea.
GM: What?
Me: Wouldn't you like to meet *Michael Frayn*?
GM: No. Why?
Me: Well, he *wrote Noises Off.*
GM: No, we don't want to meet him. We want to meet Alan Bennett.
Auntie X: That's why we're staying here, not at the Piccadilly.
GM: It's called le Meridien now—it's terribly nice.
AX: Yes, but we're not staying there because we wanted to meet Alan Bennett.

I tried to convince them that it would be great to meet the playwright of the actual play they would be seeing that evening. But they had their hearts set on AB.

Me: Well, OK then, I'll ask him to come over, but he might be in a foul mood.
GM: Is he moody?
AX: *(looking anxious).*
Me: He can be very prickly if disturbed.
GM: Oh, he seems so reasonable when you see him on the box.

I rang him from upstairs.

Me: Would you mind coming over to say hi to my granny?
AB: Well, I'll say hello *(pedantic)*—when?
Me: Let's get it over and done with, but don't be too nice. And don't hang around too long.
AB: I'll do my best.

Soon, AB arrived in his coat and was *very* nice to them (too nice). They fawned round him like the two old ladies do with Basil Fawlty. GM quoted some of the Cambridge Footlights stuff to him and he encouraged her by laughing and then remembered he'd sent her a "Get well" and she was charmed that he'd remembered and told him about it (being ill and recovering) and he made a health enquiry and then Auntie X joined in and said about when she'd been ill and they ran through their illnesses and then both said they were never ill— touch wood.

GM spoke about seeing the great Joss Ackland in *Lloyd George Knew My Father* and Fenella Fielding in *Hobson's Choice* at the Haymarket Leicester and how that theater really has some marvelous shows etc.

After AB had gone.

GM: Well, he was *charming.*

AX: Not at all difficult.

Me: You got him on a good day.

GM: He was *lovely.*

AX: What a lovely, lovely man.

GM: Would you be able to get hold of the other chap?

Me: Michael Frayn?

GM: Who?—Oh no, Jonathan Miller.

Me: No, he's moved away.

GM: Has he? Where to?

Me: Derby.

GM: Jonathan Miller's moved to Derby?

Me: Yes, he wants peace and quiet.

AX: In Derby?

Me: The Peaks.

GM: What a shame, we'd have loved to meet him.

Love, Nina

～

Dear Vic,

Will says his school motto is "slowly does it," which can't be true, they're constantly at them to work harder.

Sam: What actually is a motto for?
MK: A reminder of the aims of the school or whatever.
Sam: The list of rules.
AB: More a guiding principle.
Sam: Oh yeah, we *do* have one of those.
MK: What is it?
Sam: Don't block the toilet or anything.

Misty is hanging out at Mornington Gym. She made up a thing where she says she's an art student and she goes and sketches the men jigging about in their vest and pants.

Her friend gave her the idea. This friend does the same thing at the South Bank theaters, "sketching" the actors rehearsing. It's a way of meeting a fit bloke or an actor.

Misty says the only problem is when the blokes ask to see the sketches her friend has done. They're just stick men.

Never know what to call Granny Wilmers. Can't call her Cesia, I don't know what it means. I'm not familiar with it (like Stella's Gunter). I can't call her Mrs. Wilmers—that would be ludicrous—and I can't keep calling her Granny, that's worse. I try to avoid saying anything. Yesterday when she came here, I started to say Mrs. Wilmers but veered off and said "Mrs. Granny" and got a confused look from MK.

Love, Nina

PS Misty has given up coffee and tea due to caffeine-induced insomnia. Sleeping like a log now, on Barleycup.

Dear Vic,

Will wants to do a sponsored thing for the school.

Will: We choose either a sponsored walk, run or silence.
Me: Which do you fancy?
Will: Sponsored silence.
MK: No, do the walk.
Will: No, the silence is the best—I can read and watch telly while staying silent.
MK: I think you should do the walk.
Will: Why?
Me: It's like the beginning of a novel.
MK: (*looks annoyed*) What?
Me: Where a child begins a sponsored silence, becomes obsessed and *never speaks again?*
MK: No, it's just too easy.

So I was thinking, that could be my new novel (about the sponsored silent kid). I've been working on my semiautobiog novel and am really wishing I could just get on with it and not have to keep writing essays about other writers and theorists. Not to mention the dissertation.

We're doing a lot of literary theory this year and it's not very inspiring. I'm not that interested in translating what a load of brainboxes think about things, but loads of students get all excited about it. They love it.

The same students who don't say a word when we're talking about something amazing, i.e. the fantastic play *True West* (about two chalk and cheese brothers). But when it's a book of someone's rambling theory, they read it and get excited and keep wanting to "debate."

Even shy red-tips Fee pipes up with the occasional snippet.

Keep meaning to make a start on my dissertation. But it's like anything you keep meaning to do—you don't and you start resenting it.

Love, Nina

PS In that chicken recipe, I forgot to say: add one wineglass of cider.

∽

Dear Vic,

Mary-Kay has two mates that we call the brainy blokes.

There's the American brainy bloke (American, beard, big, brainy) and the English brainy bloke (English, stubble, small, brainy).

Sam and me reckoned the English brainy bloke was the brainiest. Will reckoned the American one. They don't come round that much and never together, so it's hard to judge them.

Sam and me think the English brainy bloke is brainiest because we never know what he's on about and he can't say his Rs (Sam thinks not saying your Rs is a brainy trait). Will says the American brainy bloke seems brainier because he speaks quietly but clearly and we can understand what he's going on about.

We asked MK which of them would come out top in a contest and she said probably the American brainy bloke. Will punched the air "Yes!" and Sam and me asked why the American.

"Because he can write," she said.

Meaning it's not how much you know but how well you communicate your knowledge. And that was a lesson for us all.

Then on Saturday the English brainy bloke popped in and we studied him.

I didn't understand much that he said, apart from "Could you let me have a teaspoonful of Bovril?" He was all over the place but MK kept up well.

I thought he'd brought a thin dog with him and left it by the bins (a dog very similar to Ted Hughes actually) but it turned out it wasn't his dog, just a dog snooping round our bins.

But then he demonstrated (a) his braininess and (b) his failure to communicate via the dog.

Me: Is that your dog out there?
English Brainy Bloke: (*doesn't look round*) I doubt it since my last canine companion died in 1967.
Me: Oh.
Bloke: (*looks out, sees dog*) Kai me ton kuna!
Me: Is it yours?
Bloke: No, but it resembles Anubis—Guardian of the Scales, Weigher of Hearts.
Me: Oh.
Will: (*to me*) An Ancient Egyptian thing.

Love, Nina
PS Then when the bloke went, he seemed to take the thin dog with him. As if it was his all along.

∽

Dear Vic,

Congratulations re your exams. God I wish I were as clever as you. I'm struggling to understand a bunch of poems and a story at the moment. I've read them and all I have to do is demonstrate that I grasp the basic ideas. And there's you... You could enter our brainy contest.

Nunney came over last night and we went out for mussels (nice but a bit gritty). Café is under new management and the mussels came with no shells on. Nunney was appalled, saying the shells are the point and that serving them without is like rolling someone's cigarette for them (if they like rolling their own).

Before we went out, had a game of cricket with S&W. After cricket the subject of the brainy blokes contest came up.

Sam: The American won, but they're both brainy.
Will: *Very* brainy.
Nunney: Hmm, as brainy as Michael Frayn?
Sam: Brainier.
Nunney: I don't think so. Michael Frayn is so brainy, he's mates with Bamber Gascoigne.
Me: OK—Michael Frayn—could he slip into Ancient Egyptian at the drop of a hat like our runner-up?
Nunney: (*tuts*) He translated Chekhov's *Cherry Orchard*—in his spare time.
Me: From what language?
Nunney: (*sarcastic*) Chinese.
Will: But Chekhov was Russian.
Nunney: That's how brainy he is.
Sam: Frayn-the-Brain wins!

Nunney explained that for people of their generation (Michael Frayn and our two brainy blokes and other forty/fifty-year-olds), being brainy is their *raison d'être* (reason for being) and they just keep learning and trying to remember everything they learn.

Will: Life's just one long game of *University Challenge*.
Sam: They're not just know-it-alls.
Me: They are, but they can't help it.

303

I think I could write a Sam Shepard–style play (like *True West*—about sibling rivalry) about the two brainy blokes. About a brainy rivalry where they end up trashing their typewriters and shouting in Ancient Egyptian and Russian and throwing lines from Chaucer and Chekhov at each other and translating the insults into different ancient languages.

Mentioned it to Nunney and he said it might not be very popular.

Nunney told me about his dissertation (again). It's a psychological analysis of how people compare themselves with other people (something along those lines, I wasn't listening that closely). He was very interested in mine but still wonders why I chose Carson McCullers.

Nunney's using an own-brand washing powder, so smells different. I told him that, and he just tutted and said, "It's all they have on campus."

It's all they have on campus. Things like that really annoy me. I said, "Get some Daz while you're off campus," but he said he'd got better things to do.

Hope all's well with you.

Love, Nina

∽

Dear Vic,

The rest of Leics trip was fine except leaving Dad's I knocked a cactus off a shelf. We were in a rush so he said to leave it. Awkward ending.

Funny traveling back on a Saturday. Football fans around and a feeling of it being a good day. As opposed to the gloomy, shut-down feeling you get on a Sunday (which would be my normal day for coming back).

Back at 55 MK was 100% tied up with getting ready for this big thing and asked me to fetch an antique white shirt that she was possibly going to borrow from a friend (to wear at the thing). So I went to the friend's flat to fetch it.

Me: Hi, I've come to get the shirt for Mary-Kay.
Friend: (*tuts*) She seemed bored to death when I was describing it.

I waited in the kitchen area while she fetched it. Blue and white cups hanging on a long row of hooks equally spaced out. "Nice mugs," I said. But she deliberately ignored me.

This friend of MK's is considered to be a very nice, jolly person (and she is, I've seen her being very nice to everyone) but she's not keen on me. Not sure why. Maybe MK's said something about me that the friend took offense at.

Friend: (*handing over shirt*) She won't want it.

Back at 55.

MK: What did she say?
Me: She hopes you like it.

Mary-Kay took one look and straightaway said it wouldn't do and I may as well take it back (straightaway).

Me: I'll take it tomorrow.
MK: Take it now, and then it's done.
Me: Ugh, I can't face going back there.
MK: Why?
Me: She'll be offended and she doesn't like me.
MK: She'll be offended tomorrow and still won't like you and it'll be a Sunday.

What a coincidence MK referring to the gloomy Sunday thing I'd just thought to myself on the train. The days of the week are very powerful—i.e. I will always hate Thursdays because of a friend of mine at Gwendolyn Junior having piano lessons on a Thursday and not walking home with me and that was fifteen years ago. I used to dread Thursdays and the ten-minute walk without that friend. It was symbolic.

Anyway, I took the antique white shirt back and the friend lived up to her jolly reputation (did a nice laugh) and seemed quite pleased (to have predicted the rejection).

Love, Nina

PS Also saw GM while in Leics. New car. She called the sun roof a "sunshine roof," which I thought was nice.

~

Dear Vic,

Yes. You're spot on. Feel a bit left behind Nunney-wise.

He's doing a radio show now with another bloke and wearing a baggy suit.

Also, talks endlessly about girls, especially one in particular, doesn't realize he's doing it. Also, mentioned that a girl slapped him round the face the other day, and that says it all.

Went to stay in the new house in Brighton, it's right on the Falmer branch line so you hear the trains, which I love. He lives with three others. They all wanted to watch Madonna concert on telly which I thought disappointing.

Nunney is working hard on his thesis (the Sussex University word for dissertation) and rambled on about it. He has devised a questionnaire so that when he states this, that, or the other psychological thing, he can back it up with evidence from a thousand (roughly) specially devised questionnaires.

I have offered to take some of the questionnaires and pass them round at Poly. N was v. grateful because one of his mates, who promised to get a load filled out, has just broken his femur.

Nunney smoked dope. I tried a puff or two and felt relaxed for the first time in my entire life. You can see why people like it.

Told MK about the girl slapping Nunney.

Me: A girl slapped him round the face the other day.
MK: That's usually an invitation.
Me: Yes, I know.
MK: He might have pinched her bum though.
Me: He's not the sort.
MK: No.
Me: It will have been an invitation.
MK: Well, he might not have accepted.
Me: But he might have.

Love, Nina

∽

May 1987

Dear Vic,

About Nick Nichols, our tutor who came over to London on a job swap and so loved London and all things Londony. Who gave us pizza pie and wine and was great fun to be with. And whose son, Scott, and his friend came to mow the lawn and watch football at Stella's house.

See the photocopy of a cutting pinned up on the Humanities notice board.

LOS ANGELES TIMES

Prescott S. Nichols, SDSU Activist, Is Dead at 55

March 06, 1987 | HILLIARD HARPER | Times Staff Writer

Human rights activist Prescott S. (Nick) Nichols, 55, a professor of English and comparative literature at San Diego State University, died Wednesday night, apparently of a heart attack, while driving home. Passersby found him about 6:15 p.m. where he had pulled his car over to the side of the road.

Nichols, an advocate for part-time faculty members at SDSU, was involved in efforts to unionize college professors in the California State University system.

I never got round to sending him the stuff on the Gin House. Or the photo of the Cheshire Cheese.

Love, Nina

∽

Dear Vic,

Meant to take Nunney's questionnaires into Poly but forgot again. Haven't got long now. I feel a bit bad because he rang and asked if I'd made a start getting them filled out and I said they were all done and dusted. Which was stupid because now he thinks they're all done.

I'll see you on Sat at the Good Earth. Will bring MK's stencil things.

They liked the fish pie. AB said the peas served separately would've been nicer. Which is true. He also said it would be nice with runner beans.

Love, Nina
PS Might bring a few questionnaires for you and co.

~

Dear Vic,

Went to the Lyric Theater to see some plays by Samuel Beckett. It was a cheap showing, one up from a dress rehearsal and in the afternoon, but tutor Vicki was thrilled to have got us all tickets to see Billie Whitelaw (Beckett's preferred actress) in the roles.

I have to admit I wasn't enjoying the show much (people talking nonsense in dustbins and making funny noises) and then, in the second half, I heard a bit of muttering coming from the (mostly empty) seats behind. I glanced round and saw, all alone, Samuel Beckett (the person). I can't describe how it felt to see the great man sitting there in the flesh.

Well, OK, it was like seeing a unicorn or a Borrower (or like when I saw that snake in the crocosmia). It took my breath away. I didn't look again and I didn't elbow Stella who was next to me because she'd fallen asleep and I knew she'd jolt awake noisily and show us all up. Also, I didn't want him to get the idea I was bored.

I don't enjoy his plays—true—but that's not to say I dismiss them as unimportant. They are/were very important (according to tutor Vicki).

In the theater, with S Beckett two rows behind muttering and possibly blowing kisses to Billie Whitelaw, I was wondering what made one person's nonsense "genius" and another's "crap"...and I wondered if it's genius if you're tall, enigmatic, reclusive, handsome...and it's crap if you're normal or short, chatty and ugly. I was just mulling it over when something AB said sprang to mind.

AB is an admirer of Les Dawson. AB says that only an extremely accomplished pianist could pretend to play as badly as Les Dawson (pretends to do). Maybe it's the same with S Beckett. He could write a really good (sensible) play that everyone would get, but he doesn't. Like Les Dawson, he's pretending to be crap. Which you can only do if you're a genius.

Anyway, no one else noticed Samuel Beckett there and I had a job persuading them afterward that I had actually seen him.

SH: (*disbelieving*) Like you saw Jackie O at Holloway Odeon?
Me: No, it really was Samuel Beckett.
SH: What did he look like?
Me: Handsome but very old...symmetrical, upright, still, slight second-class occlusion of the jaw...(*SH wanting more*) a well-groomed fisherman.
Tutor Vicki: (*convinced by description*) Well, how thrilling for us to have been at the same performance.

Then we went to a pub by the river and tutor Vicki spoke interestingly about Beckett the man (i.e. his nonsense is all about trying to express himself). Then we all crowded round the Quiz-Master and had to keep going to the bar for more 20ps. I thought to myself that the Quiz-Master seemed more popular than the plays and that was the modern world.

No one wants to be puzzled in a theater by questions that don't have answers, they want to be puzzled in the pub by questions from a machine that does have answers. The Quiz-Master was very popular, and soon after we went on it a little queue formed (people who'd heard us having a good time).

You could tell tutor Vicki would have preferred to talk more about Beckett but we'd had enough of Beckett for one day and whenever Quiz-Master asked us a literature question we shouted over to tutor Vicki—even if we knew the answer—and soon she came over and joined fully in and forgot all about S Beckett.

It was a great day out. The only thing being, I forgot to take a batch of Nunney's questionnaires and the deadline (Nunney turning up and asking to see them) is looming.

Hope all's well with you.

Love, Nina

PS If you see a Quiz-Master in a pub or service station, have a go. It looks like a one-armed bandit but isn't. But beware, it's addictive.

ᦕ

Dear Vic,

Thanks for canary life-span information. To be honest, the whole canary thing is out of date now because Stella has shelved Gunter and started hanging around with a bloke (called Dan) who wears a black and white checky scarf which gives off a smell of onions. He left it (the scarf) on the back of a chair in the 5th floor coffee bar and it was noticed and commented on by Stella's hippie friend Ruth. Then the fire alarm went off and we all had to dash out efficiently by the back stairs.

Later, hippie Ruth said (to Dan) that it was his smelly scarf that set the alarms off. He admitted that the scarf might have a "foody" smell because of the Bender Brunch he'd had in Wimpy at eleven. He thought that made it better.

Was telling MK.

MK: What's this one's name?
Me: Dan—he wears an Arafat scarf.
MK: On his head?
Me: No, round his neck.
MK: Does he look nice in it?
Me: It's just weird.
MK: Weirder, or less weird, than owning a canary?

311

Me: A bit less.

MK: Well, that's good, then.

Didn't mention the Bender Brunch or onion smell. They already think I'm overcritical.

Anyway, the worst thing about the fire alarm going off was that I left Nunney's questionnaires on a table in the 5th floor coffee bar (you weren't allowed to take extraneous items with you on the dash out even though it was a drill). I'll have to go in tomorrow and get them.

By the way: Stella is even off Dan now and is hanging around with a bloke called Plenty O'toole. His real name is Something O'something but I can't remember what because he's always known as Plenty O'toole among us. It's become normal now. Nothing's "happened" according to Stella (she just likes him because he's ironic and has the kind of spiky hair that she's fond of in a man—which I hate).

Love, Nina

PS About the questionnaires. Suppose they're not there?

～

Dear Vic,

Me and Stella ended up filling out ALL Nunney's psychology questionnaires ourselves. It took forever.

I've made Stella swear NEVER to tell him. He would be so angry and it would confirm some extremely negative ideas he has re my character.

Anyway it was a nightmare but we managed them all.

Afterward, we realized we'd done them all in the same two pens. Stella so drunk she couldn't even disguise her handwriting.

Still. It had to be done. It's like a weight's been lifted off my shoulders.

Love, Nina

⁓

Dear Vic,

Nunney collected the forged questionnaires and we all went to play snooker at Plumstead snooker club while Stella was working there.

Stella kept looking guilty whenever the subject of dissertations or questionnaires cropped up. She even offered to make Nunney a microwaveable snack—free of charge (to atone). But he said thanks but no thanks due to the off-putting smell.

After a while we witnessed Stella calling, "Jim, could you come forward please?" and a bloke strolling up to the microwave shelf area.

Then Nunney and me came over to 55 and all the stress about the questionnaires was forgotten as we played snooker again and watched *Carry On Up the Jungle*.

Nunney didn't stay long as he needs to begin the collating and analyzing of his psychological data.

Love, Nina

⁓

Dear Vic,

Should have been working on my dissertation yesterday but not in the right mood. Watched the brilliant *Return of the Pink Panther* with Sam and Will.

Then it turned out Sam had homework to do that he'd forgotten all about and MK was due home any minute.

Yesterday was very unusual homeworkwise. Sam had some. Will had none.

Sam had to write a poem about nature. It was funny seeing Will advising/commiserating with Sam on the subject.

Sam: I hate poems.

Will: I hate homework.

Sam: I hate nature.

Will: Just get it done, then you've done it.

Sam: Does it have to rhyme?

Will: No, but the teacher will want it to.

Sam: Does it have to be long?

Will: The teacher will want it to be.

Sam: Shit, shit, shit.

Will: Is that the poem?

He got his poem done just as MK arrived and he read it out as she stood at the top of the stairs looking amazed and impressed.

Birds, by Sam

Birds don't like rain
They don't like wet feet
They can't fly in rain
They can't tweet
Birds don't like wind
They get blown about
Birds only like it when the sun is out

MK: It's brilliant.

Will: (*to MK*) It could be about you.

Sam: It's meant to be a nature poem.

MK: It's great.

Sam: Is it natural enough?

Will: Are you kidding? It's cram-packed with nature.

Sam: I want Mr. Biro to like it.

Will: Mr. *Biro?*

Sam: Yes, he's a temp.

Will: Mr. *Biro*—are you sure that's his name?

Sam: Yes, it's Hungarian for jug.

Sam then told Will he liked homework and wished he had it more.

Then Will told us *why* he had no homework: Some homework last week had been v. difficult homework (coastal features). Will had protested, saying he'd never had a lesson on it and didn't understand a word of it. MK insisted and said he should listen more in class. Then today, the teacher admitted she'd given out the wrong papers (meant for 5th formers) and is very impressed with the few boys who tackled it for "showing determination and a willingness to have a go." And said they would not have to do any homework for the rest of the week (one day).

Will delighted. MK too. I would've been annoyed if it were me.

Love, Nina

෴

Dear Vic,

Dissertation needs to be finished. This should be a very short letter.

Already thrown away a whole afternoon meeting Stella's mother ("whistling Jill") who is down here to see Agatha Christie's *Mousetrap.* She kept saying, "If you know who done it, don't tell me." And saying it made her chuckle.

She was much nicer than Stella had made out. She (whistling Jill) told funny stories. Including a clearly made-up one in which Stella trains their dog ("Patch") to jump through a flaming hoop.

Jill: And she got him jumping through a flaming hoop.
Me: Are you saying flaming as in flaming hell? Or do you mean the hoop was alight, as in "on fire"?
Jill: It was on fire. It was two coat hangers with a rag wrapped around and she'd lit it.

Stella denied it. And I believe her. She's not the type to light a hoop and make a Jack Russell jump through it. It was probably just a hoop. Stella says her mum is mixing two separate memories together. One of the unlit hoop and one of a circus trip where there *was* a flaming hoop. It's what happens to older people.

Can't show MK my dissertation, it will infuriate her. She'll say it's too wordy. Especially now I've gone on to longer words—it's the norm at college—everyone does it and I don't want to be the only student saying "use" when everyone else is saying "utilize."

MK will hate it.

Have shown it to Nunney though, who asked the terrible question: "What are you trying to say?"

Me: I'm trying to say the critics didn't like McCullers.
Nunney: But you don't say that.
Me: I'm driving at it.
Nunney: Just say it.
Me: Just saying it doesn't use enough words.
Nunney: (*reads on*) Oh, here we go...why do you say "critics of the day"? Get rid of "of the day."
Me: That's three less words.

I hate it now and can hardly bring myself to look at it. I wish I'd

316

done a quirky subject like "the Lyrics of 'Jolene' by Dolly Parton" or something.

Letter too long. Back to the Amstrad.

Love, Nina

PS Nunney is going great with his (thesis), though the questionnaires are throwing up some surprises.

⌢

Dear Vic,

Crisis with dissertation. I've written the whole thing along the lines of Carson McCullers had to live a reclusive life because no one liked her gloomy portrayals. But she didn't care because she was disabled with ill health and reclusive and didn't need approval of the bigots...

These ideas were based on my reading about CMC in a couple of books on Southern American writers. And reading between the lines in her novels.

But now, just as I'm finishing the dissertation (albeit hurriedly) and have enlarged a portrait of her face looking miserable and odd to put as a cover, I've found a book in the library which may as well be called *Carson's Fun Life as a Popular Writer.*

This book implies that lots of people actually enjoyed the books and famous people of the day wanted to be friends with her and invited her to glittering events. And critically acclaimed films were made starring Elizabeth Taylor and Richard Doobrie and she was always gadding about on film sets with her husband, Reeves, and Montgomery Cliff. It was only a few boring bigots that didn't like her. Basically this book contradicts all the major points in my dissertation.

317

I say McCullers was a recluse. The book says the idea that she was a recluse is the common misconception of the ill-informed.

I say she was disabled due to ill-health. The book says she made light of her illness and smoked and drank and socialized.

I say the public resented her portrayals and critics panned her morbid interest in the grotesque. The book says the books had instant appeal and ignited a whole new interest in the ordinary and marginalized in society. And that critics of repute were quick to praise.

And so on. It pretty much contradicts everything I say and not only that. It says anyone who thinks what I've said is true is an idiot.

Told Stella this.

Me: So according to this new book Carson McCullers was the life and soul.

SH: Oh.

Me: And mates with famous people of the day.

SH: Oh, that's not the impression you give.

Me: I know.

SH: What are you going to do?

Me: Steal the book.

Stella was critical of my solution, saying it was immoral. But I don't care. I've worked hard on my dissertation and don't want to look an idiot just because some MA student has chosen McCullers' life for their dissertation (and put a glossy spin on it) and some publisher has published it.

It's all right for Stella. Her dissertation just states the obvious about what a grump Philip Larkin was and how he seemed a bit anti this and that but was good at adding shocking twists to his poems. And chucks in the odd line or two for illustration.

318

I'm determined to finish mine (dissertation) by end of Tuesday and hand it in on Wednesday. Then Finals start next Monday.

Hope all well with you.

Love, Nina

☙

June 1987

Dear Vic,

Nunney came over. His Finals are all over and he's feeling confident.

He is particularly pleased that his thesis supervisor was positive about his thesis and very pleased with the methodology.

Nunney: He liked my research methods.
Me: What are they?
Nunney: The way I gathered research and then handled the data.
Me: Oh, you mean all the questionnaires?
Nunney: Yeah.
Me: So all the questionnaires were fine?
Nunney: Yeah, but I had some surprising outcomes.
Me: So you keep saying.

That probably means that Stella and me filled them out wrong. Maybe we varied our responses too much—or something—when we should have had everyone ticking the same boxes. Nunney has mentioned the "surprising outcomes" a few times. He might be giving me meaningful looks when he says it, but I can't tell because I deliberately look away when we're on the subject of his thesis.

Nunney can't decide whether to stay in higher education and do an MA or get a job or go traveling some more only in a van (to avoid the hitch-hiking, I suppose).

It depends on many things (his words).

I haven't given much thought to what I'll do after the summer. But definitely not an MA or traveling in a van. I might get a job.

Hope all's well with you.

Love, Nina

Afterword

Mary-Kay still lives near the zoo but in a different house. Sam lives there too and is an actor and rock climber. Will is now a director. He lives in Brooklyn with his wife and children and is still an Arsenal supporter.

Vic gained numerous nursing qualifications and in 2011 received a Gold Pin marking twenty-five years' service in the NHS. She still lives in the same Leicestershire village and still doesn't go to London unless absolutely necessary.

Stella never quite left higher education and now lives near Edinburgh with Sparkie the dog and her partner and son.

After traveling some more, Nunney is now a writer and Internet guru.

I ended up in book publishing and now live in Cornwall with Nunney and our kids.

Acknowledgments

Thanks to Mary-Kay Wilmers, Sam Frears, and Will Frears. Also to Mary Mount and Keith Taylor at Penguin and to Reagan Arthur and Pamela Marshall at Little, Brown.

About the Author

After leaving her work as a nanny and graduating from university, Nina Stibbe worked in book publishing. She lives in Cornwall, England, with her partner and their two children.